Fishermen

The Rise and Fall of Deep-Water Trawling

*by Austin Mitchell
and Anne Tate*

*Hutton Press
1997*

Published by

The Hutton Press Ltd.,
130 Canada Drive, Cherry Burton,
Beverley, East Yorkshire HU17 7SB

Printed by
Image Colourprint Ltd.,
Grange Park Lane,
Willerby, Hull
HU10 6EB

ISBN 1 872167 87X

Dedication

*To the fishermen and their long suffering
wives and families.*

Contents

Fleetwood fishermen's registration photos.

Preface

Today Grimsby is Europe's Food Town. In 1977 when we first worked together, Anne from a Grimsby fishing family and Austin fishing for votes, the Borough proclaimed itself "The World's Premier Fishing Port". Icelandic fishing had ended the year before but the town still rang with tales of fishing and of northern lands and waters which even wives had visited, and the first job of a new MP was to be educated in the mysteries of that most basic of industries by good friends and guides such as David Chatterton, Don Lister, and later Dollie Hardie and Tom Jacombe.

Fascinating, but in vain. Fears about the future of distant water fishing turned to gloomy resignation as the lack of alternative fishing opportunities, the sale of the big boats then rusting on the North Wall, the transfer of others to North Sea oil work, the drift of fishermen to other jobs, other industries, other nations, and above all the failure of British government to provide any help beyond burial grants, all meant the death of distant water fishing. Indeed, hopes of saving anything from the wreckage faded as the Common Fisheries Policy became ever more constrictive. For the first time in generations a Grimsby MP had no distant water baptism on a large trawler, merely a North Sea trip on a seine netter.

Twenty years after the death of distant water this book is a posthumous tribute to that industry and the men who made it great. Talking to Fishermen, Skippers, Owners and Merchants, to wives and to all the others in the self-contained, almost ghetto-like world of fishing's "race apart" helped us to understand what we have lost and our hope now is that this book can make the distant water industry live again for a generation whose world is smaller and more circumscribed. They won't again see the great vessels coming through the lock gates, the glories of a full show on a market flooded with fish, the colour, character and humour of the fishermen, or the massed power of vessels crowding the fish dock - at least not until we take control of our own destinies and get out of a Common Fisheries Policy which has killed all that. The fishermen deserve to speak before it's all forgotten so this book, the industry in its own words, is intended to give them the opportunity. Before it's too late.

The book wrote itself as the fishermen talked. We have edited their words to cut out irrelevancies and digressions so they tell their own story in their own way. We have added as little commentary, amplification or explanation as possible because fishing was their life and this is their book. Trawling was a great industry so this book is dedicated to those who made it so. We've tried to do justice to the three main ports of Fleetwood, Hull and Grimsby, (though not Aberdeen on distance grounds), but if we've been a little over-partial to Grimsby, forgive us. It's our home. We dedicate this record by those who sustained fishing to those who still hope to see it revived.

We each did the interviews though in a man's world Anne did the great bulk of them. A few of the extracts, such as Michael Sparkes and some accounts of injuries, were published in the Grimsby Evening Telegraph which has long campaigned for a better deal for trawlermen. Pat Murray and Joyce Benton transcribed the tapes and coped with the invidious job of drafting and redrafting, ordering and re-arranging whilst Tim Grewal did the proof reading. Janet Tierney helped with the photographs. The Grimsby Evening Telegraph, the National Fishing Heritage Centre, Charlie Board and several other fishermen opened up their own photograph collections. Richard Doughty and the staff at the Heritage Centre encouraged and helped the project. Yet our biggest debt is to the fishermen who gave so unstintingly of their time, their hospitality, and their memories. This is their book. They wrote it.

Austin Mitchell
Anne Tate
Grimsby, 1997

5

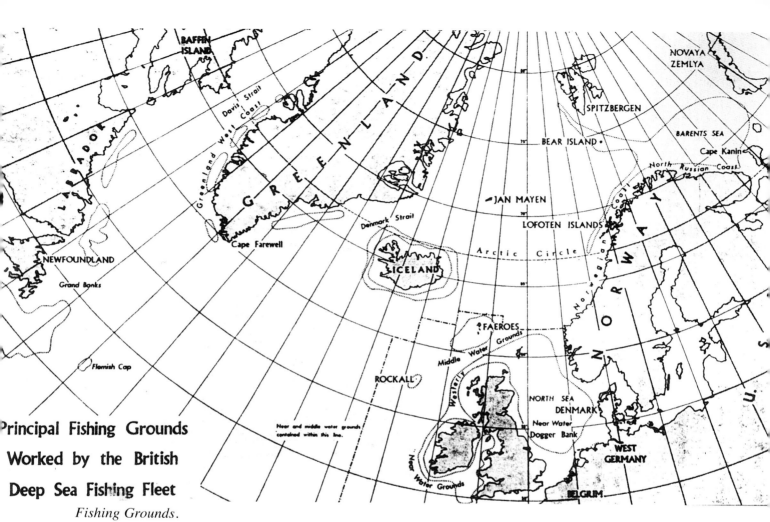

Principal Fishing Grounds
Worked by the British
Deep Sea Fishing Fleet

Fishing Grounds.

THE PRICE OF FISH

The price of fish is very dear,
Two hundred men were lost last year.

Two hundred men in a watery grave,
That was the price, the price they gave.

Up in the land of the midnight sun,
Where the endless fight is never done.

Tired and weary, drenched and cold,
They strive to fill the iced up hold.

And many a man's gone over the rail,
Lost in the teeth of an Arctic gale.

I only hope my point is clear,
The price of fish is VERY dear.

Chapter 1

Down to the Sea in Ships

When Ernest Bevin said that "islands built on coal and surrounded by fish" could never starve he could hardly have envisaged today's Britain. Not a starving country, but one which has closed most of its pits, lost most of its territorial and distant water grounds, and given up so much of its fish catch on the altar of "Europe" that most of the fish we once caught for ourselves is now imported. The shrinkage of fishing has been greater than that in the other basic industries, textiles, steel, shipbuilding, engineering and cars on which Britain's industrial strength and the way of life of its people have been built.

This is the story of the toughest and most dangerous of those lost industries, distant water fishing, through its post war pomp when it caught more than two thirds of Britain's white fish, to its pathetic decline. The story is told by the fishermen themselves, a unique breed, reared in the closed fishing communities of the three great trawler ports of Fleetwood, Grimsby and Hull, perhaps ten thousand fishermen in the Fifties, falling to just over seven thousand by the late Sixties, but with ten times that number dependent on their efforts and their catches.

Theirs is a working class epic. Not of worker power, still less worker control, for fishermen worked in an almost feudal industry and in appalling conditions, yet at sea they were their own masters, teams of mates all working together for a common purpose, to catch the maximum possible amount of fish in the shortest time. Fishing shows the much abused British working man at his best, pitting his courage, ingenuity, comradeship, and skill against the hostile elements. The fishermen weren't well educated, and not particularly well trained. Their attitudes would today be dismissed as chauvinistic, even aggressively working class. They learned their skills on the job, led by other working men, Skippers, who'd risen through the ranks and honed their hunting instincts, and

they won through against the odds because each vessel was a team in which everyone knew each other, their strengths and weaknesses and each depended on the other. Jack really was as good as his master. Indeed, in an industry where talent could rise and usually did, Jack often became a Skipper himself.

Thus fishing combined intense competition of each against the others with close-knit sustaining community and team skills. At sea fishermen were a team, on shore a community. This combination made fishermen unique: loners but companions: hunters but working men, proud but defiant towards a world which they felt curled its lip against them. In their towns, and in the media their treatment varied between romantic admiration and social disdain, for even their fellow citizens hardly knew the tough realities of their lives, and never respected them or their achievement enough.

"Fishermen" is their story, and that of the industry they loved, but which never loved them enough, because it treated them as serfs, and ultimately discarded and dumped those who had given their lives to it. Industries are about economics and politics. Fishing was too, but it was also part love affair, part adventure in great waters, and part the sociological chronicle of a unique way of life we'll not see again.

You was born a fisherman. It's hard for you to believe, but you had the salt in your blood. You was a fisherman or you wasn't a fisherman. It's very very hard to explain to somebody who's never experienced it but you didn't know any different. You'd left school. You'd gone on a trawler. And you didn't know anything different. You never even dreamed. The fellers you'd been to school with who worked ashore was home every night. You didn't realise that. You just did the trip, come in happy with what's happened and you went back. It was just the way you was a slave of the sea. You was either a fisherman or you wasn't. There was no such thing as half-baked. A lot of people same as me left school and thought, "Oh I'll be a fisherman." First trip they come back and said, "Oooh I could never do that. It killed me." I went and I loved it. Even though I'd gone through three days, no sleep, no wash, nowhere to go on the toilet, no contact with home, no radar, no wireless, I just loved it. (Tom Jacombe - Grimsby)

It`s addictive, the sea. When you`re at sea you want to be at home, when you`re at home you want to be at sea. That's the only way I can explain it to you. It is addictive. It was a terrible, terrible, hard life and even as a Skipper, you should never be asked to put men through what you had to put them through. But at the end of the day if you didn`t, somebody else would. (Don Lister - Grimsby)

What else could they do. They went fishing. They earned a lot of money and they worked very hard in all sorts of conditions and they knew nothing else. As soon as they left school they were off as Galley Boys, Deckie Learners that was their ambition. They didn't want to be anything else but a fisherman. Some of them went through to Skippers and earned a lot of bloody money but not all of them. These fellers were earning money that they had no chance of getting otherwise. If you were any good at your job you had no problems at all about getting a job at sea. (Charlie Board - Grimsby)

I came home and I thought I was the finest thing since sliced bread came out, but fishermen have got a habit of normality. They bring you down to earth with a thud. "Who the bloody hell are you? Shut your mouth," and all this, until you learn the ropes. But there was many a time I used to think to myself, "Yes, I am a man." Even though you`re only a young kid, you`re doing a man`s job. You think, "Yes, I am a bloody man." I used to think to myself, these people are not doing the things that I do and that I`ve seen. It didn`t used to last long, but there was something magic in our job to keep making men go back trip after trip, month after month, year after year. I`ve never been able to put me finger on it, but there was something there. (Ray Smith - Grimsby)

I'd go for the camaraderie. It was great. Especially when you got on a regular crew. You all knew each other and there was a bit of banter with the crew of other ships. The camaraderie was smashing. (John Pickett - Grimsby)

You had to sympathise with `em because it's an industry on its own. I don't think people realise. They talk about the coal miners and the fishermen being of equal par. But the coal miner was in his bed every night. He could be down at the local for a pint after he'd finished. The fisherman was washed about and living in squalor. I mean I've known of ships, and I've known it of experience, and particularly in the early days when we used to sleep in what they used to call the fo'c's'le and the galley and the mess deck was at the back of the ship, and I've known many a time that we've not been able to get from forw'd to aft to get some food because the waves and everything had been so bad. And the number of people that have been lost overboard attempting that. (Gordon Cockerill - Grimsby)

When you got home you washed your hands with Dettol and soap and strong soda water. If you got pricked with a fish bone it stopped it going sceptic. And it also got rid of the smell, because your hands stank like nobody`s business. You`d go to the Gaiety at night time and you start getting hot and your hands start sweating, God! You stank like a pole cat. You could always tell when you danced with a girl who worked in the fish house because her hair smelled of smoke. (Joe Linfitt - Grimsby)

You used to go down the dock and everybody used to have miserable faces going to sea. You'd go in the stores, Coalbridges or the Red House or Dobbies, and get your bits and pieces - really miserable - come out - but as soon as we used to get round Spurn I used to be as right as rain. When I was at sea the only time I ever felt miserable really was when we used to pack up and stow the gear. I always felt a bit down when we was coming home. I don't know why it is. You was always passing trawlers. If you was going home you'd pass trawlers going to sea. And they used to say to me, "Oh look at him going home. Lucky devil!". And I says, "No he isn't." He's going away to come home. We're going home to go away." (Les Bowden - Grimsby)

What kept me going was thoughts of home - what a good time you was going to have when you got in dock. If you was married and had a family that was the main thing you

Gutting and throwing the livers into the Liver Basket. Copyright: Grimsby Evening Telegraph.

thought about. That's what kept you going. There was many a time when you felt like saying, "Bugger it, I've had enough," but the thoughts of your family kept you going. (Peter Wright Wilson - Fleetwood)

Aboard a trawler you`ve all got your own set ways, you`ve got nobody behind you telling you, "Do this. Do that." You`ve a job to do once you get to be Deckhand. You know what to do, how it's got to be done and you do it. You`re more close knit, everybody sticks together. You`re all for one. The Merchant Navy - there`s too much class distinction. When you`re on a trawler, all right the Skipper and the Mate gets more than what you do, but you`re all one. (George Brown - Hull)

It was the most hard done-to industry. It was their life. You accepted it, and you knew they always had a mistress - it was the sea. Frank used to say sometimes when he went on deck and was going through the lock pits, when there was all these strikes and things, he said "You left it all behind." It was a love-hate relationship. I always used to say it was like the Lorelei, you know, mermaid calling them back. One thing, he got a grave here. He didn't have a watery grave. (Josephine Gibney - Cleethorpes)

Chapter 2
Born to the Life

In the old industrial world which shaped British life right up to the 1970s we were what we made. Different industries shaped different ways of life in communities built round the basic local occupation, be it coal, steel, textiles, shipbuilding or, in the trawler towns, fish. There a unique industry shaped a unique way of life for fishermen were neither followers of a vocation, nor drawn by romance, or even high pay. They were really bred to fishing in the tight-knit working-class fishing communities within Fleetwood, Grimsby and Hull, the towns which fishing made and which in turn made fishermen.

Some, perhaps as many as a third on the estimate of Jeremy Tunstall, a young Hull sociologist in 1962, were the sons of fishermen. Many more, probably most, came from fishing families, and the great majority lived in communities where going fishing , or at least "down dock", its half-way house, was the norm. Indeed, there was little else. So the sons of the trawler towns were fulfilling a destiny rather than choosing a job and for most there was no choice to make. They went into fishing at seventeen or younger either straight from school, or from dead-end jobs, many of them on the fish docks itself. Usually they went because they could earn more at a younger age in fishing than anywhere else. Once in, they usually stayed.

If you was in Grimsby and you was a young lad it was all fishing in them days when I left school. I left school in 1953. I had six brothers and they all went to sea bar one. My father was a fisherman, grandfather was a fisherman, uncles were fishermen and me brothers. I went to Elliston Street and I should say, looking back now, that 90% of them went fishing. I wanted to go to sea because everybody did it. You saw them come in with plenty of money and thought it was a great life. When I left school I went in the Merchant Navy for three years because me father wasn't keen on me going fishing. He said it was a horrible life and he didn't want me to go. There was thousands in Grimsby - and when you was a young lad you are impressionable and you used to see them coming in with a bag on their back and think it was brilliant. And they had a few bob. I mean they never had a lot of money really but you thought it was a lot of money. I mean they'd spend it, get drunk in pubs and all that and it was, "Oooh that's what I want to be" and really it was all wrong, all different. Very different. My mam wasn't very keen in them days. She'd seen me dad and said, "It's no life". But it wasn't really was it? (George Mussell - Grimsby)

Mostly my generation of fishermen came from fishing families. Your father did it so you did it. I started off as an office boy. A junior clerk. I was getting £1 a week and Ben Jackson, my pal when I was young, he was an apprentice Deckhand aboard the Frobisher. He came in from sea and I had my 5 shillings spending money to his £3 odd from three weeks at sea - a fortune - and I decided I was going to get some of this big money. So I chucked my office job in and went to sea. I was keen then, keen. It was a way of life and everybody you knew was involved in fishing. I liked it and if you had anything about you the opportunities were there. You work hard and if you see the chances and you want to be the best you go for it. Some had ambition. Others just came in to earn their beer and they were quite happy with that. (Derek Reader - Fleetwood)

I was only fifteen or sixteen. My dad was fishing then. He'd come out the Services. He came home and asked if I'd got a job to me mother. She says, " No. He's been fishing where you are". He says, "He's been what?." And when I came home I was never ever going to go back. But then you forget about it when you get home. Every time when you're fishing you think, "I'll never ever do a trip on a trawler again." But then when you start sailing for home, you forget about it and you're back again. In them days you were lucky if you made £30 odd for three weeks. (Bill Ellerington - Hull)

I started off supposed to be an apprentice radio mechanic at 12s. 6d. a week and all my friends were all working on the pontoon getting 30s and to me that was a lot of money. So I didn`t stick it that long `cos all it was a name for was a glorified shop assistant. So I finished up going on the pontoon with the rest of the lads, pushing a barrow and filleting fish as most of us did, and was attending the Nautical School in the evening. We were in the Sea Cadets. We lived for it. We were waiting for the day we could be sixteen and go. Then we got our Deckie Learner's ticket and took it from there. (Stephen Drever - Grimsby)

Most of the kids from my school went to sea. Barcroft Street School was the ground, that and St. John's. Where St. John's Church was there used to be an ordinary school as well. Most of the kids who went there lived in Thorold Street and all round the docks. Like living in Sussex Street you weren't far from the docks. And I wanted to go to sea - always wanted to go to sea - so I went. The old dear created. (Charlie Board - Grimsby)

On my father's side four went to sea. On my mother's side two, including my grandfather. They were both successful Skippers. I always wanted to go fishing. I went pleasure tripping from the age of ten years with my father, who was a Mate with my uncle for twenty odd years. They had a very good relationship. I used to go in the summer holidays, though my dad made me go one year at Christmas just to see what it was like - and I still wanted to go. I don't believe that you go fishing just because your family have done it, I think there's got to be something in the blood. (Ray Jones - Grimsby)

I always wanted to go to sea. I'd been to sea from being twelve. I used to go to sea with my father during the summer holidays. The brother next to me, George, we both went for the first time with my dad and he was seasick all the bloody trip so he never went any more. From that time on until my father was too ill to go to sea I was at sea all the summer time. We was working in the North Sea. Meggying they used to call it in those days. I was just going out in the North Sea and being away about five or six days and going back again. (Charlie Board - Grimsby)

Clive Finn and young Galley Boy, Othello 1956.

Ray Smith's Album.

We got lots of people wanting a start. They was predominantly sons of fishermen anyway. We did used to go round to schools later on in the Fifties and give `em a talk on fishing and how to get the industry going and you'd probably get one or two then. And then of course later on it became necessary that they had to go to school to get a Galley Boy's Certificate before they could go. But in the beginning anybody could go. I was fourteen. You could go to sea when you was fourteen. I went on the 28th of March and I was thirteen and my birthday was on the 14th of April. Well I don't think I really was eligible but it was work. Because my father was a Skipper and it happened that Jack Mawer who was Skipper and Hez Allard, who was the Outside Manager for Consolidated Fisheries, was a big friend of my father's so on their recommendation I went because I would have been fourteen when I got back. (Gordon Cockerill - Grimsby)

My granddad was a fisherman, my dad was a fisherman, I've got four brothers, fishermen. I mean I'm the eldest son, got six lads, and my dad, he came home from a trip when I

was nearly fifteen and he says, "What do you want to be when you leave school?" My dad was one of the top Mates in Northerns out of Grimsby, and I've seen him come home and throw £300 of the old white five pound notes when £5 was a lot of money, and my eyes used to pop out. I said, "I want to be a fisherman, dad." He said, "You`re never going to do what we did." But he knew just the same as all of us knew, if all the sons wanted to go to sea they'd go to sea. Out of all my class I'm the only one who carried on at sea. All the rest wouldn`t have it, because the kids who went for their tickets with me, none of their parents had ever gone to sea. (Ray Smith - Grimsby)

Before you left school we used to have what we called a Careers Officer who used to come to the school and say to everybody in the class, "Stand up. What's your name.? What do you want to do?" And you used to say, "Me name's Tom Jacombe. I'm fourteen and a half. When I'm fifteen I want to go to sea." These career people came from the Education Department and as soon as you said, "I want to be a fisherman," they used to phone up the Trawler Owners and say, "Mr. So and So, I've got you four Deckies here, four Deckie Learners." They used to send you a form to go to the Nautical College. Old Alf Hodson was an old retired Skipper. He learnt me the compass, he learnt me how to splice rope, how to splice wire, how to mend a net, how to make a drop of gravy in the galley, how to make a cup of tea. All the basics. Then when you went to sea you picked things up. (Tom Jacombe - Grimsby)

I'm the only one in the family that's gone to sea. I didn't go until I was twenty five. I worked on the docks until I was twenty five, on the pontoon, filleting, driving, kipper house and things like that. My father and grandfather had a fish curing business and I worked for them. Then I went to sea. My brother in law was a Skipper at the time and I went with him on my first trip. It was in October when I went, and I thought, "What have I let myself in for here?" Halfway through the trip I thought I wouldn't go again but when we came in dock we made a good trip and I went back again and that was it. I finished up doing twenty three years at it. (John Gilby-Grimsby)

I'd done a couple of trips in the North Sea as a Deckie Learner and I'd been violently sick for about six days on the first one, awful experiences, I mean washing about in the North Sea on these open ships, there is no fo'c's'le head on them, they are awful ships, and it was a twopence ha'penny company that we were sailing in as well, and I thought that that was too hard for me. So I went Galley Boy, signed on the Dunsby and that was a wonderful experience because the Cook, he was Maltese, and the first thing he taught me to do (after I had got over the sea sickness again I was still violently sick on the first couple of days) was to bake bread. By the time I was fifteen I had become a very accomplished baker of bread. I could turn a wonderful batch of bread out which meant there was a bit less for the Cook to have to do. You worked as a Galley Boy from something like five or six in the morning until midnight. That was quite regular, though you'd maybe get a chance in the afternoon for a couple of hours, but on average it was a fourteen hour day, but time seemed to pass very quickly because you were always occupied. You'd get

up and bake the bread and you'd do 'Busters' as well. 'Busters' are little buns, and the deckies absolutely loved them, so if you could bake a good 'Buster' you were very popular. The other things that the Galley Boy did was to prepare all the vegetables and cook them, although I'd never previously had any experience of cooking at all, but by the time I'd done a couple of trips to sea I could cook a good dinner and do the roast, the lot. I could certainly fry fish because every meal had fish in it. No matter what else you had you always had fish on the table. And the other things that a Galley Boy would do - you would roll the cigarettes for the crew. I used to sit at night and roll cigarettes for the crew, packing them into tins, ten, fifteen or twenty at a time. I would sew buttons on and do all sorts of things. I would go down and help clear the fo'c's'le up, and things like that. You would always make sure you took the Skipper a pot of tea or whatever he wanted at any time, and the same for the Engineers as well. So you'd do lots of things over and above the Galley Boy's job. (Alec Bovill - Grimsby)

I was born out of wedlock, a bastard, and my first memory was of the workhouse in Wolverhampton. From there, at aged five years, I was put in an orphanage, the Cottage Homes, Wednesfield, Wolverhampton. From there, at aged 11 years, my mother got attached to another man and I came to live in Grimsby. When I was fourteen there was nothing much else in Grimsby other than the sea. I did two or three trips as a Pantry Boy on the "Midnight Sun" Boats - they ran from Immingham to Norway. The job paid twenty five shillings a month and I realised I wasn't going to get rich at that, so then I went into fishing. For the money. It was really hard. I mean, I'd been on a 28,000 tonne liner to a little trawler throwing you about on the sea. I was sea sick for two years. But I stuck it out. There was nowhere else to go. (Bill Hardie - Grimsby)

Galley Boy work was washing up, helping the cook. All you were doing was general dogsbody really. You were there to do the cleaning up, preparing the veg` and that. It was a nothing job but it was half pay so it was a start. Then it was a case of doing so much and then going Deckie Learner, then for your Deckie. You could sign straight on as a Deckie

John Meadows on Bridge.

Learner but I was about eighteen months as a Galley Boy before I did that. My first wages was £3.00 odd, but you never see your wages 'cause they went straight home. At that time the first thing you do with your wages is to treat your family and buy some new clothes. You had all your own sea gear to buy. You took your flock bedding with you. (Graham Howard - Grimsby)

I went in the Merchant Service and I served four years apprenticeship. We docked in North Shields and they said there was a fire on board the ship so you're not going away for another month. I was getting £30 per month as Third Mate and my uncle he was Third Hand on the Lacerta, and I asked him if he could go for a pleasure trip to see how he worked. On the way down to Iceland one of the Deckies was sick and we had to put him ashore in Aberdeen and the crew wanted to get back for a football match, there was a cup match or something, and the Skipper wanted to go as well, so they said, "Look, can't we sign him on as Deckie Learner or something?" So the Skipper approached me and said, "Don, they want to know if you will help them and sign on Deckie Learner." So we went down to Iceland. We were fishing off North East Iceland and it was tough, believe you me, and I got more in the way than anything else. Anyway I came back and landed and for a Deckie Learner, been away for fourteen days and I think I landed 1400 kit or something like that, I got £40 for fourteen days. I signed off the ship as Deckie Learner and was waiting to go back into Merchant Service to join the ship and one night there was a knock at our door. It was a Runner for Bacons and he said he wanted a Deckie for a ship that was out in the river and had put somebody ashore. I said, "I ain't got any fishing gear or nothing." So he said, "I'll buy you a full set of fishing gear and I'll give you £10 in your hand." I said, "Give me the £10." So I went back because my ship still wasn't ready. That's how I started fishing. Because when I came back in dock, you see, I was picking up twice as much as I would have been for being a Third Mate of a 10,000 ton ship with all the responsibility of that. (Don Lister - Grimsby)

It was rough as a Galley Boy. On the Hull City there was a galley pump for fresh water. I'll always remember that it took three or four hundred pumps to get the water to fill the tank, which you had to do two or three times a day for the galley. The lads used to come in off the deck, to wash and the tank used to empty quickly. So I turned the valves off one day. They're a rough lot and the next thing was a clip across the ear and a boot up the backside and "You little so and so." When I was Galley Boy you got two tins of Lyles' treacle for three weeks for twenty men, one for the cabin and one for the ten or twelve men in the mess deck. I hid the treacle one day and there was a chap called Chunky Dales, a big chap. He gave me a right leathering. Little things like that just stick in your mind. It was a rough job. I only did about seven trips then I went Deckie Learner. I can remember my first trip settlings as Galley Boy. £17,777 we made, and I picked up £37.7s.7d. Me mam said to me, "What're you going to do with it?" I said to her, "Five pounds for you." "I don't want five pounds," she said. I said, "There's something for our Jack (he was still at school), and put that in the bank mam." About seven or eight trips later I came staggering in the house and she said, "Where have you been?" I said, "In the Clee Park with the lads." There wasn't much saving done after that. (Ray Jones - Grimsby)

I never ever thought I would ever do anything other than go to sea. It came quite natural and I can remember when I came in from my first trip when I'd been Deckie Learner on the Commander Nasmith. Coming home at two in the morning and going upstairs, me mam and dad were laid in bed and the usual commodity at the side of the bed - the rattling bucket - and you sort of heard the tab end snuffed out in that as you came upstairs, and knew dad at least was awake, and sort of waking them up feeling very grown up and thinking, sort of, "I'm home and I'm a big man now," this being my first

trip, and they sort of said, "Yes, we'll see you in the morning." To them it wasn't so much but I must of thought they should have got up and celebrated. In fact dad probably just rolled over and went to sleep. It was just everyday life, a family just going to work, so you got used to the ten day or three week pattern, with your brothers doing the same. You were something special. You felt marvellous. Big wide bell bottoms. Sixteen years old. I was running about in pubs and all that sort of stuff at fifteen and sixteen. I was the big man. (Alec Bovill - Grimsby)

Me grandfather, all me uncles, me father, was fishermen. He was in the Navy and he got killed in '41. Bombed at Lowestoft. Living with me grandparents - me uncles coming in all the time talking about fishing. I was twelve when I first went to sea with me grandfather as a pleasure tripper. July, when the school was closed and I did another pleasure trip with him when I was thirteen, fourteen. I lived with me grandparents out at New Waltham and Toll Bar School. So I started at the Junior Nautical School, you know, Lock Hill. Old Alf Hodson the teacher he had wires right across the room all to wall and you had to braid your piece of net. And then he'd come and slash a great hole in it like and he'd say, "Mend it." Or learn to cut out first. You bent your needle on there, your twine on there and then you'd go to a mesh, another mesh, then side knots, but your first thing was to cut that out ready for mending and then he'd come and check and if it was right then you'd proceed mending it, but you did splicing ropes, splicing wires, the compass, everything you needed to go as a starter. You wasn't allowed to go to sea then unless you could. Some of the fellers they'd go to sea all their lives and they can't splice wire. I could do it when I was fifteen.

I started in the Hargood with Uncle Tom Evans. I did one trip there because that ship was going to stop to be changed from a coal burner to an oil burner, but we was full up with fish and I wasn't quite fifteen then. Not hours on the deck, days on the deck. Couple of days or so - no sleep. I can remember going down the port side, just leaning against the casing, the outside of the engine room, and just sobbing my eyes out. I thought,

"Never again." This is my first trip working and never again. I was so determined at the end of that trip that I was going to sign off. I got in the queue at Derwent Trawlers, and you all queued up to this little wicket, and I always remember this guy in front of me, Sammy Reed. He'd just done a trip on a North Sea ship, just out the Humber for ten or twelve days. You used to have a huge piece of paper and there was all what you had to come for a start and then your deductions and Whitehead said, "That leaves you with the sum of one shilling." He just grinned at this Sammy Reed. Well Sam just pulled him through the hatch and he said, "Don't laugh at me you so and so. I've worked twelve days for that shilling," and he just put it in the lifeboat box. That made me more convinced that, "Right, I'm out of this job like." But when I went for my settling I picked up £2 5s a week - that went to me mother - and I picked up £28. I was a millionaire - well it felt like one. First trip. That was a fortune in 1949. I was able to go and pay for all me sea gear, a new suit, shoes, all sorts of things, take me mother out for a meal and put money in the bank. On £28 and I thought, "God all this money." I couldn't earn that ashore so I thought, "Well right, I'm going back but my target is the Bridge." No way was I going to stick the deck. (John Meadows - Grimsby)

I am from Grimsby but not from a fishing family. It was a case of going to make some money. That was the original thing. I was working ashore. I'd been married three months before I first went fishing, and it went on from there. I went as Galley Boy on the Ross Kelvin, in September 1961, with Snowy Chapman. I can remember being sea sick for some time, and I spent most of the time helping the Cook in the galley. I did get down the fish room a few times when they had quite a bit of fish on the deck, chopping ice and doing stuff like that. Learning what to do on deck was a matter of watching, asking questions and just mucking in. They used to take the Mickey as well. That's an old fisherman's trait. You would put a pair of boots on and find coal in them, or grease, or you'd put your gloves on and find treacle or sugar in them, things like that - going down the Bridge for 'a long weight' or going on the Bridge and asking the skipper for 'a sky hook'. I was away at sea for about seventeen to eighteen days that first trip. I can't remember what I was paid. I was

undecided on the way back whether or not to continue, but it's strange that, when you come in the river and are getting up towards the dock tower and you think, "Oh, I'll give it another go." (John Pickett - Grimsby)

I started at the Cordage as a fourteen year old. When I came nearly sixteen I decided to pack it up and go to sea. My mother didn't want us to go to sea. My father didn't want my eldest brother to go to sea. He said it was treacherous. He said you could go over the side. I went Galley Boy for two or three trips, that was all, then I went Deckie Learner in 1939, in the Ampulla with a Skipper called Harold Brennan. Brilliant Skipper he was. I was sick as anything that first trip as Galley Boy. You tried to get on with it. You still had to work. You had to do all the cleaning, help the cook with the potatoes and all things like that. Clean the mess deck up, lay the plates out for the meals for the crew, depending on how she was rolling, put the battens in place, so they didn't roll about. All things like that. That was your job and I was feeling sick most of the trip. It was a horrible feeling. Food tended to set you off. They used to give you dry biscuits for sea sickness. Didn't drink tea because it would all come up again. They'd make you eat dry biscuits. It used to work. (Roly Webb - Grimsby)

When I was on the Nellis that first twelve month some nights when the weather wasn't too bad when they was fishing - I mean there wasn't no washing machines then - all the fish had to be washed by hand and chucked down the fish room. After tea when I'd done my jobs, washed up, and things like that I used to go on the deck, two or three hours, help 'em washing the fish and chucking it down the fish room and stamping on it. Borrow a pair of big boots, thigh boots. I used to get into trouble because sometimes I used to stay up there on the deck until about one or two in the morning and the Cook used to call me at half five. He used to call me and when he'd gone into the galley I used to go to sleep again and he'd say, "You've been on that deck again haven't you? Wait until you're proper on the deck. Do your job here." (Les Bowden - Grimsby)

When I left school at fifteen you used go round the offices and if there was any deep water ships landing go to their offices and see the Runner. He used to be outside, like a superintendent. "Oh. Is there any changes?" And he used to say, "No. Not today, son." You'd go round them offices what was landing and then if you got a job you got a job. I kept going round and I went down to the Premier Steam Fishing Company and the Runner was Owen Davidson. I knocked on his door. "Is there any changes?" He went, "Have you been to sea before, son?" I said, "Yeah." He said, "What ship?" and I said, "The Valafell." It was only because a mate of mine his uncle was Skipper of it. That was the only thing I knew like. He said, "Who's the Skipper?" I said, "Billy Hardie," which was the name like. He said, "What's he like then?" I said, "Oh, big fat bloke, big fat bloke." "All right," he says, "Give us a look in the morning." So the next day I went down. He says, "Yes. We've got a job for you. Galley Boy of the Nellis. She's going away tomorrow. Sign here. Sign on. Pound Sub." And he said, "You clean this and you do the brasses here and you do this and do that." I said, "Yeah, yeah." And he said, "Well you know that don't you with being on the Valafell with Billy Hardie?" I said, "Oh yes." He says, "Oh and by the way, Billy Hardie isn't a great big fat bloke." Which he wasn't. He was only a slim chap. I went and signed on, and told me mam. "You haven't." I said, "I have, I have. I've signed on." "Oh heck." I packed my gear up and went down in the morning. Early morning it was. About three in the morning we was sailing. I went on it and I never had a clue what to do. I went on and the first bloke who ever spoke to me on a trawler was Cyril Cole. He was a Fireman and I sat down in the little poky cabin and he said, "What are you son?" I said, "I'm Galley Boy". "Oh. Right. Your bunk's there." It was a little thing and you pulled the doors back. Like a bread locker it was. He said, "You get your bed in there. That's where you sleep." We went away for Christmas and New Year. I always remember I was sea sick. Oh it's horrible. It really is. You just feel like dying. Any fisherman will tell you. Anybody who's been seasick will say it's worse than any feeling. 'Cos you're just sick and sick and sick. They keep saying, "Get some of this down you." But you can't. I remember the day that was the first time when I never felt sick. When we came in the river we dropped the anchor. I was blackleading the stove. Sometimes the tug used to come alongside and say, "Is anyone going ashore?" 'Cos we had to

wait maybe five or six hours for the gates to open. I was all mucky. The tug came alongside and apparently one of the crew members his relation or brother had hung himself on a North Sea trawler - an Engineer. He'd hung himself. And they'd fetched his body back in the river. And they was waiting for the tide. Anyway they come and told him so he was going off on the tug ashore. So the mate says, "Do you want to go ashore with him?" I was all black and mucky. "Go on. The tug's going now. Get your bag." I just banged everything in and off and I come home just as I was, like. My mother said, "What the heck?" I said, "Oh you're all right. Here's your cigarettes. I've fetched you some." She said, "Oh lovely."

I went down the next day to settle. The Galley Boys used to get half poundage or summat, but you used to get down there a bit early. You'd get your money and then you'd stand at the door and when the lads used to come up and get their money - if you'd been a good lad and you'd made the tea for them and things like that - then they used to treat you. "Here you are son." A pound here, each one, and maybe the Skipper'd give you two or three quid. And that's what you used to do.

We'd made a real good trip we did. I picked up eighteen pound something. That was a lot of money. I always remember the cashier, they called him Ernie. "Now look son," he says when I went to the wicket to get my money, "This is a lot of money this. Do you want me to keep some 'til next trip?" "No. I'm all right." He counted it out. Do you remember them big white fivers? They'd be about that big. He counted three of these out and a load of brass and I went home and said to me mam, "Here you are." She went, "What's this?" "That's yours". She said, "You want me to keep all this." I said, "Yes, yes."

I had three sisters younger than me. Me mam couldn't afford any new bikes or anything. Well there used to be a shop on the corner of Humber Street - Wolves and Stamps they called it - sold bikes and prams. I said, "Come on." We went there. She'd always wanted a bike, my sister, and we're looking in the window like at the three wheeled bikes. I said, "Right. Which one do you want?" 'Cos I think they was only about £3 or £4 then. She said, "Well I like that one." "Right. Come on then." She said, "You can't." Even though young as she was she knew, she didn't really think she could have it.....I can't, I can't have that." I said, "Come on," and I went in and I said, "I'll have that bike out the window, please." The bloke didn't half look at me. I got the bike and I got my other sister a big tea set, and I bought me other sister a great big dolly. A lovely thing. (Les Bowden - Grimsby)

The only time you got any money you had to stand outside the office and it was working practice among the men that they used to give you, as the Galley Boy, half a crown for duties that you'd done at sea. I think I walked off with something like £1.20 and I went straight to the tailors and brought myself a three piece suit. It was an ordinary suit with a waistcoat. I went straight in the pub, then to the Gaiety where I was the envy of all the girls 'cos I was a fisherman. That's how fishing was. (Tom Jacombe - Grimsby)

When you all settled up you stood there at the Paying Out Office - you got there first because the poundage you got was a quarter of the Deckie's rate. So the Deckies in those days got £6 to the £1000 and the Galley Boy got £1.50 to the £1000. As ships, like the Dunsby, would average £4000 - £6000, because it was about that time that the first trip came to £10,000 (that was the Sletness), so that's how much you were earning. But of course, having done all these jobs for the crew during the trip they would all drop you ten bob each, and the Engineer would give you a pound, the Mate would give you a couple of pound, but I always got £5 off the Skipper. I would often finish up with more money than the Deckie. (Alec Bovill - Grimsby)

I used to look up to the Bridge and I used to think, "There's only one bloke got a good job aboard here and that's the Skipper. So I think I'll have some of that". (Peter Newby - Grimsby)

I was ambitious to go to sea, to go on trawlers. Once I got to sea I worked my way up from Deckie Learner. There were no Galley Boys when I first started in the war - the lowest grade was a Deckie Learner. Then I went off to do National Service, then come back and worked my way up. I

wanted to wear a glass sou'wester. You don't get wet on the Bridge - the Bridge is protected from the water. When I was on the deck and the sea was rolling you all over I used to look up and see him, the Skipper, up there on the Bridge. I decided that's where I wanted to be. That's the best job. (Jack Tripp - Hull)

You did four year actually on the deck, as Deckie Learner, Deckhand - and then you go for your Mate's Ticket. And that consisted in them days - its longer now - but in them days it was about three/four months of schooling to get your Mate's Ticket and then you had to sail as Mate for one year actually on the deck employed as Mate, signed on the Log Book as Mate, for one year and then you could go for your Skipper's Ticket, which was another three or four months, all depending on how brainy you was. Three or four months to get your Ticket. Once you got your Skipper's Ticket you would just hope. Hope for a ship. But usually we stopped in the same firm. I went Deckhand, Third Hand, Mate and Skipper in the same firm. That was Northerns. That was about the top share firm in Grimsby at that particular time. They had all the best ships, the biggest ships. (George Mussell - Grimsby)

Chapter 3

Business in Great Waters

To casual observers, holidaymakers, painters, photographers, and other landlubbers, fishing is romantic and its practitioners depart on a great adventure. Yet deep sea fishing was an industry organised on capitalist lines, not a playground for the potterer or the self-employed. The five to six hundred vessels engaged in the industry were major investments, particularly the two hundred or so over 140 feet long and specifically designed for long trips to distant waters.

So fishermen were departing to do a job made different by the fact that they did it at sea and were confined to their floating factory not just during working hours but for three weeks. They changed around often; only a quarter sailed on the same vessel all year, half changed ship between one and three times. Their workplace was a 600/700 tonne vessel tossed on the high seas. They usually set off to work at night. Drunk or sober, dragooned or volunteer, escaping home or missing it, full crews of twenty-five on the freezers, twenty on the bigger wet fish trawlers, and fifteen on the "middle water" vessels which also battled up to Iceland and the Faroes, left the Trawlertowns night after night to a task which was a unique combination of boring routine, physical exhaustion and great danger. They averaged perhaps twenty days a trip including three to five days of travel to the distant grounds, a week or more of hectic fishing with long hours working on exposed decks then home, repairing the gear as they went, to market a catch which averaged around 80 ten stone kits per day at sea.

When the ship sailed then we used to have to go round and collect the crew - if it was early morning tides we used to go round and knock on the doors and get them up and very often we would find that they hadn't arrived home and we had

to wonder whereabouts in the town we might find them. In them days it was called the Klondike. There was houses of ill repute and what have you and it was a case of putting it in your mind and saying, "I wonder whether Bill Smith's with Mavis tonight," or vice versa and of course we had to go round. We very often knocked at the wrong door and found out that the husband was home and we didn't know that. (Gordon Cockerill - Grimsby)

The crews lived in different parts of the town. They used to say, "Would you like to be picked up in a taxi?" The taxi would come, knock on the door and you would go down to the dock. The Runner would be there with a list of names and as you got on the ship he would just tick you off. If there was no problems on the ship the Runner would stand at the lock pits as you sailed out of dock. When you got out of sight he would stick two fingers up and say, "That's it." But that's a Runner's life. I suppose they had to be bad. (Tom Jacombe - Grimsby)

Many times we've had to drag 'em out the bed and they've been absolutely out of this world, drunk as a lord, not only during the night but many a time when the tide time was, from when the pub was open. And we used to stand on the Humber corner, that was a favourite haunt of ours, and the majority of them used to come down there before they used to go on the North Wall and it was a case of going in and dragging them out and, "I'm not coming unless you buy me a quarter bottle of rum" and, "I want a rum to take with me." And I used to go in and see the old landlord - Bob Stratford was landlord in the heyday there and we would buy them a quarter bottle of rum and kid them on and carry 'em down, bundle them in the taxi and we used to virtually carry 'em aboard the ship. And they would wake up twelve hours later and they would be on the high seas. It wasn't press ganged. They'd signed the Articles. It was just that they was in dock for such a short time. (Gordon Cockerill - Grimsby)

I never missed a ship, never. I daren't anyway. If I'd missed a ship my father would have killed me. He said, "Sign off by all means, but don't just not go." The worst thing you could do was not go. You did get the odd few idiots in the pub who would say, "I'm not going," but most of them you could talk them out of it. A few idiots did jump ship. I was in my early teens and we went across to Hull me and a friend of mine, a barrow boy on the docks. He said he wanted to go to sea so I got him signed on the Hull City which is a ship I was in. But he didn't like it. Anyhow, we came in dock and he suggested we go across to Hull, we did and went to the Green Dragon. We missed the ferry and we were due to sail at about 5.00am the next morning. It was panic stations. We got a taxi to take us all the way round. When I got home my dad was sitting up. He paid the taxi, about £6.00 which was a lot of money in them days. My bag was packed and he said, "It's a good job you made it lad." He'd have never forgiven me if I'd missed my boat. He was like that, my dad. (Ray Jones - Grimsby)

I've known the time I've gone to a dinner and dance at the Winter Gardens and left there at 1 o'clock in the morning, and the taxi's been picking you up at two to go to sea. You'd come home and take your monkey suit off at one o'clock in the morning and be climbing in the taxi to go to sea within the hour. We had to take our own mattress - talk about pick up your bed and walk! (John Gilby - Grimsby)

You used to just go and sign on your ship, get your stores chit. You're supposed to be aboard the ship two hours before she sails, but usually it was two hours after she was going to sail by the time we got down there. Go to the stores, get your gear, go aboard the ship, let go with your head ropes and stern, out the dock, put your life lines up, man ropes up, finish your party off, have a good booze up for the day and then the next day you're settling down to work. You didn't know whether you was going to Iceland, Greenland, Bear Island, White Sea or what. Then it was supposed to be a secret to the Skipper - why nobody knows to this day. You had an idea, it was a guess, but nobody ever used to think of saying to him, "Where are we going?" He'd say, "What the fucking hell's it got to do with you?" Even though you were sailing on the ship it had nothing to do with you where you were fishing. The Skippers didn't like you asking. (George Brown - Hull)

On board entertainment.

You used to take some booze out with you. In the old boats, to Iceland, it used to take you three days to get there. The first day you're dying anyway after being out the night before. That first day you'd just start coming round. You'd share a few cans, if somebody's got half a bottle you'd have a dram of that. Then the second day you get the nets ready and everything and you're fit as anything then. (Tom Bagnell - Fleetwood)

Steaming down to the grounds you worked about an eight hour day, but the little bit in the middle was an eighteen hour a day job. You wasn't working fish all the time. If you were in what you call rough ground you might get all the fish gutted and put away in an hour, then you had two hours off. But when you had heavy fishing you did your full eighteen hours. Sometimes in bad ground, every time you hauled you might have to change the trawl, shoot away again, get the fish out the way and then you had the trawl to mend and one thing and another. Part of your time would be taken up gutting and the other part mending,. You can still work an eighteen hour day when you're doing a lot of mending. The Skipper's on the deck during this time because when you change the trawl, if your trawl was split, all you do is take the trawl off, put another one there, shoot away. He's up in the wheel house. Odd times, you know, if you wanted to change the trawl quick he'd come down and give a hand on the deck. Sometimes he'd probably dodge up to the other end of the tow while you was changing gear, and he would probably steam the ship up to the other end already for shooting again. If he thought there was some better fishing two or three mile away he would steam somewhere while you was changing the trawl over. (John Gilby - Grimsby)

Steaming down there was three watches, Mate, Third Hand and, invariably, a Deckie's watch - a bloke capable of taking a watch under the supervision of the Captain. He'd oversee you, pop out on the deck to check everything was all right, but there always had to be a Deckie who was quite genned up on navigation, a sensible chap who knew the 'rules of the road'. Then you had what you called 'Day Men.' Three or maybe six 'Day Men' who worked from half seven to maybe four in the afternoon, getting the gear ready. But once

you got fishing it was the watches then. In later years you worked eighteen and six. With my uncle it was sixteen and four when we first worked a watch. You'd shot the gear and were towing, and if there was nothing to do there'd be a watch on, three men up, then you'd tow for an hour or two. A good Skipper would tell you how long you was going to tow. Some Skippers you could ask, some you daren't ask, just daren't - he'd say, "Now," just "Bring down now." But a reasonable Skipper would give you ten minutes or quarter on an hour for a drink, then you'd all go to your proper stations. You'd have a Winchman, a Mate, two men on the fore door, two men aft, men amidships to work the ropes, wires, things like that. Everybody got stuck in. You had fish room men, the Mate and a Trimmer who'd trim the ice. The fish room man was obviously responsible for the fish when the Mate was relieving the Skipper up on the Bridge, and that was quite a responsible job when all said and done, if the fish was turned out wrong it was the Mate who took it in the neck. You would haul, put your fish on the deck, when the cod ends came up you tie the cod ends again and you'd shoot away again. Once you got towing again you'd be gutting the fish. You'd generally tow for two or two and a half hours, then you'd haul again. If it was a big haul we wouldn't have finished gutting before the next load, and what the Captain would sing out was maybe, "Boot 'em from forward to aft," and you'd lift the wooden deck boards up and kick 'em all aft because that's where you'd first start gutting again. Then you'd put the fresher fish further forward. So the decks'd be covered in fish guts, there'd be fish all over the place, port, starboard side, in the middle where the washer used to be etc., but eventually there'd come a time when he was catching so much fish he'd just have to lay and gut. Get everything away and clean up, then start again. (Ray Jones - Grimsby)

It was a recognised thing that you worked eighteen hours and you had six hours off, but in those six hours you had a meal at the beginning and you had a meal at the end. So you're talking twenty minutes for your dinner, twenty minutes for your tea. You're talking four/five hours sleep a day. I've seen people, especially when it's been cold - and the black frost and the cold gets to you - and as soon as you sit in the mess deck having your dinner and it's nice and warm, the heat gets to you and I've seen people fall asleep straight into their dinner. That's true. You tell people ashore about that and they wouldn't know what you were talking about. If fishing got heavy the Skipper used to shout out of the Bridge window. "Stop the watch below". Say you had been looking forward to going to bed at midnight and he used to shout that, you couldn't go. So that was your six hours gone and you had to go right round the clock again before it was your turn again. So that's three days and you perhaps never got any sleep until the fish slacked off a little bit, or the skipper got too tired, then he used to say, "Right son, go to bed for a couple of hours." I actually laid in my bed with exactly the gear I'd been working in - me frock and me sou'wester and me boots. I've been that tired I've just collapsed in me bunk and you seem to just shut your eyes and the next minute somebody's shaking you saying, "Come on son, start again." You used to think, "Christ."

Down in the Fish room

Me hands have been that sore with welts, cuts and you name it I've had it on my hands, and it was a recognised thing before you started work you used to have to pee on your hands to free 'em because your hands was that sore. I don't suppose there's a fisherman ever gone to sea who's never done that. You had to do it. That was the only way you could get movement in your fingers. There was no such thing as saying, "Oh, I want to go to the doctors 'cause I've got a

headache, I've got this, I've got that." There wasn't anything like that aboard a trawler. Didn't matter if you had whatever you had. You still had to turn out. If you never turned out to start your work correct on the dot you was sacked. (Tom Jacombe - Grimsby)

When I was a Skipper we used to work eighteen and six. We got more civilised. If, say, we was towing three hours and we never had a lot of fish and it only took an hour to clear all the fish there was two hours gash time before you hauled again. Sometimes if it was light fishing the lads got quite a lot of sleep but then you weren't getting no money were you? Because you weren't catching no fish. So you was sleeping and not earning'owt. But numerous times and everybody's done it trawling you pray for no fish so you could get a little nap, an hour's sleep. (George Mussell - Grimsby)

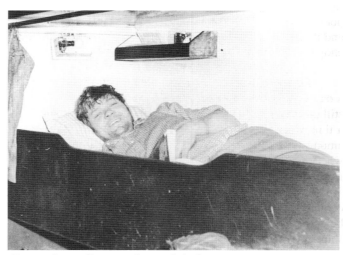

Start of a well earned watch below.
Copyright: Grimsby Evening Telegraph.

All the ice was in pounds forward and the ice had to be cracked, chopped and thrown aft, so you could put it on your fish. When you got to wherever you were fishing it used to be rock solid and you had to crack it with axes, chop it then shovel it aft. The fish room man put the fish away spread with the chopped up ice. The Mate used to treat him for that because the condition of the fish was the Mate's responsibility. He would get sacked if he let the fish deteriorate. So a good fish room man was important and he did all right. (George Waudby - Hull)

The fish room was all in separate pounds boarded off or sheeted down with aluminium with your boards in them. Every so often there was a little board, a shelf was what they called it, with ice and fish in between. So you put the boards on the next one up and you did the same again, ice all on it, fish on it, chucked some ice on the heads, cos that's where the gills is, to keep them good, and put your boards on top of them again. And that's what you did all through your trip. You sometimes had a thousand kit of shelfers, when it's shelved with boards and ice all the time. Your normal fish when it was bulked you went to about fifty kit of fish, or maybe twenty five kit, and you put your shelf across. That preserved your fish from being crushed by too much weight of fish in the pounds. And that was your fish room. You had two Trimmers and if one of them was below - they used to send one down to chop the ice. (Roly Webb - Grimsby)

In those days the lads could be working eighteen hours a day with six hours sleep which is hard work when they're still on the deck. Especially up at Iceland and Norway. Many a time when we fished Iceland up at the North Cape you're amongst the ice and you can imagine the lads on the deck when you're iced up. They're gutting fish and the fish is nearly frozen before they can get round to gutting some of it. We've towed a few ships out of the ice because we were big enough. When you're fishing in the ice and you roll in your bunk for a sleep you can hear the ice hitting on the side of the ship. You get used to it but the first few times its murder trying to get to sleep because you think the devil's coming through the side. (Colin Donald - Grimsby)

In those days the average trip was three weeks. But in the summertime there'd be fine weather and plenty of fish at Iceland. I've been thirteen days dock to dock. I think the record trip was about eleven days. Of course you could also be away twenty four if it was slack fishing. All depended on the fishing and the weather. In the summer you was always in with the chance of making short trips because you had the weather. In the winter I would say the average trip was twenty four days. A long while wasn't it? (George Mussell - Grimsby)

On the way back you'd perhaps be half a day squaring the decks up and then perhaps you would get a day off - what we used to call a rest day - and then you had to think about scrubbing the ship, making it presentable. You can imagine what a trawler was like after three weeks at sea. You had to start washing walls, scrubbing your berth, making your berth presentable. Every part of that ship was scrubbed from one end to the other. Many a time I've even known a Skipper get the sack because the ship wasn't up to the Owner's satisfaction. They used to stand on the lock pits and say, "I'll see you when you get to the number one berth." That was a sign that they didn't like the appearance of that trawler. You could guarantee the next trip there'd be a different Skipper. (Tom Jacombe - Grimsby)

On the way home it wasn't so bad because you had time to unwind. If, say, you was at White Sea, you was five days steaming home. Then you were just doing normal watches, what we used to call steaming watches. You'd go on about dinnertime 'til teatime and then you never went on again while the next morning. You used to have about twelve hours off, 'cos there was not much to do. You was all cleaning the ship and getting the gear ready for the next trip. You might do that for five days steam. So you got plenty of sleep coming home. (George Mussell - Grimsby)

When you're towing a trawl you don't go full speed. It's only when you're coming home. In fact, the worst part of the trip for a Chief Engineer is coming home. You'd think it would be the good part, but they always used to leave barely enough time to catch the tide for the market. If they were having bad weather they'd try and ease it on a bit. You were always flogging it and that's when the trouble can start. We had a three bladed propeller on that Ross Revenge. It was what they call a variable pitch propeller. The engine was a fixed speed but how we altered the speed of the ship was by the propeller, the various pitches on it. We were about twenty four hours from home, and we clouted something and knocked a blade off. You couldn't stand a cup of tea down on the messdeck on the tables because it was vibrating that much. That ship it had to go in the dry dock in Immingham to clean the bottom. It was too big for the slipways in Grimsby. We brought the ship in, landed and it came back to the quay opposite Ross's office, which is Tom Sleights now. There was just a skeleton crew, the Skipper, myself and what they used to call 'the Steamers.' They used to start the ships up in the morning - ex Chief Engineers. When the ship started they could see the vibration and they called down on the air to the Skipper to tell him not to run it over half speed and go as slow as possible. They didn't want to shake the rest off . The propellers were massive, each blade, and all that was left on it was the boss. Took the lot off. We used to carry a spare propeller so they put that on but it must have been a fair old clout. (Colin Donald - Grimsby)

When I first started fishing it was a recognised thing, especially Bear Island, White Sea, where you could go down and fill one of the old Northern boats, Northern Spray, Northern Duke, in about a week. I'm talking about 4,000 kits. It was a regular occurrence where there was seven or eight deep water ships, all from the same place, landing on the same day - the market was flooded. In them days it was the regular thing where there was up to forty or fifty North Sea ships landing every day of the week. There was a glut of fish. I always used to think to meself when I was laid in bed - being at sea for three weeks - I used to pray for rain because I used to think that if it rains the market will jump. But if the sun comes out and nobody wants fish you've just worked three weeks for nothing, and I mean nothing. There wasn't any guaranteed fall back. It was just a case of you owe me, give me it. If you was earning a lot of money you would come in dock and you would land on a Monday. You'd dock Sunday and land on Monday. You'd have a day free and then you would sail - so you're talking about two days actually. In the North Sea ships you used to come in, land, and go away the very next day. You'd have about eighteen hours perhaps in the dock and then you was away. (Tom Jacombe - Grimsby)

They would always want to try to land Monday, Tuesday, Wednesday - Thursday wasn't so good. All aiming for show day which was the Wednesday. But, of course, they couldn't all land. One of the big problems we had running ships which I haven't touched on was the availability of landing. There was a certain Lumper force and there was rules - shortest trip got its labour allocated first. There were special complicated rules. There were complicated landing arrangements - if you weren't careful you could be 'shot out' for labour as it was called and have to land the next day. To keep your fleet in tune with the landing requirements was a problem. In about 1970, or a little later I think, three people were responsible for setting up (the principal people were Vernon Green of Boston, Nigel Marsden of Consolidated and myself) a Planned Landings Committee and we used to have various people responsible, whoever was the designated representative. We used to meet every day at two o'clock and try and sort it out and we did it very well. To everybody's surprise it worked very well. The shortest trip had priority for labour. This was done to maximise quality. I don't think they had the same system in Hull, so if you had gone to Iceland and you'd made a fairly quick trip, seventeen days to landing, you would be allocated labour before somebody who was nineteen days and so on. (John Butt - Grimsby)

In them days you always started landing at midnight. No matter how much fish you had in you could settle about ten or eleven o'clock the next morning. You was all squared up and everything. You relaxed off the ship, you had a few beers. Say we docked at ten o'clock, well the pubs were shut in them days, but say you docked at eight you'd have a couple of beers. In them days the Deckhand got a wage. He got that no matter what you made, he used to get his wage. Then for every thousand pound the ship made the Deckhand used to get £6, the Bosun £12, Deckie Learner only half, he used to get £3, half pay. Twice as much work and half pay. But the Skipper he used to be on about £50 to a thousand. So a Deckie's on £6 and a Skipper's on £50. I think the Mate was on about £35. That was the same when we packed up actually. I think they got a decent wage when we finished in them days, I think they got about £30 a week. That was there every week and I think it went up to about £12 for every thousand. Bosuns always used to get double that. Us Skippers we used to get £50 a thousand, but then if we made a good trip we used to be on a bonus. So we was on good money, very good money at times. You take a Deckie on £6 to the thousand and a Skipper on £50 and there's a lot of difference. But if you're in charge you're always paid more. You also had the responsibility if you came in with no fish. You got the sack didn't you? (George Mussell - Grimsby)

The first thing that I had to do in the day of course was to be on the market to look round the trip, laid out in squares of 250 or 300 kits each. Took a lot of space on the market and the Mate always had to be down and we used to go round the trip together. I had to say whether it was satisfactory or whether it wasn't, and the poor chap and his crew had been washed about for twenty one days and I had been sitting in a warm office but that was the job. Then the fish was sold, and we use to go for breakfast in the Northern Trawlers' canteen, followed by our morning conference which started at half past nine every morning where we used to go through the requisitions and the engineering report of the ship's performance with the Superintendent Engineer. Then mid-morning we would be given a Sale Note which set out what the trip had made, what the fish had made and then the rest of the morning was taken up interviewing Skippers who'd landed, discussing the trip and where I thought we should go the next trip and so on. (John Butt - Grimsby)

Chapter 4
It Takes All Sorts to Make a Trip

Fishing was a team effort. Fishermen mostly came from the same background in what used to be called the "rough" but also the "respectable" working class. At sea they depended on each other and worked hard together for their common purpose well before Volvo discovered the benefits of workplace teams. Fishing's teams were small, fifteen to thirty depending on the size of the vessel, tight-knit and organised in a rigid hierarchy in which everyone knew their position, their role, and their job, and got on with it with little instruction and less coercion. Authority was earned not conferred, asserted through skill and strength, and dependent on neither uniform nor qualifications but respect.

The pinnacle of the hierarchy was the Skipper, absolute master of his ship, and often at a young age, for their average age was only forty-two. The Skipper was the man on whose skill, knowledge of the grounds and willingness to take risks everyone on board depended, as indeed did his own earnings geared largely to the value of the catch. Under him came the Mate and Bosun, each in their independent little spheres, the mechanicals, Chief and Second Engineer; two Firemen in the coal burners; the Radio Operator and, all important though uncertificated, the Cook and his Galley Boy. Most of these ate and lived separately from the deck crew, headed by the Third Hand, a human resources manager in more dignified settings. He organised eight or more hands working in shifts, plus the Deckie Learner, learning on the job.

Each vessel was a team, a community, a male preserve, and a man's world, rather like the army except that all were working together for a simple common purpose: to catch the maximum amount of fish in order to make as much money as possible, and so to get home quickly and

profitably. Problems of survival, injury, health, accommodation, even morale, were all secondary to that common purpose of maximising the money.

I was coming home and we were reaving a set of bobbins and I caught my hand in the winch, so I couldn't go fishing no more. I lost my little finger. They put me ashore in Norway, and when I came home I went to the Firing School and you learned about how to change burners, boilers and things like that. It was for about three weeks to a month. Then you got your Firing Ticket, then you went firing. St. Norman - that was the ship I had my accident in. That stopped me being able to gut. Still, firing meant that I was still at sea. Mind it was a bit better because you didn't have to go on the deck. You got the same money as a Deckie. A Deckie you'd maybe get a day off steaming but you didn't in the engine room, six on six off until you got home. You had a Chief, Second and two Firemen. They were just small ships at that time. When they turned to diesel you started getting your big ships. It wasn't hard work. Just very uncomfortable. The stoke hole was red hot. Only a little cramped space, and you had to be battened down all the time for bad weather, nearly always battened down. We used to be roasting sometimes. So we stripped off even in the winter. Mind we did used to get a bit of ice down in the engine room in the winter. I've seen the galley iced up, even with the fire going. You had to chip the ice off in order to cook, it was freezing that hard. (George Waudby - Hull)

Carmichael, the drunkard, was the finest Fireman out of Grimsby. Records would say he's been in court for drunkenness and vagrancy three hundred times or whatever. There were some ships would probably burn ten ton a day but there were some ships would burn 15 or 20 ton a day and that was a lot of work. But Carmichael was the finest fireman. It wasn't just a case of throwing coal on the fire, it was a case of raking and making sure in the old fire place that your bars were clean so your ash could get underneath it, and the more flame you got the more power the ship got, but Carmichael could work any ship possible. His only trouble was you couldn't get him to sea. I mean he was noted for it. We had a ship called the Hekla and she was a twenty ton a dayer and it would kill firemen. They just couldn't cope with it. Yet he could go on there and it would be a toy to him. But we just never signed him on because we knew he wouldn't turn up. I mean I've took Carmichael up to North Shields and to Aberdeen when a fireman has been ill to replace him. In them days I was always going up to North Shields and to Aberdeen where the ship had put in because of an accident and taking a replacement crew member up. It was a case of knowing that I'd got him because he was in the car with me and as sad as it may seem I had to get him drunk to get him in the car to kid him up to go up there. I mean, you get driving up to Shields and Aberdeen with a drunk in the back of the car, giving all this, it was a bit horrendous at times but we had this to do to get the ship to sea. I didn't want the ship to come back to Grimsby because of the cost of bringing it back in coal and dock dues, plus the fact when it got back to Grimsby the crew would probably jump it anyway. So it was easier and quicker and cheaper for me to take a car and to go. (Gordon Cockerill - Grimsby)

At that time we kept the coal in the fish room, so that you could do twenty one or a twenty three day trip. That's about all you could do. So if the fishing was slack you'd try and lay up. If you were on the West Side where you go for the flats, the plaice, you tried to keep going 'cause you could make a trip with a few plaice. It was just before Christmas, 1962, and we hadn't been making a great deal of money. The money stakes at home was a bit short and it was coming up to Christmas, and we were away about sixteen or seventeen days. There was nothing in the kitty. We were all desperate. I'd gone up to the Skipper, Bill Spearpoint, because I'd taken stock of the coal and told him we were on the 'gypsy's warning', twenty four hours fishing coal left - and we'd caught nothing. He said, "Aye, all right". Well that night we pulled over 220 kit of plaice. He said, "It's terrible that we've got to leave it now. One more night like that and we'd have cracked a bundle". I said, "Oh go on, let's do another night and we might just scrape home with the coal situation". So we fished again for another night, and it was another buster night for the plaice. I was thinking that the kids would get plenty in their Christmas stockings this year after all.

So we steamed home and of course the weather was perverse and put a gale of wind on our bows and there was nothing we could do about it. So when we was getting towards the West Coast of Scotland I told the Skipper that we would have to go in and get coal. We went into Oban and took on about thirty ton of coal, and the Skipper told me he would back me about saying that we'd have enought coal to get home to stay that extra twenty four hours. When we got into the dock the Manager sent for me and told me I was in trouble. I didn't care. I'd got me kids' money in. We sold the trip off and we made the highest trip that had ever been made in Fleetwood. And we were an old, 1930's coal burner, and we'd outdone all these fancy new diesel ships. (Chris Fisher - Fleetwood)

There were some very very good cooks but they were very few and far between. It wasn't the case that we would send anybody. We would pick the best out. We would know that Joe Smith was a good cook or a bad cook by the times that he'd signed on ships and got the sack. Everybody can't be wrong. We would try to pick the best out because at the end of the day it wasn't just a case of getting your ship away it was making it successful and a cook was like a woman with a husband - the way to look after her husband is through his stomach and it was the same with them, because if they hadn't got a good cook and they hadn't got good food, in fairness, they wouldn't be able to do the work as well. They was very very well looked after, quite truthfully. They were better looked after than they were at home, possibly because they weren't sober enough when they were at home to have a meal. But no, they didn't go short of much. They didn't have the cream cakes, but then again I don't think a workman particularly wants them, but they had good meat. There was always fresh fish daily when they were on the fishing grounds. There was always a good pan of "shackles". It was a soup, and it was a case that when everything was cooked and anything that was left it used to go in the pan of shackles, so it was there to thicken it up. Most cooks, whether they were bad cooks or not, would always do a pan of shackles. But you wanted a cook that could make good bread. The most important thing aboard the ship was having a good batch of bread. (Gordon Cockerill - Grimsby)

There had to be a routine and the routine was different for each type of ship. As a Cook you used to get up at 4.30 or 5.00 am. You'd have a wash first. Cooks had to be clean. Deckies didn't bother washing. You'd go down the cabin and get the tables ready for breakfast. Go in the galley. Going out of dock, in some firms, you got bacon. You'd put a pan on for the 'beargoo' (porridge). They used to have different names for different things at sea. Like, what is called a pan of 'scouse' in a trawler is called a pan of 'shackles' on a crabber. 'Scouse' is a pan of stew like hotpot. If they was at table they wouldn't say, "Pass us the fish" they'd say, "Give us a Lilian Gish." First couple of days out of dock you'd have for breakfast, porridge, bacon, fried bread, tomatoes (red lead). After breakfast was finished you started making the dinner. You put the soup pan on. You always had a good pan of soup on the go. You had roast potatoes, a roast and vegetables. You lived well. They didn't skimp. They did on old fishing ships. When I first started to go to sea everything was rationed, but when rationing went things got better. There'd always be a sweet, like a steamed pudding, a duff. For tea you'd have a pan of shackles and you'd have fish. When you was fishing you always had fish with the meal because they all used to like it. At night time we used to put a snack out. It would be cheese, corned beef, sardines, something they could use to make a sandwich. That was when we were sailing home waters. The food was different when you sailed to Iceland 'cause you was on bondage stores. You got more food and, after the war when food was rationed, you only got National flour at home, but on bond you got white flour. That was much better, especially because you had to make your own bread. You got so many joints of beef for a trip. When you was running Iceland and it was cold weather the meat used to keep very well but in summer you had to pickle it, salt it in a barrel called a harness cask. You would get a potato about as big as an egg, put it in the harness cask along with four buckets of water. You'd add a big block of rough salt, brine. As soon as the potato came floating up to the top of the water, you'd put the meat in. Then you got a packet of saltpetre in with the water, swilled it round and left it for about two weeks.

The main thing was to satisfy the crew. On a Sunday, if you was in a good ship, I used to save bacon and egg for the Sunday breakfast, and at dinner you always had the same thing. That was pea soup, a leg of lamb, roast potatoes, boiled potatoes and carrots or whatever, and they always had a currant duff. Someone once said to me, "Why do you always have a currant duff on a Sunday?" and I'd tell 'em, "So that the crew know what day it is." On a Saturday night you used to get 'em a big ham for Sunday. You'd have to lock it away in the pantry so the Deckies couldn't get at it or they'd pinch it. For Sunday tea you'd have the ham with chips and onion rings and that, and I used to make a trifle, cakes, biscuits, all sorts. After that they got whatever they could scrounge. Don't forget you had to bake your own bread. I used to bake that at about 11 o'clock. You let it rise over dinner time, then knocked it back down, and cooked it after dinner. In Fleetwood ships, they used to make what they called 'busters'. You rolled 'em up and let 'em rise, baked them and they ate them hot. In Iceland there would be big crews of twenty two or twenty three. You would have an assistant. Mind you, knocking up a batch of bread is an easy thing to do. I was very good at making bread. There were some who couldn't make it. But my father was a Cook for many years and he taught me the job proper.

You had to be a little bit of a diplomat working in the galley because all the ship's gossip went through the galley. They'd tell you the tale, talk to you, and you just said, "Oh yes, right" and that'd be that. I didn't allow anybody in the galley if I wasn't in it because they used to make a mess. My law was, "Galley door is as far as you go." I would pass their tea out to them but not let them in. You always had this set routine, even with tea. They had a kettle of tea for their breakfast, another one at about ten or eleven o'clock in the morning, one after dinner, one at tea time, and three brews out a night. Sugar and tea in a tin, and two tins of milk. So they could only brew the tea as you gave it to them. They couldn't just make a brew when they wanted. If they used all the milk they couldn't have another tin. They had to drink it as it was.

When you was cooking in bad weather you used to have battens on the stove and on the table to stop things falling off. So you'd have your own little place battened off at the table. When you was working on the galley top, like a bench, if you was cutting meat up you got a wet dish rag, put that on the surface under the meat. That would stop it slipping off. When you'd finished with the pans you put them all together battened down on the shelves so they didn't slide about. Everything had to go in its place so it wouldn't move. Of course, you couldn't fill a pan up to the top with water or 'ought like that, you could only fill 'em so far, depending on the roll of the ship. If you got a bucket of water - you used to wash up in a bucket in the old coal burners - and you couldn't waste water if you was at sea, and you used to get the water out of the engine room, out of the condenser which was always hot. Water was a very special thing if you were at sea, you couldn't afford to run out of water. (Claude Couch - Fleetwood)

Cook and Crew in the Messdeck, 1966.
Copyright: P. Horsley.

We'd a cook with us. Well actually he was an excellent cook. You know the Kingsway Hotel, well there was a large family of them there and one of them was a plonkie and he was Cook with us. He was a fantastic Cook. He'd been Head Cook at the Kingsway Hotel when it was the tops and they chucked him out because he was never bloody sober. So when he came to sea they'd bring him aboard and chuck him in his bunk. Then for two bloody days he'd be completely lost to the world. So the cry would round, "Can anybody make a batch of bread?" And the Deckie would say, "Yeah, I can."

So they'd go make a batch of bread and they would see to the grub while the Cook come dry. When he finally came round he'd be trembling, but when started he was a fabulous Cook. We'd got the same sort of food as the Kingsway Hotel. I must say this about the Trawler Owners, they never skimped on food for the crew. We had the best of everything. We needed the bugger an' all to be honest. (Charlie Board - Grimsby)

Ninety percent of the cooks were bad ones, especially after the war aboard the Hellyer ships. You lived worse aboard a Hellyer ship than any other company on the docks. The Cooks had a problem because they hadn't got any decent food to cook. They just got the bare minimum and there were no fridges in those days. The meat was kept in the fish room and you got the cheapest and the worst meat imaginable. When you started fishing the meat would be just chucked on top of the ice in the fish room, and as you were using the ice they'd just chuck the meat into the next lot. By the time you were ready to use the last of it it was black. They'd just take it out and wash it in sea water. Terrible. It was usually green by that time. Those days you used to have a wooden brine cask on the boat deck, aft, and the cook would make up some brine and put in half a dozen pieces of meat to soak in the brine during the time you was at the fishing grounds. Then he'd cook it for the journey home. Some of the cooks could do it beautiful. They all had their own ways of making brine. (Ken Robertson - Hull)

You were never bored because in a Sparks' job, you were hunting for information all the time. You didn't only have to keep all your equipment going no matter what happened, your gear had to be going, your radars, your giros, your sounders, and also your navigational aids. The whole top and bottom, you was there for information. Weather forecasts, we used to get a lot of them, but you was there primarily for information for the Skipper because he had to decide where he wanted to go. If you was with a top man he might say, "All right, we'll go to Iceland this trip or we'll go to Greenland or we'll go to Bear Island, Spitsbergen or the White Sea." But if you could go up to your Skipper and say, "There you are, Skipper, there's the information at Greenland, Iceland, Bear Island and Spitsbergen," then he had an idea where he wanted to go, that's if he hadn't got his mind made up before he left dock. When you was running off you was getting all this information all the time and you was collating it and the Old Man was checking it. We knew where the group of ships were, and we'd either go there or if the Skipper had a bee in his bonnet, he wanted to go where he wanted to go, you'd go there. There'd be no ships there, but the Skipper had that feeling and he'd go. A lot of our top Skippers - we always said that God held them in the palm of his hand - because some of our top Skippers would catch fish in Cleethorpes Boating Lake, and I mean that literally. You had to be a technician all the time. You had to keep his gear going for him. Because there was no way you could turn round to a Skipper and say, "Oh well, that's it, can't do 'owt with that." Because you'd be looking for a ship when you got home. (Ray Smith - Grimsby)

Basically Engineering is the same sort of job on all boats but on the bigger boats a lot more is involved. Bigger machinery. More powerful engines. But when you got into the deep water fleet, into the big ships, you carried more crew down below. On the smaller boats there was just a Chief Engineer and a Second Engineer but occasionally you got a trainee, like I was to start with. Later on when you got into the deep water ships you had what they called two Greasers. The Second Engineer had a Greaser on watch with him and the Chief had one on watch with him. So you did six hours on, six hours off, all the time. So it was twelve hours a day from when you left Grimsby to coming back to Grimsby. The Greaser was like the labourer of the engine room. They call 'em Greasers but we all used to muck in together but basically the Greaser was the painter and if there was any greasing to do on the deck machinery they'd go out and do that. They were there more or less as a back up for the safety, because when you are down there on your own in the engine room nobody on the deck thinks to pop down and see how anybody is. You could be dead on the plates and nobody would come down So it just gave you a bit of back up. (Colin Donald - Grimsby)

What was I responsible for as a Chief Engineer? All machinery, everything, galley stove, the fridge - you name it,

if it moves it's the Chief's responsibility. All the electrical work, everything. Breakdowns were a rarity with the diesel ships towards the end but if you got a major thing, like we had a shaft break in a gear box, there was nothing you could do - in fact they towed us all the way home from Iceland with that when I was a trainee in the Ross Stalker. (Stephen Drever - Grimsby)

I liked the job. You was independent to a degree. You were subject to the Bridge and you had to perform good enough to satisfy the Bridge and the company. Provided you gave satisfaction you had no problems. You've got to have a Skipper but by the same token you've got to have an Engineer. The line of command should be down. The Skipper tells you what he requires and you supply it. No disagreement about that. (Harold Dawe - Fleetwood)

The Skipper never interfered with what was going on in the engine room. He was in charge but then the Mate and the Chief Engineer was more or less on a par. I've never sailed with a Skipper who ever interfered with the engine room. On the Kelvin she was like a Bridge Control ship, where the Skipper could control the engines from the Bridge 'cause it was linked to a gear box. Now if you thought they was being a bit rude with your engines you used to fix things so that you'd make it a little bit hard work for them to learn them a lesson, just to calm them down a bit. It was easy for them. They could swing the ship around a bit, but it didn't do the ship much good so we used to slow 'em down a bit. On the way home they'd put it on full. They might ask you "Can you get a bit more out of her?" and then you'd see what you could do. The engines was governed but there was ways round that if you were trying to catch a tide or was racing the tide, you could get a bit more speed out of her. But, in bad weather, diesel ships are governed by the engine temperatures and we was allowed to 800 degrees Fahrenheit on the exhaust temperatures. Anything over that and we had to start easing the ship down. If we was in bad weather it's hard work for the engines, the temperatures start to shoot up and you're telling the Skipper, "You'll have to ease her down because of the temperatures." Normally they would comply because otherwise they'd cause damage anyway. But if you was racing for a tide you'd fiddle it, you'd probably go up to 850.

Deckies Gutting.

The crews didn't like the Engineers because they thought they got it easy, but whenever they got wet and wanted to dry their gear they were more friendly so they could hang their frocks in the engine room. I used to have one area where I'd lay down a cover so they could hang their frocks so they didn't drip on my engines. (Graham Howard - Grimsby)

On the first trip I did in the Ross Revenge, we were fishing and a brake went on the winch. They were big brakes and the lads used to have to help me to carry them 'cos they were forward of the ship. We were steaming at the time, changing fishing grounds, probably going to be four or five hours something like that. I'd never actually changed one of these brakes but they were a similar sort of arrangement to the other ships. Well a couple of the lads who went to get the brake they'd done it before. So they knew which end to take off first and set it up. Meadows, the Skipper, had his head out the window and he shouted down to me about the job, "Do it this, do it that" and I ignored him. We did the job and carried on steaming. It was afternoon when I should have been watch below. And I rolled in. Well the phone rang in the berth 'cos in that ship I had a telephone from the Bridge and the engine

Fred Quinn – Bosun.

room. It was the Sparks. He said, "The Old Man wants you on the Bridge". So I says, "OK I'll be there in a minute". I went up and he said, "You ignored me when I shouted down to you." I said "Yeah, well what did you want doing - the job doing or did you want me to come up here and have a yarn with you?" After that we got on like a house on fire. You'd never interfere with the Skipper anyway. That would be fatal. Skippers, they were tin gods . A man like him could earn you a good living and you respected him. It was a happy ship for me. I was with him just over three years. I was nine years on the Ross Ramilies. (Colin Donald - Grimsby)

They were all fishermen who spent their lives fishing. Some of 'em hadn't got the ability. They remained Deckhands. Now the Third Hand is in charge of the deck crew. The Mate's in charge of all the crew and the Third Hand would be in charge of the labouring work when they're gutting 'cos the Mate would be down the fish room. That was his job. So if anything went wrong with the fish when it was turned out it was the Mate who got the sack. The Third Hand was the foreman of the crew. He saw that everything was going all right. The Mate was in charge of the whole thing, but you had to have somebody who was going round among the crew and telling them. That was the Third Hand. He got twice as much poundage as the Deckhands did. The bloke we had was an excellent fisherman. The Mate's responsible for the net but the Third Hand is responsible for keeping it in order - keeping it going all right. (Charlie Board - Grimsby)

As Bosun you took your orders from the Skipper. But the Bosun was the main man on the deck. He was responsible for making sure all the gear was ready, keeping the Skipper happy. You was more or less like a foreman. You had to be at the forefront of everything. If it was just picking a matchstick up off the deck it was your job to make sure it was done. You had to have respect from the crew. You used to have to rule them with a rod of iron sometimes. You did get the odd one that was out for trouble, but you had to 'play the game' with them, and they would 'play the game' with you. The Bosun had to be in the forefront of everything, setting an example to the crew. That's how you earned their respect. (Peter Wright Wilson - Fleetwood)

The Bosun was like a Second Mate. If there was no fish you would perhaps go up on the Bridge in case the Skipper wanted to do anything. At midnight the Mate would go on the Bridge and the Skipper would go below. The Bosun was on the deck in charge of it from tea time until 6 am the next morning, while the Mate was on the Bridge hauling and shooting and the Skipper would be having a sleep. That's how you normally worked it. (Ken Robertson - Hull)

The Mate's in charge of 'em so that's why we always had a big bloody Mate. There was never any need for physical discipline at all. The Mate used to say, "What do you think you're doing?" Everybody knew the Mate was in charge. If the Mate said, "Jump down there", he jumped down there. There was no messing about. If there's anything went wrong the Mate got the blame. The Skipper'd say, "If you can't do the bloody job I'll have to get someone else who can." That's how it was. So you gradually built a first class team. The Skipper never picked the crew. The Mate did. So if the Mate picked a bum the Skipper would say, "Where the fucking hell did you get him from?" "Well," he'd say, "We'll have to carry him. We can't chuck him over the side but make sure when we get in dock he don't come back again." The Mate used to go on the Bridge. Say we were coming down the coast and we hit the Spurn light vessel to turn into the river, the Mate would come on the Bridge and the Mates were all great bloody big ten foot blokes, eight foot wide big fellows and they'd come and see to the Old Man and the Old Man would say, "All right what you doing then?" "Well its like this, Skip. I'm going to fire him". And the Old Man used to say, "Well if he's no bloody good, fire him. Get some bugger else." (Charlie Board - Grimsby)

You got a lot of Skippers who sacked people because their face didn't fit. They was tret like animals anyway. One of the favourite stories was of an old Skipper. They called him Hutchinson. His name was Hurricane - Hurricane Hutch. And he was Skipper of the Stoke City which was one of ours. They used to go to the White Sea. There was so much fish that we used to pick 'gutters' up. That was Norwegians or what have you. It saved the firm paying a weekly wage for

*Clockwise from Top left:-
1-Wireman, 2-Winchman,
3-Net Mender, 4-Gutter.*

one thing. It saved them giving a percentage of the ship and they just used to get paid so much a day. And it was absolutely blowing a gale of wind and the riggings and the Bridge was full of ice and the men was on the deck gutting the fish and Hurricane called out to the Mate, who was a chap called Fred Chatterton, and said, "Fred. That scrob. He's sat on the hatch. Go and wake the bastard up." And he went over to the hatch where he was sat and tried to wake him and he'd died. And Fred called up, "Skipper. He's dead Skipper". And Hurricane's first words and his reaction was, "Why the tired bastard. He'd rather die than gut my fish." And he meant it. He meant it. He was a terrible man. All he was interested in was his fish. On the dock there was a lot more like him. As far as the crew was concerned they were just animals and they would swill 'em about. When the weather was really, really bad and I'm talking about waves coming over, they would still shoot the gear and try and fish in it. Others in fairness would pull into board and say, "That's enough now we'll dodge into the wind for a couple of hours while the weather subsides." But some of them, they was vicious. Non-stop Norman - he sailed for Consolidated pre-war - but he thought a lot about his crew. Your Billy Hardies, they was out for a good living but they'd also got their crew at heart. Your Len Browns and people like that - Jack Mawer - who I was with, he was very good, but some Skippers, they'd fish in anything. (Gordon Cockerill - Grimsby)

I used to get away with murder with the Skipper I was with, simply because I'd been with him sixteen years, something that was almost unheard of. I think I must have been the only one out of either Hull or Grimsby that stopped with the one Skipper - and he was the devil incarnate when you started fishing. The nicest bloke in the world the rest of the time, like a father, but once that trawl went over the side he just wouldn't stop. He'd never stop for weather or anything like that. He had no nerves. So he'd fish when everybody else was weatherbound. I'd known him since I started fishing. He was just a Deckie Learner then, but you knew he was going to do well, even in his teens you could see that. He got all his Tickets very quickly and when he got his Skipper's Ticket he asked me to go with him. It was a rat race at that time, dog

eat dog. He got a start in the oldest ship in the company, a coal burner. He couldn't keep a crew he was that bad. He fished through any weather and being an old ship as well he couldn't keep a crew for long, they'd leave as soon as the ship came back in dock. I don't really know why I stayed with him. Maybe it was because we were coming home, even in this old ship, with a bit of a load and beating the big ships. So he was soon doing well and the bosses weren't bothered how he got the fish just so long as he got it. He got better ships as his career went along and he was making a lot of money, so I stayed. But when he was on fish he really was a devil. He wouldn't even tell his wife the truth about how he caught fish, and he loved her. He was the biggest liar that ever walked was Mal. (Ken Robertson - Hull)

Say you didn't like somebody you wouldn't have 'em. I had a regular crew for a few years actually. I changed firms and they followed me in that firm. I was with Northerns and then I went into Consols. I was pretty successful in Northerns but I got a divorce at the time and I went off the rails a bit. On the booze and that. And I missed a ship, a ship called the Northern Princess, and I was drunk and I wouldn't go to sea, so I didn't go. Well no Skipper did that. When the Gaffer sent for me he said to me I was unique because he expected when you went down dock that so and so hadn't sailed because there was no Deckhand, no crew, but he said not a Skipper. No Skipper's ever refused to sail. (George Mussell - Grimsby)

There was a lot of competition between Hull Skippers. The Company bosses used to tell us that we were to work together for the firm's benefit, but you all tried to beat each other regardless. That's because the better you did the better ship you got. There were some good ships and there were some poor ships. Later the ships were all generally quite reasonable, but before that you could get some poor ships. But the better you did the better the ship you got, and the better the ship the more you could do. You tried to work together but when you were in Hellyers, or B.U.T as it later became, there was one time, when they first combined, that they had upwards of forty ships, and the best ones were the best ships in England at that time. So if you were in one of them you were at the top of the tree, and that's what you

BOYD LINE LIMITED

SKIPPERS' POSITIONS

1ST OCTOBER, 1971 TO 30TH SEPTEMBER, 1972.

Trips	SKIPPER	1972 Position £	Kits	1971 Position £	Kits	1972 Days	1971 Days	1972 Kits Landed	1971 Kits Landed	1972 Total Earnings £	1971 Total Earnings £	1972 Av. Kits Per Day	1971 Av. Kits Per Day	1972 Av. £'s Per Day	1971 Av. £'s Per Day
7	S. BARWICK	1	1	1	2	155	178	13691	18519	113,014	135,413	88.3	104.0	729.1	760.8
3	C. HAMLING	2	7	6	6	64	255	4283	21753	44,162	166,001	66.9	85.2	690.0	650.9
11	J. WILLIAMS	3	5	5	4	218	279	17474	24563	155,688	181,961	74.6	83.0	649.1	669.4
10	C. GILL	4	4	3	3	217	212	16604	19706	139,935	145,724	76.5	92.9	644.8	687.3
12	C. WALKER	5	6	2	5	263	279	18295	24520	166,744	200,579	69.5	87.9	634.0	719.0
9	C. PITTS	6	7	-	-	191	-	12786	-	119,543	-	66.9	-	625.8	-
5	G. KENT	7	11	7	7	115	278	6407	23307	70,770	166,660	55.7	83.8	615.3	599.5
5	T. THRESH	8	2	-	-	107	-	8499	-	65,378	-	79.5	-	611.0	-
11	P. GARNER	9	10	8	8	247	284	15622	22839	15,093	163,617	64.0	80.4	610.9	576.1
5	W. LEWIS	10	9	10	10	114	159	7345	11642	63,634	81,760	64.8	73.2	558.1	514.2
3	R. GRAY	11	3	4	1	68	130	5227	11795	36,255	87,028	76.8	130.8	533.2	669.4
5	B. HODSON	12	14	-	-	107	-	5106	-	56,527	-	47.7	-	528.3	-
13	R. McCARTHY	13	13	11	11	286	145	15598	9588	143,307	68,897	54.5	66.1	501.1	475.00
5	R. JOHNSTONE	14	11	-	-	106	-	5900	-	51,589	-	55.7	-	486.7	-
7	G. CHEEVERS	15	15	9	9	158	219	6899	16763	66,249	125,811	43.7	76.5	419.3	574.5

Skippers' League Table.

wanted. They wanted you to work together but it was really just impossible to get forty people to co-operate with each other. (Sid Morrell - Hull)

On the catching side, it is a competitive industry but you have to realise that the top Skipper got the best crew and hopefully he got the best ship and the earnings in those top ships were higher, so there was always pressure from youngsters to shoulder their way to the front and shoulder their way to the top ships. A lot of rubbish has been talked at times that this competition caused accidents. I think in the top ships it was certainly not the case because if you're fishing at Spitsbergen you have to steam back to Norway to land an injured man. That's the end of the trip and you would find that the top Skippers had a wonderful record of low accidents and low injuries. It's where you got into the less efficient Skippers with the less efficient crews who tried to emulate the performance, because it was a competitive industry and they wanted to show how good they were, that risks were taken which Skippers at the time were unqualified or inexperienced and unable to deal with. (Tom Boyd - Hull)

We used secret channels and all sorts. So we'd been fishing on the east side and this fish took off so there was about ten ships all steaming round Iceland and there's Eddie St. Pierre in his ship. Anyhow, the ships are going along and I'm gradually shaping away, sliding off, sliding off. I just flicked on Channel 12. I said, "Are you there you Bill?" He said, "Yes, you Mick ... give us a shout a bit later." Then we used to put it on reduced power or take the aerial out so they couldn't hear you. So anyhow I got closer to him. I said, "Now then." He said "I've got a buoy down." He'd put a buoy down to mark the fish and he said, "The fishing's good." "Oh", I said "Right." So anyhow this little voice said, "Now then, Micky" It was Eddie St. Pierre. He'd followed us through. All the others went away. So with that there was three of us fishing.

They lied summat rotten. There's our Bill in this little Ross Puma and I mean we're in bigger ships. And he filled his ship up. I think he had about 1,400 kit in this thing when he went home. So there's me and Eddie then. He said, "Well we've got to start unloading some of our fish, tell them that we're catching fish. How do we do it?". Eddie said, "Well I'll put it out tonight that we're inside the limits and we keep coming in and out and that." So if of course they think you're too far inside they won't come. So we got our trips in and with that a Yorkie come up - one of Marrs's. He said, "I'll have to tell our firm about this fish." So Eddie said, "If you tell them I'm going to tell our firm." And he did do. And do you know who was the first ones there round us was the Germans. It's amazing how they knew our code isn't it? It was all in code when you tell your firms ships, all in private code, but the Germans were there before the British ships. It was a cut throat game. (Mick George - Grimsby)

One of the main problems I had with Skippers was making sure the Skippers were honest on the schedule. We had a twenty four hour report for the office but we also had an inter-ship schedule about every four to six hours. If you just shot away following some fish or something and you hauled a hundred baskets, say two bags, and again a hundred baskets, well you had to be very careful on the air as the world and his wife was 'wigging,' as they called it. Because some Skippers were straightforward, others weren't, and there was some who would deliberately mislead - that's a masterpiece of understatement. (John Butt - Grimsby)

A Skipper was only as good as his catch and your top Skipper was never out of a ship whereas the others was struggling and they learnt as they went on, but if you came home and you'd no fish, been away for three weeks and you hadn't caught the capacity they're looking for or to clear their expenses etc. then that was it. (Bill Ellerington - Hull)

We were in the Pentland Firth when a storm blew up. One of the Deckies was on the Bridge and he says to me, "Do you think we're going to make it Skipper?" I says, "'Course we are!" You see when you were on the Bridge you had to try and give your crew confidence, and you had doubts in your mind yourself, but you couldn't show it, could you? It was a very lonely life. The seas don't just come at you head on, they come at you from all angles. Anyway I managed to get

through. The Lord was with me again. You assert your authority on the crews, don't you? I always used to try to treat them with an iron hand in a velvet glove. I took the Aston Villa but she was no good to me for the simple reason is I used to fish in bad weather, terrible weather, so therefore I had to have good ships, that was my way. (Don Lister - Grimsby)

Most skippers had a steady backbone of their own crew, with three or four others coming in or out at any one time. About two thirds of your crew was regular. A third were shipped up by the pool office. Skippers wasn't allowed to socialise with Deckhands. You did to a small extent. I've been out many a time with my Deckhands. I've taken them out for meals and that, as friends, but the general instructions from your boss was not to socialise with the crew in order to save trouble. I know one or two Skippers that have been banged about by Deck Hands. That's not stuff for a book though, I think it happens in any port. (Derek Reader - Fleetwood)

I used to tell 'em - just what I wanted to tell 'em on the radio. Say, for example, you are fishing off the south end of Iceland. Everybody who wanted to go to the North Cape of Iceland passed you, so if you were to tell everybody you was on fish, you would finish up with everybody there and, once they had had their fill, they would then carry on to the North Cape, so you would just tell them what you want to tell them. It was all in good fun. The Skippers, they knew what each other was up to. They used their own common sense to decide whether or not to believe what you said on the radio. They weren't fools. They'd decide to assign the boat for a couple of hauls just to have a look. (Jack Tripp - Hull)

You've got to be apart from the crew. Steaming down to the fishing grounds I'm talking to them and friendly and all that, but as soon as the gear goes over you switch to being another person. That's the business side of it. That's when you become your other self. (John Meadows - Grimsby)

We had eight ships at our peak and I think we had about nine or ten Skippers who we would call upon. What we used to try and do was that if a Skipper had a trip off, as of course they did, then we used to try and put either his Mate, or another Mate in, to give him the chance. Some of them did well, others fell by the wayside. But basically your top earning Skipper went into the new ship. That was expected. (Bill Letten - Grimsby)

The first boat I took out as Skipper was the Wyre Vanguard and I was a 'Christmas Cracker'. I had my Skipper's Ticket then and the regular Skippers were staying off for Christmas. That was when they gave the 'up and coming' Skippers the chance. So the chance always came in the winter months with the bad weather. I did two trips at Christmas. I didn't do brilliantly, but I didn't do bad. They were just run of the mill trips. That was the same time as Victor Buschini got his start. It was 1957 I think. We were both 'Christmas Crackers,' Victor and I, but he had the better ship. Victor developed into the top Skipper in Fleetwood. After that I went back to sea as Mate in the same ship. Then, six months later in June, Mr Wheildon the gaffer took a shine to me, that helped a lot (if the boss like your face you was in), gave me the Wyre Majestic, and I never looked back. The second trip I had I made a very good trip. I remember it because it was the time when my son was born and I was given the news as I was coming through the lock pits that I had a son, and I crashed into the bloody lock pits. At least I gave them a good bang. Anyway, I'd made a good trip so I didn't get told off for that. (Derek Reader - Fleetwood)

At one time you had a lot of Skippers, the old Skippers, who, if the weather got too bad they'd go in and drop anchor and wait, but the younger generation who came along, who were competing against each other, they'd work all weather. They might have thought it was alright but you're talking about young kids. The Skipper might be saying it's all right, but if he's only about twenty odd or summat, and you might be forty with more experience regarding weather and all that.....I mean they had to do it. After all, if they went in and dropped anchor and another boat is carrying on fishing the gaffer would want to know why when they land, and they could have got sacked. There were some hard Skippers. Hard case Skippers into fisticuffs, but they were good blokes who really understood the job, and you seemed to work better for them than for the other ones. (Thomas Bagnall - Fleetwood)

Some people used to fish in ridiculously bad weather. We all used to fish in bad weather but some of them used to go to the extreme. Some of them got a bad name and crews just wouldn't go with em. Mind you they always got crews. I mean the most successful Skipper I should say and one of the most successful businessmen that Grimsby's seen for years was Bunny Newton. I never had the misfortune to sail with him but they reckon he was a pig at sea. Well everybody couldn't be wrong. (George Mussell - Grimsby)

August Ebenezersson was a master mariner and a perfect gentleman. God must have been smiling on me when I went with him. A wonderful fisherman and a fantastic navigator. When we took sights I had a sextant and he had a sextant. I learned all that for nothing. He was kindness itself. I was one of the top spivs - Radio Officers - in the company. I'd already been in there before the war so I was one of the top spivs then - big headed bugger. I stopped with him for about eight years. Unfortunately, his wife was an Icelandic woman and he was earning quite a lot of money - so was I - but he was earning a lot more money than me and he had a weakness for booze. When we went in dock to land his wife used to feed him as much as she could because once he got Brahms and Liszt she helped herself to his money. She destroyed him. He was still earning good money but, of course, the thing was that he began to drink a bit at sea, and then he turned into a plonkie at sea. As long as I could get him onto the Bridge by the time we were passing Faroe we'd have him sober enough by the time we got to Iceland for him to do his work. That's how we did it. The Mate and I got her as far as Faroe - nothing difficult about that - and we gradually stopped his tap and he would be very ill for a couple of days or so, but by the time we got to the north side of Faroe he was alright. He was a fantastic sailor, a real seaman. A marvellous navigator. But it got so that after two or three years you couldn't do anything with him at all, so I left him and went in another ship. (Charlie Board - Grimsby)

Bunny Newton was very well known in Hull because a lot of them lost their trawls through him. If he was on fish and you got on his track after the same fish, and he was coming back, there were no rules of the road for him, no give way or anything in the way most Skippers would. He'd just go straight across your trawl and chop your trawl off if you didn't get out of his way in time. Oh he was a beast. (Ken Robertson - Hull)

The best Skipper for money - he wasn't the best to sail with though - he was a bit of a prat really - but for money was Vic Meach. He was in Northern Trawlers. He was the most successful. He could find the fish. He did that with experience and a portion of luck. You had to have luck to go with it. No matter how experienced you was a Skipper - I mean you could go to one place one day and there wouldn't be no fish. Another the Skipper would come and there would be tons of fish. You could be that close and that near. (George Mussell - Grimsby)

I was on a ship called the Northern Dawn. Bunny Newton was Skipper of a ship called the Lifeguard and his fish room man had signed off Bunny's ship and signed on our ship. We were laid up at Iceland mending our nets and Bunny came steaming alongside us, jumped aboard our ship and started fighting with this man. We all wondered what was going on. It was in the days when television first came out and this feller had bought a television off Bunny and paid him two or three pounds a trip for it. This bloke thought I'm not paying any more and he'd come to us on our ship. Bunny had got to know by talking to the Skipper and he came straight alongside us, clambered aboard and hit him. His eyes were black and blue and his nose was bleeding. Bunny then went back on board his own ship as though nothing had happened. Skippers were the law of the sea. (Tom Jacombe - Grimsby)

I was with this Skipper one time. He had a lady aboard in his berth. A Norwegian woman whom the agents supplied to some Skippers. I'm not saying what she was - a loose woman, put it that way. He used to do it through the agent. And the crew, he'd give them all a bottle of rum each. And they all went drinking in the cafes. Then the Pilots come aboard, which you had to have two Pilots see. "If they're not

aboard in an hour we're walking off." So I said to the agent, "Go in that cafe and get 'em out." He was the agent in Norway for the ships. We got 'em out and some had had a really good drink. They had their heads down. The Skipper had had a good drink and this woman had gone off the ship. I chucked the ropes off with the pilots and I was six hours at the wheel on me own. I was seeing stars more or less, and a Danish lad who was the only one who hadn't had a drink he came and relieved me on the Bridge on the wheel. (Roly Webb - Grimsby)

Bunny Newton on the Brandur.
Copyright: Grimsby Evening Telegraph.

Bunny was a character of his own. He was a bully. He could be nice, he could be a very jolly man, but his character was just that of a bully. But even Bunny could not do as he liked with the Trawler Owners. He was still under their thumb, for all his character and what he would tell people. He was still controlled by the Trawler Owners. He could be nice, but at times he wasn't very nice. He was an absolute bastard to his crew. A Chief Engineer once told me that Bunny called

Graham Howard and his Mates on the Northen Chief. Laid in the river waiting to dock.

him up on the Bridge and, thinking he wanted to give him some orders, he went. Bunny said to him, "Those revs are not right". The Engineer said,"They are Skipper". Whereupon he said, "Don't argue with me," and he just punched him in the face and the Engineer was then walking back with his nose full of blood. Of course the Engineer could have complained to the Board of Trade who could have taken away the Skipper's ticket, but Bunny was a record earning Skipper, and the Engineer would never have got another ship. Every man who was badly treated by a Skipper had the right to complain to the Board of Trade, and the Board of Trade was very serious about discipline, but of course, if men took this route they wouldn't get another ship. There was one man on board one of Bunny's ships. Bunny had treated him very badly and he did report Bunny to the Board of Trade. Bunny was disciplined and the next day the man (Arthur Bland) was walking down Fish Dock Road and Bunny drove up, got out his car and beat him to a pulp. The man never got another ship. (Bill Hardie - Grimsby)

I don't really know why I loved the sea. I think mainly it was the comradeship that I found at sea but never found ashore. When you were at sea, no matter what you were doing anybody standing near you would give you a hand if you needed it. If you was lifting something heavy, those nearby would just stop what they were doing and give you a lift. You was always there for each other. Even though you was married and loved your wife and family, you had such good mates when you was at sea that it was something else. It wasn't quite the same when you got to Mate or Skipper but when you was just a Deckie, if one of you had a row with the officers and decided to sign off, then two or three of your mates would sign off with you so you could all go to another ship together, and you stayed together like that for years. That's how it was. (Jim Quinn - Fleetwood)

Chapter 5

Those in Peril on the Sea

Trawling was the most dangerous of occupations with more deaths and injuries than any other industry, be it construction work, mining or any of the other occupations which generated headlines about death and danger. Heavy equipment, worked in stormy and icy conditions on exposed decks cluttered with machinery and crossed by running warps, with men over-worked and tired by an eighteen hour day, leaning out-board to haul and cast nets in all weathers, while fishing in the world's worst waters, all combined to ensure that the price of fish was paid in limbs, lives and lingering debilitating diseases such as arthritis, eczema, heart disease and asthma. Safety was more a matter of fatalism than an obsessive concern. Stability was not a major preoccupation in the design of vessels, machinery could not be protected or covered, surveys and safety inspections were lax, life saving rules were those applicable to the Merchant Navy requiring the carriage of rigid life boats which often could not be launched safely or quickly from fishing boats in rough weather, and working hours were not limited by law as they were in Germany and France. British fishermen had to fend for themselves.

The Holland-Martin Report of 1969 calculated that the standard mortality for trawlermen was seventeen times that of the male population as a whole, while those aged from fifteen to forty-four were twenty times more likely to die as a result of an accident at work. In the ten years before that report 208 trawlermen had lost their lives, most of them in individual accidents, the most common of which was loss overboard, many of them in years of tragedy such as 1954, when Grimsby lost five vessels and 55 men, or 1968 when three Hull trawlers and 57 men were lost in a matter of weeks. That tragedy led to a campaign on safety and to the Holland-Martin Report itself revealing to a horrified world just how dangerous

fishing was particularly distant water. Yet not all of the danger was due to wild elements. Of ninety vessels lost or seriously damaged, forty-seven were in strandings or collisions due to negligent navigation with a third of these vessels being navigated by uncertificated men at the time. Self-inflicted, or imposed by circumstances, danger was the fishermen's constant companion.

I've known me life being in danger but you never dreamed about it. Many a time you thought to yourself, any minute and it's going to happen. Something's going to happen. You sensed danger. You lived with danger all your life. You knew either you was the master or the sea was the master. And if it was the sea's turn to be master people got killed. They put it down as an Act of God. I was in one of the Roderigos when them ships got lost at Iceland. It was blowing a hurricane. Ships shouldn't have even been there at the time. The weather came, caught 'em all unawares. The people got killed - it was ice, it just turned the ship and there was nothing you could do about it. Even though you're alongside of 'em you couldn't do anything to help 'em. You used to think to yourself, "Poor souls." And it was out of your mind. People who you knew all your life. That's what happened to 'em. And it just went out of your mind. You never thought about them people again. That's how a fisherman was. (Tom Jacombe - Grimsby)

I mean we used to look at it this way. You used to get knocked down by a bus when you was ashore didn't you? I think I've been through every weather condition that you care to imagine, and some of them you couldn't even imagine in your worse nightmares, but I always felt confident in my ship and the Skipper. He might have been the biggest basket in ten towns and all that but I still had confidence in my ship and my Skipper. These ships of ours, were the finest sea ships in the world, because they had to be for the conditions that we had to work and sail under. I always felt confident. I always came back. A lot didn't admittedly. Me old man as well. And me father in law, he was lost at sea, and my wife's brother he was lost. It's just part of the job. It was a hard job, it was a dangerous job at times, but nobody ever thought of it that way. (Ray Smith - Grimsby)

ate letting go of the Codline - bottom of Cod ends.
opyright: Grimsby Evening Telegraph.

I was about twelve year old and me and my friend at school was going home for dinner and there was a special paper out saying there was a ship down and crew lost. It was the Golden Deeps. My friend didn't come back to school in the afternoon and we realised that her dad must have been lost on it. The Skipper had gone ashore and one of the Croft Bakers was with him and they'd gone ashore in Norway I think. The ship broke anchor and the ship ran onto the rock. I think one or two were saved but the majority of the crew were lost. It was very sad and we all sat and cried. Then the same thing would happen again and again. It became a part of your life. It was a very cruel life and a very cruel sea. (Dolly Hardie - Grimsby)

It was pretty frightening at times. I don't think you was ever terrified or scared or 'owt like that because you wouldn't have gone again, would you? You was just pretty wary and while you was all busy at the rail heaving the trawl in you could hear "Water." You knew it was the sea coming and you'd all scarper like, but you had the Skipper up there watching you all the time. You'd get the sea rolling towards you all the time because your starboard side was the weather side and that was the side what you was working because the trawl was over the side and the wind was pushing the ship away from the trawl. While you was busy you couldn't be watching the water too much and watching what you was doing. So the Skipper would be watching the seas. (John Meadows - Grimsby)

Most people didn't mind a head to wind. It was uncomfortable but that was all. When I was in the Ross Kelvin we was running before the wind and she laid over and she'd leaned over so far that where you used to fill the gear box to the oil filter the oil was coming out and the Bridge side was in the water. I was a little bit frightening but she came right again she was a good stable boat. It seemed endless but it was only a couple of minutes. Trawlers were well built. They was good ships and you never really felt frightened. You did get iced up but you took that as part and parcel of the job. You didn't mind wind on its own, you didn't mind the cold on its own, it's when you got the combination of the two that it got a little bit worrying. If you couldn't get on the deck to chop it away then in the end she was going to turn over, but mostly you could get out of it, just the odd one was caught out. (Graham Howard - Grimsby)

It was a dangerous job. I have seen three people killed. I saw a feller virtually get chopped in half. He was just bending over the warp. In those days the warps ran across the decks where you were working. He just leant over the warp to get a liver basket and we came fast on a wreck and it pulled the warp. It went sliding through the deck and through the big rollers and it just virtually chopped him in half. I'll always remember another feller who had his head chopped off through a silly mistake in real bad weather. We came fast and we had a real nasty trawl to mend. It was real bad weather and this feller got a wire around his arm. In the panic to get the wire from around his arm (he managed to shrug it off but it got round his neck) and with the movement of the ship, the ship went one way and he went the other and it just guillotined him. That feller was only about twenty five or twenty six. He left a wife and two kiddies, but the Trawler Owners said it was just an Act of God. How can you say that to a wife and two kiddies? If it happened in a factory you'd have the factory inspectors round - you would have Board of Trade people round. But the Trawler Owners just used to say it was an Act of God - sorry - and there was nothing for the poor wife. She never got any compensation for losing her husband. (Tom Jacombe - Grimsby)

I've seen a bloke lost his head when the messenger wire, which is what pulls the trawl wires together, and a splint in the wire caught on his frock, dragged him and of course, went across his head, and that was it. You usually put them down the fish room and then put them ashore. They are then sent home in a lead lined coffin because of the distance. You never see that many lost at sea. For the way you worked there weren't all that many injuries really. A few finger ends and that but not what you'd call really serious ones. It was a case of you knew what you was doing and you looked out for one another. If the Skipper was to sing out "Greener", you just dropped whatever you were doing and just hung on because you knew there was a good lump of water coming at you. That's why they don't like green aboard ship you see, cause

it's a green sea. It's an unlucky colour. (Graham Howard - Grimsby)

An awful thing happened on the Jowitz when I was sailing on her. We were fishing and the Mate, I'm nearly sure his name was Figgy Moraleck, he was a great guy in his mid twenties, maybe a bit older but not much more than that. This day I came out of the Galley which was under the Bridge on that ship - a magnificent trawler, magnificent - and I just stepped out of the galley door as they were hauling. Normally I wouldn't have done that so I turned straight round to come back in as you don't want to be getting in the way on deck as they were hauling and equipment is flying all over, and Figgy must have looked over the side when they 'knocked out'. When they 'knock out' the trawler one warp actually flies up and down and vibrates violently, and his head was literally chopped off. I saw him, he walked for two or three yards, I saw him, and there was no blood - I don't know what I thought at the time, but you could see an oilskin walking towards you as his head went over the side. (Alec Bovill - Grimsby)

The only fellow I lost was chap called Dick Dennis. He was a Fireman on one of the boats out of B.U.T. We was working the westward, the north of Scotland and he was ill with ulcers. We were due to haul at half past nine at night and the Mate came up about twenty pasty nine and said, "Skipper, old Dick is rolling around in agony." So I says, "Watch the Bridge and I'll go have a look at him". So I went down below and there he was rolling around. He said, "I can't stand it Skip, I can't stand it." I says, "OK Dick" I says, "We're hauling now." I said, "We'll go straight to the nearest oil rig." 'Cos the Cormorant field, was right up north there and we only had about three hours steam. We got hold of the doctor and he suggested giving him a drop of morphine for the pain. When we got within half an hour from the rig he died. His stomach just blew right up like. So the rig says, "Well what you going do now Skipper? Are you going to take him into Lerwick?" I said, "Well I'd like your doctor to come aboard to confirm him dead because there's ninety mile to go there." Which he did. We wasn't qualified to say the man's dead even though you surmise. We took him to Lerwick and then we went out fishing again. But it really broke me up like that because you like to take the full crew back all the time. (John Meadows - Grimsby)

There's not many fishermen you see with a full set of fingers. I lost half my thumb at sea fishing. I just trapped it. You was hauling and shooting about eight times a day, which was a big operation actually. It wasn't for us because we got that used to it but looking back it was a big operation. And it was all heaving, heaving on wires all the time. So you wanted it doing in the fastest time. If they could do it in an hour you wanted it going in forty minutes. Do it in forty minutes you wanted it doing in thirty minutes. It was a race. Speed, speed was the essence. There was no safety in them days.

They had to take me in because it was crushed. They took me in to a place in Norway and they took it off and then I came home on another trawler. I was off about three or four months after that. I was nineteen year old then. I hadn't been fishing long then I know that. That's the most common injury for fishermen. Fingers, one or two hands off. Same thing getting trapped and that. There was that much heaving. It used to normally take you half an hour to haul and shoot. Well you had to heave all that gear in and then heave it out and the safety aspect was nil. It was all speed. You wanted that gear up - cos when that gear was on the deck you weren't catching no fish were you, so you wanted it up and over again in the quickest possible time. Looking back it was absolutely ridiculous. Looking at the safety factors at sea now and then looking at how the way we performed we was crazy. No doubt about that. Mad. (George Mussell - Grimsby)

At Bear Island, I've seen people with their fingers off and having to steam to Norway for about 200 and odd miles at say seven or eight knots with nothing to help but try and keep them calm with their fingers off. While you was hauling, bringing the nets in, they had one look out to shout "Water." Everybody used to jump out the way, but one chap couldn't. He was a biggish chap and he grabbed hold of the gallows and as he grabbed hold the sea hit him and left his hand on the gallows. Oh! there were some terrible conditions. (Bill Ellerington - Hull)

And these boils. It was the muck getting in the pores. Salt water boils - they used to be terrible those. You'd get them on your hands and on your fingers mostly. They used to come up. It wasn't just like you'd got a boil. There used to be maybe four or five cores inside of it. You used to get haddock rash. That was all a rash on you from touching the fish. Some blokes used to get this if you was gutting a long time - Jumbo Wrist. And that is absolutely agony. What it is if you're gutting and you're moving your wrists and you're doing it all the time then your wrists start to swell up. There wasn't no sympathy. There was a Cook and he got a boil on his finger, a big boil on his finger, and we took him in Faroe. We just anchored off and the boat come off - a little boat - to take him to the doctors. And I went with him to the doctors. His finger was really up. He was in agony. Anyway we went into the doctor's surgery and he sits there. The doctor looks at his hand. I mean the Faroese and the Icelanders they was noted that if you went in for a toothache there was none of this anaesthetic. They was cruel. The doctor got his scalpel and he cut it like a cross. The poor bloke nearly fainted then. And he had an implement with four things on it and he dug it in this thing and then he pressed it so that it widened and then he got these tweezers and he dragged these cores out of his boil, and the poor man. He said, "Water, water". And the doctor said, "No water. No water. Head between your legs". He just wrapped it up and went back and banged him on the trawler. (Les Bowden - Grimsby)

The whaleback is the covered in part. Well just behind of that the rigging goes up and when they heave the bag in it could be as high as from here to the top of that tree. That's all fish. Sometimes it comes in and knocks everybody. One of the lads had hurt his leg. So I have to go and look at his leg and I thought to myself, "Christ almighty. His bloody foot is turned round the other bloody way." So I had to get me knife out 'cos he'd got long boots on. "What the fucking hell are you going to do?" I says, "I want to get down there." "That's a new pair of bloody boots. Pull it off". I said, "Don't be so bloody stupid". He said, "No pull me boots off - its a new pair of boots this." But I didn't, I just carried on and cut down there and pulled it off and his leg was broken and if I'd have pulled his boot off as he wanted I'd have pulled half his bloody leg off. (Charlie Board - Grimsby)

I was Third Hand of the Lord Beatty, December 1971. Whilst hauling the trawl I let go of a bag of fish and a huge stone came out of the cod end and knocked me down. I ended up with a dislocated hip which, in turn, dislocated the lumbar region of my spine, with four fractures of the pelvis. I was put ashore in Iceland, flown to Scotland and my pay was stopped as soon as I landed on British soil. After five months in hospital and twelve months convalescence I was paid £750 for total disability. I was granted a lawyer through my Union but it was decided that the firm I worked for (B.U.T.) could not be held responsible and that it must have been an Act of God. (Edwin Glenton - Grimsby)

I had my left shin bone broken when a loose deck board sprang up and hit me. I was taken into Greenland where I had an operation and a steel plate was put in. I was in hospital for three months. When I was finally flown home I found that my pay had been stopped as I was no longer a crew member. My wife had five children and was expecting the sixth. She couldn't get a sick note as I was out of the country. After a month with no money Dr Lanney got in touch with Northern Trawlers and issued a certificate without seeing me, to help her. I was another year out of work - with no compensation. (Edwin Hall - Grimsby)

I went over the side in one ship. I was Mate of the Sisapon in Northerns and it was a February trip. I married a woman with two children. I wanted the money else I would have stopped at home because she was expecting twins to me, though she lost them when I was at sea. In the Sisapon we came out in a Force 8 to 10 gale wind. We shot our gear away as best we could. Comes to haul it. I didn't realise there was a great big stone in the belly of the net. With it being Force 5 wind there was a bit of a swell and I was the one with the Third Hand that had to put the ropes round the belly to draw the net in. But the stone took all the net out and chucked me over the side. The ship drifts away with the wind so I was drifting away from it but I grabbed the net and got to the ship's side, but by the time I got to the ship's side one arm had gone numb with the cold weather and the other one was going gradually. I put my arm up to grab my wrist and a few of the lads yanked me aboard. I couldn't speak to nobody. My heart was chug, chug, chugging like a train. I laid there for ten minutes gone numb. "Leave me alone." I come round and I went aft and the Skipper sent me a tot of rum. I didn't know that in the meantime the crew said, "Don't we get a tot of rum Skipper?" He said, "You'll have to go over the side like the Mate." (Roly Webb - Grimsby)

Four of us got washed overboard and got washed back again. It was blowing very hard and there was mountainous seas and we was struggling with the gear. Trying to get the net in and the gear aboard when this big sea rolls up and she hit the ship both sides. She just tipped over and filled up with water. They have got hand rails round the casing and all that but we never got to it. We've also got handrails underneath the veranda. We used to have monkey bars where we used to jump up and hang on to it in case. We couldn't get up there in time and she washed us all over. Luckily, we were still hanging on to the net and I busted me foot, I got me foot caught under the rail and twisted me ankle so when we did get the gear aboard and when we did get into harbour I had to have me foot looked after by the doctor. I still remember going overboard. When the ship tipped and the water comes up it fills all the deck up, fills all the ship up, and it pulls the trawl up - of course you're pulling the trawl in, it just takes you with it, we're all hanging on the trawl, but of course when she tips back again she fetches water and some of the trawl back again see and lifts you back aboard. But with me being so small and having a busted foot as well she tipped again and I was going to go over again but one of the lads who had been washed overboard he'd got hold of the ladders, I think, and he grabbed hold of me as I was passing. He pulled me back again. So I might not have been here now if it hadn't been for him. It's all in a day's work really. You just take it in your stride, it's part of the job. (John Kirk - Grimsby)

We lost the Wyre Majestic on the rocks. This was blamed on one of the crew ignoring standing orders, and the vessel was stranded. It ran onto some rocks at a time when it was a high tide. Once a boat goes onto rocks on a high tide and holes itself there are lots of problems getting it off because the next high tide is a month later. We made attempts to get it off which all failed, and when the insurance assessor came the cost involved was so great that he said it should be regarded as a total loss. The insurance value then was something in the region of about £120,000 for the full vessel. The cost of obtaining tugs and the repairs involved in trying to re-float her would have been in excess of that, so they wrote her off. She still stands there, proudly painted. If I'd been at fault and had been a major cause of the stranding I'd have hung my head in shame and shrunk into a corner, but my orders are all written down in the log book about what to do and when to call me, but these had been totally ignored. The Bosun thought he had the knowledge to take her through but that was bravado and I don't know why he did it. I've never spoken to the man since because I think we'd fall out. I think I was the only Skipper in Fleetwood ever to lose a vessel totally and still go back to sea. People have run ships aground and got them off and gone back to sea, but to lose a vessel totally and go back to sea - I can't think of anybody else in Fleetwood who has done that. (Derek Reader - Fleetwood)

You've heard the saying if a ship takes three waves she'll go on the third one. Well there was me, Frank Clarkson, and Harold Beaumond and we was all stood aft side and it was really bad weather and she just went over like that and you could see a big white wave was coming towards you. She hit it and she went right over. Me, Beauie and Clarkson, we leapt on top of the boat deck, and we were saying, "If she takes another bleeder this is going to go." Her Bridge was practically in the water and we were just going to let go of the life raft when she took this third one and it was shaking like hell. I said, "This bastard's going to go!" We were just going to let go and she just seemed to come up and shakes all the water off it, and all the water just run out of her. Our hearts were in our bleeding mouths, but the third one hit the same starboard side and she righted herself. She just come up out the water like that, like a big sperm whale. (George Brown - Hull)

We went to Bear Island in January. We'd got good fishing. One of the crew came up to me, "I've got heart trouble". I mean I was stuck out on Bear Island. I says, "Yes, you've got heart trouble all right, the bugger's not big enough!" We got a storm warning and really heavy swell, and

I thought, "We're going to get this," so I battened down all hatches and thought we'll just ride this storm out. And it came on to blow terribly and we got iced up. I couldn't get men on deck to chop it the weather was that bad. And the ship turned on its side and shifted coal, just turned over on its side. I sent out Maydays and everything and they wouldn't answer, nobody was there, only one ship answered. Charlie Sleet was Skipper and he was at the North Cape of Norway and they was getting very, very bad weather there, and I thought we was going to lose the ship. Anyway I got all the crew out, the Cook, everybody - she'd turned over that far all the Bridge gratings came up, so you could tell how far she laid over, and I said, "We've got to shift this coal, we've got to shift it back again." Anyway, all Hands went down there and shifted the coal with their hands. Everybody was down there, except the Engineers and myself. I was on the Bridge. We got this coal shifted and she came up a bit and righted herself and I said to everybody, "Right, strap yourselves to the deck, I don't care what you do, get that ice off this ship, chop it off or we'll go over again." And we chopped and chopped, we was 36 hours chopping ice, continually chopping ice. I often sit back now and think well if you'd been more experienced would you have got out of it before it started to blow. But you learn, and I never made the same mistake again. And we got the ice off her and I put her before the wind and run her and I was on the Bridge, well it was five days. And I run her towards the Norwegian coast and I was going to start fishing on the Norwegian coast and I thought, "Oh sod it." (Don Lister - Grimsby)

The last big trawler I was on was a ship called the Robert Hewett. We'd gone to the White Sea, fishing in a place called 'Archangel' which is forty miles from Mermansk in Russia. I was Second Engineer. I went on deck and looked round and thought, "My God." I was fishing with forty Russian ships around me. They had a big mother ship there. It had everything aboard, cinema, even a brothel. Coming home we were going for the plaice, there was a glut and we was bringing it aboard like it was out of fashion. It was near Christmas. We came home via the Norwegian Fjords, guided by the Norwegian pilot, and just as we was going through I asked what the weather was like out there. He said it was howling, which it was, a Force 9 gale. Unfortunately,

Wyre Majestic-

*Wrecked in Islay Sound,
October 1974.
Copyright: Peter Horsley.*

*Riding the Waves.
Copyright: Grimsby Evening
Telegraph.*

Icing Up.

someone had forgotten to put the fore hatch down and it went unnoticed because it is only a small hatch where they fetch the nets, bobbins and that in. The water filled it up to the top. We'd seventeen feet of water in there. I'd been on watch and turned in. At about 8.30 I thought, "What the hell's wrong?" I was listing over to one side in my bunk. I got out and the first thing I noticed was the slope of the deck. I put my jeans on and went out and all the lads were in the rest room. I said, "What's up?", and they told me the fore hatch was full of water. We'd put the pumps on down the engine room but the fore hatch had got gear aboard, nets, bobbins etc., and they all had tags on them. This was underneath the pipe that was sucking the water up so, consequently, it was sucking up hardly anything. I got behind the winch to go across the deck to the fo'c's'le head, and the water, instead of coming over the side, hitting the deck and running through the scuppers, was hitting the deck and going over the other side. That's how low we were. It felt like we were on a submarine. Eventually I got across, I was wet through, and the lads were all there, bailing out with a bucket. Seventeen feet of water, the fore hold is about seventeen feet square, and they're bailing it out with just a bucket. In about eight hours they'd got down about two inches! That was all. But all this, the pressure of things like, was just about enough for me. I don't know if it was that but about twenty four hours later we started moderating, went into Aberdeen to get pumped out and the office said that while we were diverted there we might as well land the fish. We did that and made £25,000, which was a record trip for that ship. But it was a hell of a way to enjoy it because when I went down to the engine room next morning as we were steaming back to Fleetwood to get paid out, the engine room seemed to be turning round and round. It was me, gone. I stuck it for two days. I didn't tell anybody. I knew then that my fishing life was more or less finished. I did go back but I always had that feeling of fear. I went to the doctor and, in fact, later he sent me to see a psychiatrist in Blackpool who told me it was due to the pressure of the different things that had happened to me at sea. (Wilf Cartmell - Fleetwood)

I always remember the night the Gaul got lost because we were dodging in a full hurricane - a Force 12 hurricane. I had been on watch with the Skipper, and the Skipper had been up about three days and he was whacked out on his feet. I always remember this particular time looking out the Bridge window and the sea roared at the ship just like, well, a block of flats. It picked the ship up and just hurled it - the ship was over a thousand ton - it just picked it up and slung it to one side. There were about four or five ships in the area all struggling to try and get to land for safety and, unfortunately, the Gaul didn't make it but we did. (Tom Jacombe - Grimsby)

All trawlers really was good sea ships, that's 90% of trawlers. You could combat any weather. Once you got the severe icy conditions you was in trouble. Say you had to keep a ship head to wind to be safe it was that cold all the time you were spraying water it was freezing. Of course it was building up, building up, building up and if the weather got too bad for people to get on the deck to chop it away you were in trouble. You started getting top heavy. It happened to two or three ships. I remember one winter time I think it was the Roderigo and the Lorenzo, both Hull ships, they capsized with it, with the build up of ice, and they knew they was going. I was ashore at the time but I was talking to people. They couldn't get in to the land, the weather was that bad, so they knew they was going to drown. There was gradually a build up of ice and then they drowned.

I think there was about three ships lost that winter. As you went Nor,'Nor'East, Norway and Bear Island and Spitzbergen you used to get the bad weather and the icing conditions but not as bad as Iceland. That was always the worst, Iceland. But it was always good fish see. You always seemed to make more money from there. (George Mussell - Grimsby)

When the Cleveland went we were all fishing off there with them. There was a big gang of ships off there, and I was in a ship called the Boston Explorer with a skipper called Harry Dingle. We all started steaming in together and we were listening to the ships and where they were going, and there was a hell of a lot of ships making for Isafjord. Harry said, "The way the visibility is going it's going to be hell in there

with all the ships. We'll carry on and go into Derrifjord." We got in there, already badly iced up, and we were dodging around there. But you didn't have the distance there for dodging like you had in Isafjord, but at least we didn't have a glacier like Isafjord. Freezing though it was for us it would have been worse still coming down the glacier. A few more ships came into Derrifjord and it began to get a bit crowded in there. Me and the Skipper were talking and I said, "Look, she's gonna bloody sink lets get her alongside the quay, at least then we can step off." He agreed. We were working, all hands, an hour on and an hour off, and on your hour off you was doing your chopping. I saw lads on the deck with blood coming out of their ears with the cold. Eventually we got alongside the quay and everybody was trying to do the same. It's something I'll remember to my dying day. The Skipper said, "What are you doing?" and I told him I was going to the phone to phone home, to phone my missus. He told me to tell her to let all the crews wives know. I rung my wife up and she picked up the phone. As soon as she knew it was me she started crying because it had been on the news about the Cleveland. She said, "Don't go back on that ship. Get all the crew together and I'll find the money to fly you all home. I don't want you on that ship." (Jim Quinn - Fleetwood)

There was a Wireless Operator - he lived in Combe Street - I've often thought about this and felt very guilty. His name was Denopolis and he was the wireless operator. And it was an early morning tide and I went round and he refused to go because he'd had a row with his wife. In fact they was having a battle royal. I'm there and I'm trying to persuade him and I'm not interested in their battle. I'm trying to get him to go to sea because I knew that particularly without a Wireless Operator we wouldn't get the ship away that morning. I eventually kidded him and kidded her to let him go and it was that trip that the ship was lost. He got killed. And when I went round with the Port Missionary to inform her she actually flew at me with a knife. She said that I'd killed him. She said, 'He didn't want to go to sea. You was the one that made him." Looking back on it I was. I know I was only doing my job but I used to think, "Did I kill him?" (Gordon Cockerill - Grimsby)

We was fishing off Iceland, it was a Force 10 or 11, full storm, and we was anchored and dodging. Anyhow we stopped her, and I thought right I'll get turned in now. I'd just been turned in about five minutes and the telegraph went, engines going ahead again, five minutes elapsed, telegraph went again. I thought, "We're aground, that's it". I got out of my bunk and there was a kid opposite me panicking. I said, "You're all right. By the way, you've got my socks and my boots on." We just went on the boat deck, we looked up, as far as you could see it was snowing, a full blizzard. "God, where are we?". The lights of the ship were reflecting on the mountain. So two or three of us got the spanners and knocked the life rafts over, the inflatable ones, put them over the side and they inflated so much, but part of them wouldn't because it was covered in ice. So we pulled up alongside and I jumped in one of them, started knocking it up and it inflated all right. Then I did the other one. I'd been down the engine room and seen this pinnacle of rock stuck through the ship itself. The rocks were underneath this life raft, so I went straight back aboard the ship then. The boat was filling with water as the tide must have been coming in. The Old Man sung out, "Who gave you permission to launch them?" I said, "Who gave us permission?" shouting at the top of my voice, "Nobody, but they're there in case we need them. I mean it's no good leaving them too late is it?". Anyhow he said, "Tell the Chief I'm going to ring and pull astern." So I went down to the Chief and told him, and he said, "These engines aren't going to move, they're stopping, it'll just rip the bottom out." An hour elapsed and you could see the water rising and this little light zoomed in out the darkness and it was this life boat from the mother ship, the Othello, and he made three journeys and took us all off on his own. The next day they said, "We're to go back aboard the ship and see what we can salvage on the Chad." So I said, "Oh you can do me a favour Tom, in that top berth in the locker there's a pot there with my false teeth in. Can you bring them back?" Anyhow, an hour later he come back with the pot. So all I got back was my teeth! (Clive Finn - Hull)

The Ross Cleveland, we was at the Cape when she went and I'm not kidding you I cried that day because I heard her and her Skipper. His nickname was Stab a Sausage. The weather was atrocious, it was freezing very hard. When conditions were like that you always used to hope and pray that the wind would either come round or else back round so the temperature would rise. The weather was bad, it was blowing very hard, but our Skippers wouldn't go and steam and lay under the land, if they could get away with it. When you were steaming there and steaming back you was losing time. We got further and further into Isafjord and we heard him, he was talking on the VHF, she was like a Christmas tree, we all were. Everybody aboard the ship was chopping ice, and he just says, "Give our love to everybody at home", and she went like that. There was three in the life raft, there was a Fireman, the Galley Boy and Harry Eddoms, the Mate. Harry was the only one who had a duck suit on, protective clothing. The others died because they were in T-shirts and jeans. The cold killed them. The Kingston Peridot had left the Cape area and steamed easterly at Iceland, at a place called Melrakka Flats. All they found of her was just a puddle of oil, and the St. Romanus as far as I know she was going North, North East to the White Sea, but she didn't have a Sparks. That was a disgrace that. She had no Radio Operator, and nobody heard anything from her. They never even found a fish board let alone anything else - she'd just gone, full crew. So that's three full crews gone within the space of about ten days. (Ray Smith - Grimsby)

One ship I was in ran onto the reefs in the west of Norway. She went down in an hour and a half. Luckily we were near a big lighthouse with a small village near it. We lit mattresses to draw their attention. She was laid over so we could only get one life boat out. We got the Engineers, Galley Boys, the Cook, the Deckie Learners, and got them into the life boat. We were spotted from the light house and this small village had a few small fishing boats. They came straight out and took us off the ship. It was a complete write off. It had gone down straight away. It didn't put me off fishing. There'd been no loss of life. I was young so I hadn't really been frightened. It would be different now, but when you're only twenty one or two nothing much bothers you. You need the wisdom of age to recognise danger. (Ken Robertson - Hull)

The Sinking of the Sargon in Iceland.

It was 1946 when I started fishing and on 1 December 1948, when the Sargon went down I was on my second trip on her. We'd tried three times to get away in the fog and the fishing was very bad. We only had about 300 kit - very poor. We were off N.W. Iceland running into Patricks Fjord and the weather was atrocious - the worst for thirty years - when we went aground. I was on watch at the time, me and the Skipper, and it was about a quarter to ten at night and he said, "Will you make us a drink, Fred?" So I'm going down the ladder and that's when she just shuddered as if she were going over. Before then we were taking soundings, we'd no radar, but we knew we was in the fjords somewhere so we took a sounding. Then they said, "Call them all out, get round and call them all out." Anyway, we were calling them out but when I got down the cabin it was filling, and the lights went out. She was full up in no time, then she shuddered again, that's when she hit this mountain, but it was freezing hard and hailstoning, you couldn't see a thing. We managed to get a rocket off, just one, the other one just hit the water, and that's all we had. No means to let anybody know where we was. Then she was chucking sea over the Bridge from her stern really bad and we see sparks coming out the fo'c's'le funnel, so me and a few others decided to get forward. We had to crawl along the deck just to do that and we gets forward. We'd got dry gear on, and that's what actually saved us. I got a bag of gear to try and take back, but couldn't make it, the sea was too bad. I was stood on top of the fo'c's'le ladder watching the water coming up, to see how far it was coming to the level, and that was just after ten, and it was eleven o'clock next morning I think it was, when we got rescued.

I see Billy Beech coming down the ladder and I ran to help him, and I thought he said to me. "The Second's dead", but he said, "They're all dead". I didn't know, because one of them stood on the Bridge window, he was just stood there while we was getting rescued, and there was no way we could get him off the Bridge. Anyway we come off and the next day they found his body on the beach, he must have tried to get off himself. Then they found the Skipper down the chart room, he'd got down there, unbeknown to them, and he drowned. He just froze to death. We were seventeen altogether and all of them that stayed on the Bridge died. We didn't because we got the dry gear on so six of us survived. If they'd come with us most of them would have been saved, because it was only a matter of thirteen hours until we were getting rescued.

I don't know much about the rescue. We never thought we were going to get rescued. When we saw them there, we were relieved like, but I was hit on the head with a rock and I didn't know much more after that. I can remember them saying to me, "Keep your legs up, keep your legs up." Then it started freezing again. By the time they got to us the weather had eased down a lot, but before then you just couldn't see the Bridge at all, such a great sea, so you didn't have much of a chance. Six of us was winched ashore and half of them got up the cliff on the first day. I remember them washing us all down like with some spirits or something, with us being cold, to try and stop the frostbite. Then they fastened us with belts to get us up the mountain. I was only half way, I think I was about the third going up, and they were dodging these boulders coming down. One of the Icelanders got hit on the shoulder. I was behind him and I got hit on the head, fractured my skull. After that I don't remember much about it. I was passing out most of the time. They took us on horses. None of us could walk properly. By that time we were really frozen. I had frost bitten toes. When I came back they put my feet in ice to cure them. When I came to I was in this farmhouse, just me and the Mate separated from the other four. I think it was in the early hours of the morning the next day. I was in bed when I came round and the Mate was in the next bed to me. I always remember seeing this young lass stood over me, farmer's daughter. Looked after us well. Then when we got over it we used to help them on the farm. We were there a week or so, I think, just the two of us, and we didn't see the other four for about a week after. We had to go and identify the bodies. They had them stretched out on the lorry. Then they took us to Reykjavik. It was about three weeks before I got home. First off I felt like giving up life at sea. Then I did go away eventually in the Arnold Bennett and when the Skipper found out who I was he sent me back off the ship, "Get ashore". That was it. (Fred Collins - Hull)

One of the tragic things that I had to do in my job was when a ship was lost, going round and notifying the widows. The Port Missionary and I used to go round. Naturally we had a duplicate of all members on board. We would be stood by the radio and in touch at the time, like when the Leicester City ran ashore, with survivors that had been picked up, and those that had been picked up dead. We notified them first that the ship had run aground. Then it was a case of waiting for verification of whether they was actually alive or dead. That was a very sad time. One was a chap called Hunt and I remember they lived in Orwell Street and he had a son, a bit of a hard case, but he would be about twelve years of age and I knew him because he'd been down dock with his father. And I had to inform his grandmother, and say that they'd lost their son, and he was playing outside. And I said to him, "You better come inside with me. I've got some bad news." And I took him inside and explained to his grandmother and grandfather that we'd just had notification that the son had been found but he was dead and of course they was crying and upset and he just jumped up in the air and started to laugh. Then he went outside and was playing football in the street as though nothing had happened. And when I went outside I called him over and I said, "You realise what's happened?" And he said, ''Yes, I know. Me dad's dead." I could have got hold of him and I could have throttled him. A few days later after we'd got the bodies home the service was at the Bethel Mission. And I remember looking at him when he came in as though he hadn't got a care in the world. On walking out - he hadn't got outside the church and he collapsed. And he was paralysed. The doctors diagnosed that was the shock. He realised what had happened and in his bravado instead of mourning or being sad he tried to put it away and then the few days that he'd had it in his mind and all of a sudden the impact of coming out the church it paralysed him. He did recover . In fact he eventually went to sea. (Gordon Cockerill - Grimsby)

Chapter 6
Different Ports and Different Grounds

The three great trawler ports were home to the great majority of the distant water fleets. Hull had the largest, a hundred big vessels over 140 foot which were the biggest catchers. Some 8,500 people, five percent of Hull's population, worked in fishing compared to Grimsby where 11,750, or seventeen percent of the population, worked in it. Grimsby had a smaller distant water fleet, half the size of Hull's, but compensated by a middle water fleet which fished distant waters too, and a near water fleet which Hull did not have. All this made Grimsby's fish market better for quality fish where Hull went for bulk and scale. Ninety percent of Britain's bigger vessels operated from the Humber but Fleetwood, the poor relation of its East Coast rivals, had ten distant water vessels in the Sixties, plus around fifty smaller, middle water, vessels which fished Faroese and Icelandic waters. This was bigger than Aberdeen with two large vessels but sixty middle water vessels, or Lowestoft also with two big and a score of middle water vessels.

The big three shared a degree of isolation common to towns "at the end of the line", a proud sense of identity and a common way of life which made them unique. Each had its fishing communities in the town, ghettos, where the fishermen lived, while the Owners, Skippers and Merchants kept a degree of distance and lived further away. Everywhere the fisherman's life was much the same. Same Owners. Same man's world "down dock." Similar pubs and clubs, and the same lures to relieve 'three day millionaires' of their money.

That was earned mainly in Icelandic waters but the industry reached out to any grounds where catches could be made. Iceland was the shortest round trip at 2,000 miles and usually provided the best and most consistent catches but Bear Island, the most northerly fishery was 2,700 miles and the White Sea was 1,700 miles one way, some of that via Norwegian Fjords. The Northern Norwegian coast was the fourth main source of fish, ahead of Greenland, the furthest and most difficult regular fishing ground. Some vessels stuck to one area, most rotated, usually on a seasonal basis, to the Norwegian coast in February, the White Sea in the second half of the year, and Iceland most of the rest of the year.

Fleetwood was such a small place. My wife's family came from Grimsby, my father in law's father had been a fisherman. My father can remember walking across from Grimsby when the coal strike was on. My mother came from Aberdeen, another fishing fraternity. One of her brothers was lost on a ship from Fleetwood, and another brother was also a Chief, so things run in families like that. (Harold Dawe - Fleetwood)

Here in Fleetwood you had the Wyre Mariner, Sam Hewitt and a couple of others. You only had about four boats. After that you could nearly get in any of the other boats - go to Iceland and maybe make £2,000. But in Hull you'd probably be making twice that. There was plenty of jobs here then, in the Fifties. At that time it got so you didn't have to go down the dock gates, you just sat in a pub and some of the Runners would come in and offer you a ship. You'd say, "I'm not bothered," because you wouldn't make much other than your wage. (Tom Bagnall - Fleetwood)

I think the problem of the fishing industry in Fleetwood was that those who were not involved looked down upon fishermen and their families. I noticed that in the very beginning there would be certain elements in the town who would have regarded them as slightly suspect and that fishermen and their families would have a certain reputation, be it the reputation for drink, for hard-living, running up debts, unreliable, swearers, whatever, neglecting your family - well of course you'd neglect your family if you're away for eighteen days and you're only home for three days, but it depends on the definition of neglect. And some of the fishing families if they were open would tell you themselves that they were regarded as lower than low. One of the other problems I discovered was that those who had positions of authority in the fishing industry, possibly Skippers, that some of their families looked down on the ordinary fishing families as well, and that when I came into the town there was the ludicrous situation where because the ordinary fishermen were shopping and serving in shops in the town, those who were Skippers' wives and whatever, they went shopping in Blackpool and elsewhere because they didn't want to be associated in the same shops. Fleetwood was always looked down upon. The rest of the Fylde coast was a bit upper class compared with us because Fleetwood was, and still is, the only working class town in the Fylde coast. It was also at the end of the line, so even to this day you do not come to Fleetwood unless you have to. And these are all part of the problems of the town so it was even a greater problem than, say, Grimsby and Hull in that sense. It was isolated because of its geographical features, and because it was a working class town, and it was also isolated because of the tradition in fishing. (Fr McMahon - Fleetwood)

There was fishing community areas in Fleetwood. I didn't live actually down this bit. I always lived back in the town, near the tram lines, that was where I was brought up, and that was a council house estate. Then away from there towards Beach Road, they used to call that 'Skippers Road.' A lot of the top Skippers lived in that area. They owned their own houses. That was my aim in life. To own my own house. That was the first thing we did. When I proposed to my wife I said, "We're not getting married until we've got our own house." And that's what we did. We were in the process of buying it when we got married. So that was one goal we achieved and it was all uphill from there. It was great. (Jim Quinn - Fleetwood)

I think there was two breeds of fishing in Fleetwood, the Icelandic and the home waters. When you start learning your seamen skills, if you happen to be a Bosun or Mate sailing Iceland it's obvious that you are going to learn all the Icelandic grounds, so if you do develop into a Skipper you'll be an Icelandic Skipper. In my case I was sailing home waters, middle waters, and I learned most of the home water

grounds, hake fishing etc. In around 1966, one or two ships started going a little bit further and started intermingling with the Grimsby fleet. I was one of them. We found out that the Grimsby men were making more money than us catching haddock etc., rather than the specialised hake fishing that we did in Fleetwood, so we started intermingling with them, picking their brains, and eventually I finished not as a hake fisherman but fishing alongside the Grimsby men. You talk to them, on ships you get in each other's way and you get talking on the wireless, you introduce yourself and find out about them. You got to know them just by being in the same grounds and hearing each other on the radio. The best Skippers keep tags on each other. Quite a few Fleetwood Skippers did it. Hake was what they wanted in Fleetwood, and it wasn't until the mid Sixties that the Owners started finding out that the mixed fish - cod and haddock - was earning more money. Money was the be all and end all of every operation for the Owners. Until then Fleetwood was a specific hake port. (Derek Reader - Fleetwood)

Hessle Road was marvellous. Nobody had anything but it was a wonderful place to live. There was nowhere else in the world like it. They were all fishing families, from one end of Hessle Road to the other. Maybe two and a half mile, from Osborne Street to Dee Street, it was almost completely fishing families, fishing or connected with fishing. There were that many pubs you could have had a drink in each one and by the time you got to the other end you'd be blind drunk. The pubs were always crowded. There was either a pub or a club for nearly every street. In those days Hessle Road was just like a bee hive from early morning. We used to get woken up by the Bobbers going down the road with their clogs on. The Bobbers would go down about midnight to open the ship's hatches up and getting everything ready to unload the fish. You'd hear the steel studs on their clogs as they went clumping down the road. (Ken Robertson - Hull)

Lots of the fishermen lived in the East Marsh which was nearer to the docks, in Hope Street, Albion Street and that area at the back of Freeman Street, the main shopping area. They lived in the two up and two down houses, six in a row with one outside tap between the six, and no bathroom. The

Skippers lived mainly in Orwell Street adjacent to the docks in great big three storey terraced houses with bay windows, but after the war there was a different type of Skipper because of the bigger ships that were coming in, and they moved to the rather select area of Queen Mary Avenue, in semi-detached houses etc. So the Skippers separated themselves from the crews.

You'd see the crews congregating at Riby Square in the Lincoln Pub, the Red Lion Pub and Cotties Pub, which were the three pubs near the fish docks that the fishermen used to go in, and also the Icelandic and Danish fishermen known as 'scrobs'. Riby Square was where the fishermen used to assemble. They would land at midnight or at 6 o'clock in the morning and they would settle up at 10, but you would find the fishermen congregated at Riby Square before the pubs opened at 10.30. Between 9.00 and 11 there would be literally thousands of fishermen around the Riby Square area. They would then drift out, get the money, get their settlings and then they would go to the pubs down Freeman Street from Monday right through the next Monday. Every lunchtime was like a Saturday night because fishermen settled up whichever day they'd landed, usually Monday. That was when the biggest landing was. So the main shopping street was a wonderful sight with all the fishermen having their Saturday night every lunchtime. You'd see the Icelandic fishermen who'd spent all their money in Grimsby. They'd be coming up Freeman Street with clothes, furniture, pianos and put them back on board the Icelandic trawlers and take that stuff back to Reykjavik. So Freeman Street and the docks area was unique.

Every Friday lunchtime the schools in Grimsby closed. They didn't operate Friday afternoons - the kids left school at lunch time. We used to take a lunch to school, have a sandwich about 11.30 a.m. and school used to finish at 1.00 p.m. We used to go home and all the fishermen's wives used to go down the fish dock to get the husband's wages because they were left an allotment and they drew that every Friday afternoon and at 2 o'clock, the first pay out was at 2.30 p.m., but from 2.00 p.m. to 4.00 p.m. you'd see literally thousands of women going down to the dock with the kids from school

and they would go and draw the money and come back and that was known as the 'Fish Dock Races.' It was a sight worth seeing. (Alec Bovill - Grimsby)

You got rats in the old ships. You couldn't avoid it because the fish dock was alive with rats. I expect it would be the same at Grimsby. I never saw it myself but they do say there was a big migration of rats in Hull one time, from the fish docks. I never saw any of it but the older men saw it. When they were building the new St Andrew's Quay in Hull they found the old fish meal factory was alive with rats. They had intended to demolish it in one go but the Environmental Health Officers wouldn't let them. They had to gas all the rats in one part and demolish that bit when the rats had been cleared, then do another part in the same way. They said that if they'd just pulled it down in one go, the rats would have moved out in one mass. The original story of the rat migration was from the fish meal factory. There used to be two fish docks and mainly they used to leave the bridge swung across, and that was how the rats came across. The rats were supposed to have come from the fish meal factory across the bridge and into the town. (Ken Robertson - Hull)

I wouldn't say the town was on the same scale as Hull. I always thought Hull and Grimsby was bigger than Fleetwood. I've heard people say Fleetwood was the biggest fishing port but Hull seemed to always make more than us. We was more a port for quality fishing, hake and that, whereas Hull and Grimsby mainly fished Iceland. They didn't have the home fishing like us. But I would have thought they was bigger than Fleetwood. When I got spragged once I went to Grimsby. Lived there for a bit. Half a dozen of us just decided one day that we'd go to Hull, then decided on Grimsby. It was even hard there. It was the same thing. There was jobs but on the boats that weren't making 'owt. But we was spragged for six weeks in Fleetwood so we went there. I finished up in some little boat. Average maybe make about £1,000 - summat or nowt. We asked about the big 'uns but couldn't get one. There was a lot of Fleetwood blokes in Grimsby, still there now some of them, married there. They got in decent boats but we never got 'owt. We was in digs in Cleethorpes, about six of us in one house. If you happened to be in one ship and they was in a different one they'd come in and take all your gear - shirts and that - using them. So you'd try and keep together so they couldn't touch your gear. I enjoyed it. It was a good giggle. I thought they were good people. I've sailed with a lot of Yorkies, Hull people who came to Fleetwood, but they was - I don't know - what you'd call the outcasts I suppose. I got on well with them, they was the same as us, but in Grimsby they seemed to make you more welcome when you went in the pubs and that. Even the women would buy you a drink if they'd got 'owt. There was no saying that you're short and out of work. They was good people and I got on well with them. (Thomas Bagnall - Fleetwood)

Hull had always specialised in bulk and their gear, their fishing gear, their style, for instance the weight of their gear and the design of it, was different from ours which was all orientated to quantity. Hull had always gone in for bulk, their ships were bigger, not bigger than the biggest Grimsby ships but they'd always gone in for Bear Island and White Sea and I don't think apart from Hellyer Brothers they fished Iceland as well as some of the Grimsby firms. They adapted their gear, the trawl, the bobbins and everything to make it more suitable for bulk and their outlook was different. I remember saying that when we took over the nine or ten Lord Line ships from Hull they couldn't have been any more different. The attitude of the Skippers and the layout couldn't have been more different if we had taken them home from Shanghai. Everything's slightly different even though we were only twenty miles away. Fleetwood, for instance, was more concerned with fishing for species like Icelandic plaice on the west side of Iceland and hake which is west coast fishing and orientated to smaller ships and smaller trips. Our older ships used to go to Fleetwood. Hull's older ships used to come to Grimsby. (John Butt - Grimsby)

Hull and Grimsby have always had a friendly rivalry. They've both laid claim to being the biggest fishing ports in the world. They were both right in different ways. Grimsby had more ships but a big proportion of those were the snibbies, the small Danish type built 70-80 footers, and they had more ships going middle and near water. I would say that only maybe ten percent of them went really deep sea fishing. By that I mean really distant water - Bear Island, Spitzberg etc. Basically Grimsby was more of a quality port, for plaice, haddocks and them kind of things. But Hull was for bulk fishing. Mostly cod, and haddocks when there was a lot of haddocks, at the breeding time between February and March, and for things like what we call soldiers, the bergaults, the red ones, and coleys. Hull was a big bulk cod, haddock and coley port. Where Hull was the largest in sheer volume of fish, Grimsby was largest in the quality fish.

The Silver Cod encouraged the catching of rubbish. Sheer volume. Most of the Silver Cod winners landed a lot of fish that they wouldn't normally have caught if they hadn't been in the top handful who were in the running for it. The Challenge Shield replaced the Silver Cod and with that everything was taken into consideration. You got awarded points for less days at sea, for volume, for how much your fish sold for, so that was a much better idea because it encouraged quality. People did take it very seriously. To be in the top twenty for the Silver Cod was quite a feather in your cap. To be in the top five towards the end of a year meant it was a race. I was lucky. In my last year at sea - I chucked it in on the 21st of May 1973 - and on the 21st of May 1973 I made £21,600. The previous year, my last complete calendar year (the competition was always run on calendar years), I'd never even started fishing until March because my ship was laid up with a huge boiler job, so I only got in nine months fishing out of that year. There were only fifty six ships out of the port then and I started up in March as number fifty six and I finished up number eleven. I was very proud of that. (Jim Williams - Hull)

I think there was more blokes lost or injured because the Skipper was after the Silver Cod. That's why they knocked that on the head. It was only going for about five or six years - I can't exactly remember which years. I was in one that won the Silver Cod, the Somerset Maugham. Billy Brown. He won the Silver Cod. Our top trip we landed 4,200 kits. That was a good lot. He was a top Skipper and he worked the crews hard. On deck all day gutting. You'd go home and make nowt, too small. They wouldn't buy it, 4,000 odd kits and they wouldn't buy it. Once I

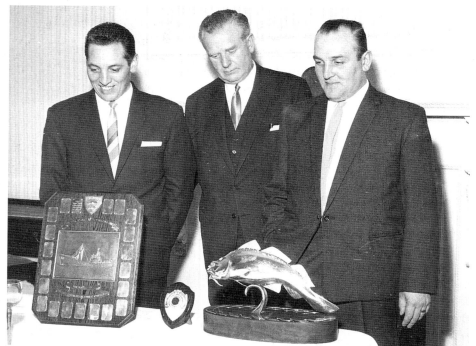

landed in the James Barrie 3,200 kit, and I picked up half a crown. All condemned. But it still counted for the Silver Cod. The Skipper couldn't care less. He still got his money. We didn't though. So did the Owners 'cause it went for fish meal didn't it and they owned the fish meal factory. It was all just a racket but we couldn't do nowt about it. If you was in a Silver Cod, taking the year in hand you must have made money to land the fish, but it was hard work. Mostly you was earning good money because of the poundage. But it was rough. Everything got weighed. Whereas, when you weren't fishing with the Silver Cod blokes, you'd dump the small stuff, save only the good fish, you could make a good market. Not the Silver Cod blokes. They kept everything and you'd be all day on deck gutting it, sometimes for nowt. It was just a silver cod, a silver fish. It's in the Dock Museum now. The winner kept it for a year. Every year somebody won it. When you won it the Skipper generally bought the crew something. Maybe a silver ash tray or something like that. We got a tankard - I keep flowers in mine. That's all it was worth really. (George Waudby - Hull)

I was the Ship's Runner for seven years and then the Ship's Husband until 1964. We used to have to meet the ships and see the Skipper and Mate to ask if there were any vacancies. In other words if there was anybody not suitable on the ship and they wanted them replacing, if anybody was coming and having a trip off for a holiday, so we knew on the following day that we had to get replacements. We was like an employment agency. We had an office and people used to stand outside and come down every day to see if there was any vacancies and we would pick the best man for that particular ship or that particular Skipper. I was responsible for victualling the ship, depending on whether it was going in the North Sea, whether it was going to Faroe, whether it was going to Iceland or Bear Island, to the length of stay that we anticipated it would be away and we had to victual the ship according to how many men was aboard. On a North Sea ship there used to be ten men aboard, a Faroe ship there used to be fifteen, and then in deep water ships as we used to call them,

Iceland, Bear Island and the White Sea, there was anything from twenty to twenty eight. We had to put enough bread to last them for a couple of days, until the Cook had baked his own bread which they used to do. But all the meats was put aboard - sausages, livers, things like that, potatoes, vegetables - enough to last them for the duration of the trip. Occasionally they would run out of food or the food would go rotten and they would have to call into Iceland or wherever possible to get new provisions. We used to order it from the Cosalt and Tanning Company and then it was my job before the ship sailed to make sure that it had all been put aboard. It was a double check on it. (Gordon Cockerill - Grimsby)

You knew that the fish would go to the same places each year to breed so you'd go there. That's nearly always been what we went by. At the beginning of the year you would plot your year out. Say from mid January to early April I would say you'd be fishing on the Norwegian coast, just above the Arctic Circle, and all the way up towards the North Cape of Norway. After that you'd go to the West side of Iceland, round the South West Coast, up towards the West Side up towards the Cape and then, afterwards, to Bear Island or the Barent sea. If they heard that fish was being caught somewhere else then the bosses would tell you to go there, but generally when you did that the fish had gone by the time you got there, so that would be a waste of time. So the bosses would say, "You shouldn't have gone then." I mostly worked by the calendar for the distant water fish. The big breeding season on the South West Coast of Iceland, we used to call that the Island Seas - the Westman Islands - and you used to get a lot of cod and haddock round there. (Sid Morrell - Hull)

The Iceland season was in the spring. The fish moves on its way from Bear Island. It moves down the Norway coast and then branches off to Iceland. The season for the Norway Coast would be February and March, then of course, Iceland, then Bear Island and then across to the Barent Sea. (Bill Hardie - Grimsby)

My first trip as Skipper we went to the White Sea. That's off the Norway coast. We made a smashing trip and I never looked back from then really. We fished all over then,

but later on I used to concentrate on Iceland, fish Icelan because I liked it. It was closer. This is when I was Skip, You could go to Iceland and you could be fishing in less tha three days but if you went Nor',Nor' East, that was all round the Russian waters, Bear Island, Spitzbergen, you was five or six days steaming. A long time isn't it? (George Mussell - Grimsby)

The worst weather, I think, was at Iceland. Even in the summer there you got some bad gales. But the ice was a terrible thing. I mean the ice on the fish. You'd be fishing in fine weather and before you'd got time to haul your gear aboard it was upon you. The winds used to just spring up and bring frosts with them. You just couldn't do a thing about it. The weather conditions were that bad you perhaps couldn't get to the land for safety. You had to ride it out - what we call dodging. Didn't matter where you went you got the bad weather, but if you got the strength in the wind plus the icing conditions, which was at Iceland, that was the worst. (Tom Jacombe - Grimsby)

My father used to tell us about when he started fishing. The Icelanders only used to have little boats for inshore fishing, they knew nothing about trawling what so ever. It was Grimsby ships that first went down to Iceland to explore the fishing grounds. What they found was so much fish that there wasn't enough marine life to feed it, so the fish were underfed and not of very good quality, but of course they caught these fish and brought them back, and the amount they brought back paid off. They were keen on exposing the fishing grounds off Iceland because it was a very rich fishing area, but it was Britain's historical fishing grounds because they explored them, they pioneered them. Men went down to Iceland in ships with no modern navigational aids. They had nothing, no sextants, no such thing as radar - they didn't have it sometimes even in the war - they were very hard men and they realised they had got some very good fishing grounds. The West side of Iceland was rough ground where they used to say, the fishermen who fished there, that they were going where angels feared to tread. (Bill Hardie - Grimsby)

a lot
...er.

d go to Iceland and you'd go to different ...ou'd go to the North of Iceland, the South, ...rever the fish was best. But always the best ...which was very bad weather. Very bad ...ad to run for shelter and run quick, or else ...or trouble. We were up there one time anchored out the way and of course there were three or four turned over. All the ice was coming down. The ice used to build up on the riggings so they were ten times as thick, and then of course you got anything you could to break it. In those days there was no way of melting it. They used to kink over and that's what turned a lot of ships over. If you were in Iceland you'd make for Norway, and once you'd got to Norway you could come right down the fjords and avoid the weather. It'd have to be very bad weather before you went in the fjords. But I enjoyed it all at sea. I didn't know nowt better. I couldn't come ashore and do what a carpenter was doing. I used to like it. (Jim Johnson - Grimsby)

There were more bad fishing grounds used by Fleetwood fishermen. We had our share, especially around Iceland. The names of the grounds tell you that: the Coffin, the Headline Pitch, The Hindenberg, Hari Kari Bank - these names speak for themselves. Harry Kari means sudden death. The Headline Pitch, the headline on a trawl, when the net parted somewhere, with a bit of luck it parted on the Headline leg so you'd just have a wire to replace, but if it parted in the middle it meant a lot of net mending. (Jim Williams - Hull)

The trip was unusually hard, the conditions off Iceland's North Cape appalling. We had gone through gales, black frost and icing problems. Most of us had developed frostbite on our lips, hands and feet. We were ready for home. We had in the hold 1,600 kits of top quality fish. So when the news came through that we were to stay only another forty eight hours before heading home we were well pleased, I can tell you. And to crown it all, the weather actually took a turn for the better, the gloom lifting to reveal a great ice field which had moved down from the north. The Skipper - a relief - decided to tow closer to the ice after hearing reports of giant cod. It was just after breakfast on our second to last day. As we hauled the trawl we were amazed - it was just bursting to the seams with large cod. But with them came the smell, a cloying stench that filled the air, causing the deck crew to pull mufflers around their mouths and noses. I have never known anything so horrible. Then we noticed it covering the net. A strange waxy substance that dripped from the trawl as we hauled it aboard, turning the deck into a skating rink. The Skipper ordered it to be swilled off and we did so using two hoses and shovels. But that was not the end of the matter. Twice more we had a similar experience, the second time finding it in such quantity that it took two hours to throw it back into the sea. As evening approached the Skipper decided to tow away from the ice field. I can still remember the Deckies lined up on the after-casing breathing in the fresh air. They even had to wash down their oil frocks and boots before going to the galley for a mug of tea - Cook's orders! Apparently two big Hull trawlers had also picked up the waxy substance. But one of their Skippers had recognised what it was and had ordered it to be put in barrels. To our surprise we learned it was ambergris, a secretion made by the sperm whale used in making expensive perfume. We, in fact, had never seen any sperm whales - I never did in Iceland all the time I fished there. One theory was that it may have been carried down somehow by the ice field. But we did learn that the Hull trawlers took it home and sold the lot to a buyer. The Skipper decided to lay for a while. We cleared the decks and got the cod iced in the fish room. It was while we were gutting in the pounds that the second amazing incident of that unforgettable trip occurred. About five hundred yards away on the starboard side the sea began to froth and bubble. We stopped and stared in disbelief as a huge conning tower slowly emerged carrying the hammer and sickle of a Russian submarine. At first we thought we'd strayed into a military training zone. The sea cascaded off its superstructure like a giant waterfall and onto green and slimy decks, making us all wonder just how long it had been underwater. When the Russian captain arrived on deck, however, his request was simple - and easily met. All he wanted was fresh fish for his crew's evening dinner! We obliged by sending two baskets of assorted fish, after which he sent back eight bottles of best vodka to be shared among the crew. I remember the taste of it today - it was like firewater. The transaction completed, he then submerged leaving behind him a huge trail of bubbles.

The rest of the day on the fishing grounds passed without incident. (Michael Sparkes - Grimsby)

You never took money to sea but you could get a sub from the Agent. But you didn't want to get yourself too much in debt. You had it to pay back. We was in Akureyri. We'd got a big job - about five or six day at least. And the Agent come down and said to the Skipper, "I can organise some outings to keep the crew happy." So he says, "That's good." So he organises these trips out into the hills and he was giving the Skipper the bill for these - it was working out about £23 a man. That was a lot of money. Then we realised that the Agent owned the bus system that was taking us out and he was also making the ship move berth every day, which because the engine was disabled meant a tug. Then we found out that he owned the tug. Then when it come to re-stocking with grub, because we used up our grub, who owned the store but the agent. Then he comes through to Dave and says, "Would your crew like to go to the pictures or swimming?" Then we found out he owned the cinema house and the swimming pool. It cost a fortune. We was there eight or nine days and they run up a bill for over £5,000. Well the ship only used to make about £6,000 for the trip. And Dave was panicking. He thought he was going to get the sack over it but he didn't realise 'til he fetched these bills and he found out he was an Icelandic Agent. He was on a good thing. The Owners used to have an Agent and no matter what firm it was, they was the Agent for the port, and they'd come down. I mean usually you used them for radar jobs or 'owt like that. Or if 'owt went wrong or the Skipper wanted a night in. Usually if you said, "Oh the radar's gone," you used to get in for a night. (Graham Howard - Grimsby)

Greenland fitted in when you could fish nowhere else because it is a horrible place to fish. The tides are so strong, the icebergs move with the tide faster than you. A lot of problems with the ground so you get your nets torn - it's not a good place to fish. (Bill Hardie - Grimsby)

I went to Greenland with a chap, a bloke called Andy Jensen. We went on the Prince Philip, a 139 footer. Me dad said to me, "You're not going to Greenland are you, in that?"

But I went with Andy, he had no fear of ice, nothing whatsoever, but I'd never been to Greenland, and when we was approaching Cape Farewell, he say's to me, "Just skirt half a mile off any of the icebergs." You just can't envisage, until you see one, just how big they are. Like a block of flats. We used to skirt round them by about half a mile, looking at the radar, and this one particular time I'd gone about half a mile when it should have been a mile off, and we hit it. There was one almighty bang and a scraping sound. My ticker and everybody else's was palpitating but Andy, he just strolled out saying, "Don't worry about it." We'd just scraped a submerged part. We went in that particular trip to a place called Julianna, I believe it was. I thought we'd never get down this fjord, it's just a mass of ice but he went on top of the Bridge, I was on watch at the time, and I was doing the steering. He gets up there and says, "What you do is you basically head for the bigger 'bergs which keep the smaller 'bergs out of the way and there is always a gap there." (Ray Jones - Grimsby)

In Greenland the fish came down and when the warm air of the Gulf stream used to go across they wouldn't go through it. It was warm water. So they used to starve. Thin, starving fish, and that's what you used to catch, bring 'em home as slinks - no good. We had 3,200 kit aboard, nearly all condemned slinks - thin cod, like razor blades, too thin, you could see right through them. The gaffer used to say, "Get 'em aboard, get 'em aboard it'll be all right," but that's when I picked up half a crown for the trip, 3,200 kit. Michael Burton was the gaffer. He was on the James Barrie. (George Waudby - Hull)

I've been in Greenland, I've been in Godshaven, that's the capital. That's a very primitive place. It was a well known fact in Godshaven in Greenland, as soon as you tied up you was surrounded by the girls. The girls wanted to get pregnant, because it was illegal for them to be living in Greenland if they was pregnant. What they used to do they used to send them back to Norway, which was another godforsaken place. It was a well known fact as soon as you tied up in Greenland all the girls of the town would come. That was their only let

A Nice Haul - Plenty of Fish in the Pounds - Certainly worth a dram. Copyright: Grimsby Evening Telegraph.

up of their way of life. There was nothing. There was a few little coal jetties, a few little shops, plenty of snow, plenty of ice. That was it. So there was no such thing as pictures, dance halls, you couldn't go for a pint in the pub, there was nothing. So they wanted to get pregnant pure and simply to get shipped out back to Norway. That was their way of life. I hope I never made anybody pregnant. I can't remember doing it but I wouldn't know because I sailed away.

I always remember when we was approaching Godshaven there was an almighty clatter and a bang. I'm talking about something which deafens you. Because a glacier was coming down the mountain. And as soon as it got to a certain height it has to break off and create the icebergs. When you see a football match and you hear the noise they make I would think you're talking about something a hundred times louder than that. I thought, "What the hell?" Then I realised what it was. If I'd have had the sense to have had a camera to take pictures of things like that - but in them days you couldn't even afford a camera. So you never had one. (Tom Jacombe - Grimsby)

When I was Mate I went into a trawler called the Churchill. She was a new trawler and the Skipper was Norman Rogers, Non-Stop Norman was his nickname. He was a hard man. We were fishing on the Norwegian coast at a place called Berlevag up on the Norwegian coast near Tanna Fjord. That's right up north. The wind was blowing off the land, there was a storm blowing very hard, and we were fishing a mile off, us and a Yorkie. We had a trip on board. We had a lot of fish. Anyhow we were catching this fish and the gunboat come round and see us. Well we hauled our net and we steamed straight out into the weather, but the Yorkie got caught. So they took him to a place called Vardeo in the north of Norway, and heard his court case. We were steaming home with about 2,400 kits and the Skipper said, "We'll call into Tromso - the cheekier you are the better you are." So we went into Tromso and got arrested when we went alongside. I thought, "This is charming." I hadn't been married long and I thought I don't know how long this lot's going to last. Anyhow we were laid alongside the quay. We'd got all the couplings and everything into the ship and there were armed guards with Tommy guns, and this officer with his revolver.

This officer and one of the sailors went for lunch and the other fellow was stood on the quay with his gun, and the Skipper said, "Now when I give you the warning out the window let go of the ropes - the head rope - and we're off." Anyhow I got the signal and I thought, "Yes, soft Mick if he starts firing when I'm letting go of the ropes." Anyhow we went full astern, took all the couplings, the hosepipes as we went and as the ship swung. We also had two Customs Officers on board the ship. They were coming to England with us they said. So off we went full speed, we were really going, and I went on the Bridge and was steering the ship. Skipper said, "Well there's nowt can follow us or anything." Next thing there's an old Catalina aeroplane flying over us. I thought, "Oh here we go" and then we got up to Yesben or somewhere up the fjord and this MTB boat comes scorching up alongside of us and he said, "Stop your ship." And the Skipper says, "I'm not stopping my ship." So we carried on and next thing he come right up tight next to us. The Skipper said, "I've a good mind to swing to starboard and sink him out the way." I said, "I don't know Skipper." He said, "When my nerve goes you'll be on your knees praying." I thought, "Aye." Next thing they open fire and there's these tracer bullets, red and all different colours, going in front of me past the Bridge window. I thought, "Oh heck." Anyhow in the end the Skipper stopped. We dropped the anchor. They wouldn't let him see the British Consul in Tromso and they put armed police aboard as well as the armed sailors with Tommy guns. I forget what we got fined - about £5,000 which was a lot of money them days - and we landed 2,350 kit. We made about £4,000 which was nothing for the trip we had. And the Skipper got suspended. (Mick George - Grimsby)

When you was at the White Sea you always called in Lodigen to pick the pilot up because the blokes used to write letters home. And blue cigarette papers for some reason they was priceless in Norway. Not red but blue ones. Blokes used to take boxes of blue and sell em. Get good money for 'em. You used to pick the pilots up at Lodigen and then they used to take you through the fjords for twenty four/thirty six hours, and then the blokes used to give him the letters to send home and for the stamp money just give him a packet of fag papers, and then when you came back from fishing and picked the

pilot up at Honisvag your mail, if she'd wrote back to you, that would be there to collect. You still had another four or five days to get home - but you'd have a letter. It was good. I wished I'd saved some of my letters. (Les Bowden - Grimsby)

The Russians were very lax in regard to fishing limits and things like that in the old days, when it was three and four mile limits. Regularly we used to fish within those limits, two or three miles off instead of four or five, and they never used to bother. I was never taken in but one of our company ships did, and the boss was on board at the time. The fine was about £250. Nothing much. I was in Marr's when the Swanella got arrested. The Skipper was a well known character, Leo Rennet. The young boss was at sea pleasure tripping with him. The Russians arrested him and they said that he'd been plotting radar towers, spying. They took him into Mermansk and apparently he had a hell of a time. They had armed guards all over the ship. They used to come and take him ashore to interrogate him until four o'clock in the morning. He'd get back to the ship, just get back to sleep and they'd come back and take him again. This went on for four or five days then they took him to the courthouse and fined him £250 and told him he could go. He went steaming out of Mermansk, it is a big Naval base, and fortunately for him he'd looked out of the window and seen the young boss who was standing out on the veranda taking photos of the Russian Navy. Stupid. The Skipper pulled him by his neck, kicked him down the ladder and told him not to come back on the Bridge until they got back home. (Sid Morrell - Hull)

In 1957 I was sailing as Bosun on a deep sea fishing trawler operating out of the port of Hull. The vessel, the Kingston Almandine, was owned by the Kingston Deep Sea Trawling Co. The Skipper of the vessel was Cyril Burt and the Mate was Gordon Shepperd. On the trip in question we also had on board a passenger, sometimes referred to as a pleasurer. At the time of sailing only the Skipper was aware of the true identity of this so called passenger. During the trip the passenger and I discovered we had a few things in common and as a result became quite friendly. We had long interesting conversations on the Bridge whilst I was on watch. It was during one of these conversations he disclosed his true identity and the reason for him being on the vessel. He said he had decided to tell me as I would guess most of it anyway. He was a young British Naval Lieutenant by the name of Andrew Marks. He was attached to a branch of the Royal Navy which he referred to as the Naval Intelligence Branch. He told me Navy Intelligence had received information that the Russians were about to sea trial a new class of warship. As the Kingston Almandine was going to the area where it was expected the trials would take place, the Navy had positioned the Lieutenant on board in order that he could photograph (among other things) the Russian Warships should the opportunity arise. Lieutenant Marks had a large canvas type bag which was heavily weighted at the bottom. In the bag was what seemed to me a very expensive camera, a telescope complete with tripod, what appeared to be a pair of binoculars, a sketch pad and two or three hardbacked folders containing silhouettes of Russian warships.

We eventually arrived at Kildin which is on the Russian coast and the island from which the Russian warships would normally appear. On our second or third day three warships came into view, one of them towing a large target. The Lieutenant took many photographs of the warships, he also told me he had recorded the rate and accuracy of the guns, he never explained how he'd done it. He frequently used his "binoculars" from which there was a lead that he plugged into his ear and I believe a microphone into which he spoke. These so-called "binoculars" were blank and he told me they were really an instrument used for the recording of the frequencies of the Russian shore-based radars. Lieutenant Marks told me that in the event of us being boarded by the Russians the weighted canvas bag was to be jettisoned immediately, and if he was closely questioned by the Russian boarding party he would tell them he was a university student gathering material for his thesis. I remember joking with him and saying he would get a medal for all the information he'd gathered. His response went something like, he didn't know about that but his superiors would certainly be pleased.

At this stage I believe it's appropriate to mention that this clandestine operation was common knowledge among the Skippers of Hull (I sailed as Skipper out of Hull for many years). I met Commander Brookes on a number of occasions and he would always ask you questions if you had been fishing off the Russian coast, e.g. did we see any warships, how many, what did they appear to be doing etc. He would then ask, "Are you going fishing off the Russian coast on your next trip? If you are would you take a camera with you to photograph any Russian warships or anything else you think may be of interest to us?" By "us" he was referring to Naval Intelligence.

Commander Brookes made no secret of the fact that he worked for British Naval Intelligence, not to me anyway. The Hull Trawler Owners were fully aware of the under-cover work that was going on aboard their vessels. I saw Commander Brookes in our office, Hellyer Bros, which later became British United Trawlers, on three or four separate occasions. (Neville Beavers - Hull)

Personally speaking, I would call what we did information gathering. Different people have different ideas about it but at the end of the day you were still doing a government job. A time or two, ships have been asked to move on, and when there's a few guns behind the request you don't ask questions. In lots of thing you knew how you stood with the Russians. Even straightforward fishing you always knew what a Russian was going to do because he would do it by the book. The Russians were the only people that ever used flag hoists to indicate that they were hauling or shooting. All those kind of things. They went by the book. A lot of it was because they didn't know anything else. All of a sudden, after the war, they had thousands of ships and it takes more than five minutes to train a Skipper or a Mate. So they had to operate by the book. They never interfered with you. They never even communicated with you. They just came along and scooped up everything that was going. But on occasions ships have been asked to move on by the Russian naval ships. I suppose they knew what was going on the same as we did. We knew what was going on with them. I was in one ship, the Galliard. That was said to be a spy ship. I was Mate in it at the time, and Commander Brookes was a lovely feller. He had a little office on the dock, Commander Brookes. This particular trip the Skipper said to us all, "We'll be all right this trip, we're taking some Navy chaps with us and we're guaranteed so much a day. More or less we'll make £10,000 whether we catch a fish or not." There were two Wireless Operators and all they did was listen with their gear, and they had tape recorders. They understood Russian and they just listened. Commander Brookes came with us and there was this other chap, I'm not quite sure what position he held, but he'd served in Embassies in various countries. He was a gentleman. I used to love to listen to him talk about some of the experiences he'd had. He would be on the Bridge with antenna kind of thing, listening round, and the wireless operator would be listening on other frequencies. They'd work six hours on and six hours off for the time we were there. Brookie would take the other shift. And it was just taken down and they'd sift through this information on what they thought it was when they got home. After that they'd leave maybe a tape recorder with a wireless operator and, if he heard Russian being spoken, he'd just switch it on. They might just have been talking about fishing or anything for all we knew. But sometimes one piece of information could be of importance. Some of us were given small cameras with telephoto lenses by MOD through Commander Brookes. He was classed as a Naval Officer and he worked for the MOD. If you saw any Russian ships, navy ships, planes, submarines, anything, you'd take photos and give him your roll of film when you got back. If you had any film left you'd use it to take photos of your family and such like. They'd print them and give your family pictures back to you. I had that camera with me for two or three years or more. They didn't pay us. They only guaranteed the £10,000 the time when they all came on that trip but they didn't have to pay it because we made more than that. We could have just gone through the motions and not really fished, the lads wouldn't have minded that at all, but as it happened we dropped onto a lot of plaice and made £4,000 more than the £10,000 they'd guaranteed. On the other hand, if we hadn't caught anything we knew they'd have made up the earnings to £10,000. (Jim Williams - Hull)

I never took any Navy personnel on my ships. I was in the Royal Navy for my National Service and one of the officers, Lt Edwards, from the last Navy ship I was on, HMS Thesius, one day he did come to Hull and he was working then for Naval Intelligence. Generally they used to come to you in the office asking you if you'd seen any activity from the Russian ships. You did used to see the Russian ships quite regularly at certain times of the year when you were working round the Russian coast and off the Finbar coast. But I've never taken anyone to sea. I know friends who did, one friend of mine got a camera from the Admiralty and I believe he still has it, to take photographs. We used to do it ourselves with our own cameras, but I don't know if anything ever came of it. You just used to pass the film to them. The Russians were pretty reasonable with us. It was only when they were doing manoeuvres off Mermansk and things like that that they used to be a bit heavy handed. Then they would come up to you and shepherd you out because they wanted the area for their manoeuvres. Apart from that I always found them reasonable to work with. They were very, very correct. (Sid Morrell - Hull)

When I took over as Manager at Consols. no Naval commander or Naval person ever contacted me to interview Skippers. When I was Skipper this Naval chap would often be in the office, although only if you'd been to White Sea, because we went to White Sea more or less in the winter months but the majority of the time we were at Iceland. He used to say, "Have you seen any Russian Naval ships?" which we saw tons passing, and he used to give you a book and there was silhouettes all in the book and it would be, "Would you recognise this that and the other?" We used to say, "I believe it could be this type." It would only be a type, it wouldn't be a ship. So there was some sort of gathering going on but not in Grimsby on a big scale. Absolutely not as I know of and I knew all the top Skippers in Grimsby, and even now I speak to them and I've asked them and they say, "No." They only had the same experience as I had. That's all. (Don Lister - Grimsby)

The British Intelligence had one Commander who looked after this dock. I don't know whether he looked after Grimsby as well. The Naval Intelligence was obviously keen to get as much information as it could on Russian ship movements, particularly Naval ships, and certain Skippers were willing to do the work. You mustn't forget a lot of our

Skippers at this time had been ex-RNR, so they had been in the Force and they'd been minesweeping. We still sent our young Bosuns and Mates on the Naval Disciplinary course at Corsham because we felt that the Services had a tremendous amount to offer in discipline and man-management. There were close ties of course and we provided what information we could on Russian fleet movements, so I would say they were information gatherers. They might have got into military manoeuvres, ship manoeuvres, but the Russians were pretty ruthless and skilful at shepherding people off, so the best we could do was gather information on the sorts of ships that the Russians were operating and from time to time we would carry a Naval team who would try and identify particular Russian ships and their characteristics but I mean there was nothing like the cloak and dagger stuff like in the last war, running spies to the French coast and vice-versa so it was an information gathering exercise really. (Tom Boyd - Hull)

Chapter 7
Poor Bloody Infantry

Fishing was a man's world and a working class monopoly. Other industries trained workers, upgraded their skills, demanded ever higher qualifications or brought in better educated youths, even graduates. Several reports on fishing advocated drawing people from wider backgrounds and training them better. Yet fishing remained an unregenerate, traditional industry, a last bastion of paternalism and traditional "us and them" relationships. Its workers were less well protected by legislation, rights or union power (a joke in fishing) than those of any other industry or the fishermen of any other nation. In France, Germany and Iceland most were protected by law. British fishermen wanted none of this being keener to work on to earn more money and get home quicker.

Once at sea the workers were in power. Not through worker control, for fishing was run on almost feudal lines and the Owners exploited everything, physical and human capital, to the limit, but because each vessel ran itself like a series of floating working-class collectives. Each crew, led by one of their own, was a team responsible for their own success or failure. Each triumphed or failed together, bound together by companionship, love of the life, a common lust for money, and a sotto voce *hostility to the Owners.*

Talent rose from the ranks. Many were keen to compete and struggle to the top. There they all competed energetically with each other. Others were content with specialised niches or happy to remain among the companionship of the team. Yet all shared the common, and hard, way of life. Perks and privileges were minimal. Everything focused on the ultimate reward: cash per trip.

To the outsider fishermen's earnings looked like big money. Yet payments per trip fluctuated wildly and large sums, spread over three weeks of intensive work with long hours of up to eighteen per day, turned out much smaller on an hourly basis. In 1968, the British Trawlers Federation calculated that Deck Hands' earnings in Hull distant water side trawlers were £32.2s.6d. per seven days, figures which would be less in Grimsby and Fleetwood but higher in the freezers. All got around £20 a week as their guaranteed minimum.

This was not a lot but more than most lads from a similar background could have hoped to make and it was paid in a lump sum each time they returned home. Always, too, there was the incentive and the hope of making more. The Skippers themselves got much better money, averaging over £130 per seven day trip on vessels over 140 feet in Grimsby, and between £20 and £80 more than that in Hull. Huge sums of money passed through their hands. Indeed one skipper, Wally Bowden of Grimsby, has kept a chart of his earnings which shows that from May 1957 to May 1970, he made 192 trips and brought in 342,089 kits of fish which sold for £1,754,451, averaging £9,137 a trip. Not a lot of that stayed with any fishermen.

I've known blokes come in and land on a Thursday and the ship's been sailing on the Saturday and instead of being a big money earner they'd said, "Oh I'm going to go to the match on Saturday." They would sign off the ship and go down the next week and get another ship. But good ships earning good money had a pretty regular crew, didn't have many changes. I mean if you made a big trip like that then financially you had a bob or two to pick up. Some people stuck in one firm all the time. You probably did while you were Deck hand but then when you come to getting a Mate's job, if you were in a particular firm and you were waiting for a Mate's job and an opportunity comes somewhere else in another firm. Or if you went in another firm and then you didn't think you were getting the opportunities that you warranted you'd better move somewhere else until you get a better offer. Although you were in different firms you're doing the same job. The pay system was the same throughout. One Trawler Owner never competed with another as regards offering better money. (John Gilby - Grimsby)

There was ships what people wouldn't go in because they wasn't making anything, just a waste of time. A lot of them used to be laid in dock for weeks waiting for crew. We even shipped a ship up once. It had been in dock about a month trying to gets crews. They had a Skipper and Mate and just for a giggle we made up a crew. We got a Chief, Second, four Deckies, Bosun, all of us who knew each other, and we all went and signed on and got it to sea. We never made much when we come in but we just wanted to see what we could do. But the thing about it all was that you never seemed to make much money, not even average money. There was no way you could get in the ones what was making the money unless somebody died, and even then you'd have to be well in because nine times out of ten the Skipper or the Mate sent somebody down. You didn't have a chance. I did know a lot of people who was in the good ships but they was at sea nearly all the time. They were a clique, even if I'd have got in 'em I might not have stayed. It was getting on with them that would have been a problem, you know, creepy crawly kind of thing. That way. (Thomas Bagnall - Fleetwood)

We're steaming along and the Bridge is above my cabin and I heard all this commotion on the Bridge so I just walked up the staircase to the Bridge and the Bosun who'd been with me for a long while, Frank, Frank Trott they called him, he was doing his bloody nut like. He'd had a good drink, I could see that. He was tormenting the watch. I says, "Frank, just come down in my cabin. I want a word with you." He said, "I'll take you on the foredeck you bastard." I said, "Well, later, but just come and have a word now like." Anyhow he comes in, he was a strong feller, used to be a boxer an' all, but that was when I was round about thirty. I shut the cabin door and he sprang at me and I grabbed him and I just heaved him over and laid him on the floor and I just jumped on him and honestly if I'd had a sombrero in me hand it'd have been like breaking a horse in the way we was flying round the cabin. I was losing me breath with trying to hold him down. He was

berserk. Anyhow I thought, "I've got to win or else he'll bloody kill me." So I always wore these big strong boots because I've broke this ankle twice so it was a support. So I just leapt up in the air I couldn't think of anything else and I just landed on his chest and cracked his ribs. So I lifted him up like and sat him in the chair and I give him a can of beer like and I said, "Now then Frank, what's the matter?" And he just sobbed his heart out. It was his wife. Off with another bloody fellow and that you know. You see a lot of that. All sorts of things like that. I used to be like bloody Marjorie Proops telling them, "Everything's all right, this that and the other." And then the bugger happened to me like. Who do I talk to? They were all right at home, it was just when they got to sea. Their minds played tricks with 'em. They started thinking all the worst like a bloody feller in prison. They're just laid there rattling on the bars aren't they? A feller at sea he can't do nowt about anything. You're four or five days steaming. That's the time when they're doing nothing. When the gear goes over the side they're occupied all the time. (John Meadows - Grimsby)

All fishermen are superstitious. I had heaps of superstitions. It was all sorts of things like not wearing a particular pair of socks 'cause they were unlucky. The worst one was whistling. You were said to be whistling up a gale. Another one was 'Grunters'. You don't mention pigs - that was a bad 'un. You don't mention them curly tailed buggers. (Fred Quinn - Fleetwood)

Me mother was very superstitious. She never washed any gear the first day you sailed, it was called 'washing you away'. The wife was a bit like that when we got married. But I was never superstitious. None of this about whistling and that. A lot of chaps were. If you were a young Galley Boy or Deckie Learner you'd get a clip across the ear if you whistled. They'd say, "Hey, stop blowing your brains out, what do you want, a gale of wind?" (Ray Jones - Grimsby)

You never washed before they sailed, you see. By God! And once I thought, "Well he's gone, he's gone early tide, and I'm in court tomorrow, so I'll get the washing done." When he come in, first thing he said was, "Did you wash?" And I said, "No, why?" He said, "Well somebody did, the Skipper's asked us all." He said, "We've had one of the worst trips, we've caught nothing hardly." I said, "No, not me." So that was the end of washing. And you didn't scrub your step, because you scrubbed them away, not the day they went. You never bought anything green - we bought a green Ford Consul once, we had nothing but trouble with it. I bought a green suit, got rid of that. (Josephine Gibney - Cleethorpes)

I was in the Hull City, we had a Cook, well I was there 5 years and I think he was there all the time I was there. He was brilliant. But there's some not so good. They had a difficult job because the food wasn't all that good when I started in the Fifties, but it did improve in the latter part, very good proprietary brands, sauces and jams, things like that. Early on it was certainly the cheap end of the market. They were always short of fat in the Fifties and the early Sixties for frying fish which was your staple diet. The cook would save the fat so when they were frying fish at night there would be mutton fat in it, pork fat, it was all mixed in. There were a lot of good nick names for cooks. One they used to call "Tins of Milk" because towards the end of the trip he would always go on the Bridge and say to the Skipper, "Can you get some tins of milk from somewhere? I'm running out of milk." It was always his swan song. Then there was "Bacon and Egg Smithie." When you left the dock all the bacon that all went. Some of the cooks used to save it for Sunday, so naturally you didn't get mixed up with the days, every day was the same. But we always used to know on a Sunday it would be bacon and egg in the morning and then at night - it didn't matter what ship you went in - it was always cold ham for tea, pickles and chips and tinned fruit. That was the only night you had tinned fruit. Sometimes, if you sailed on a Saturday and it was a longish trip and you had four Sundays at sea, the last Sunday you didn't get tinned fruit. There wasn't enough to last more than 3 weeks. Then there was another one called "Tiddley-oggy Ted" because he used to make these individual meat pies and they always used to call them "Tiddley-oggy pies." And actually if they met each other in the pub they used to refer to each other as the nickname. I remember going down to the White Sea. We called in Tromso with a welding job and there was another Grimsby trawler in there. We tied up along side him for the fitters to come aboard to do this job and the cook come aboard and he said, "I'm Tiddley-oggy Ted". (John Gilby - Grimsby)

When I started going to sea the food wasn't very good at all. That was with the Owners putting it aboard. But after a bit it got better and better. And when we packed up, especially in Consols, I don't think you'd have eaten better anywhere. But then it all depended on what cook you had. There used to be some brilliant cooks trawling. I had a few cooks, Gordon Hamsley, Lenny Keightley, they was all brilliant cooks, marvellous they were. You always got a three course dinner, soup, dinner and a sweet. Then they used to have their specialities. Fishermen used to have onion duffs. You don't see them ashore. A duff, like a suet duff but this had onion in. They were brilliant. They all had their specialities, like with the different fish they used to use. Halibut soup that was brilliant. You don't see that now because you can't afford halibuts. Mind you, you got some bad cooks. If you got a bad cook the whole ship altered. Because I always said a good cook made the ship. If everybody was feeding well at mealtimes, then everybody was happy. You used to get some really, really good cooks, marvellous cooks in fact. I mean they used to make all their own bread, what we used to call busters, you know hot buns. Yes, we used to get hot busters in the afternoon. (George Mussell - Grimsby)

On the Ross Revenge we used to boil our own livers. What they call a 'liver man' used to get extra money. We had a shoot to put ours from the deck and they used to get blown aft to the boilers. We used to have a big boiler and make steam, throw the livers in, get the steam through, leave them so long to settle, get the oil off. You used to open a tap 'cos the oil was at the top and the rubbish was at the bottom, drain it off and get the oil into a big tank. You got extra money for that - liver oil money. We never had colds any of us, 'cos what we used to do was keep a jar in the liver house, put pure cod liver oil in and have a couple of spoonfuls of that a day . You never had a cold and your hands you could move 'em. Beautiful. (Colin Donald - Grimsby)

I used to give them a dram a day, and I used to give the Mate the bottle ('cause I didn't drink rum). I'd never give them half a bottle. I'd give it to the Mate and he'd give them a dram. If, say, you'd been mending 'cause you'd got busted, and it was cold and freezing, the Mate would ask to take the bottle round. You see, with a lot of them, if you gave them the bottle, or half a bottle, they would swap it with someone else for sweets or something, and of course those who swapped with them were those who loved rum and the next minute you'd find they were drunk. They're absent from their job. It was the first twenty four hours that were the problem. When you left the dock going to sea, that's when you got those who'd fallen out with their loved ones and they used to really take it to heart. They were softies really, but they couldn't cry on anybody's shoulder, they had to be macho, so they hit the bottle. That was natural, but that first twenty four hours was the worst for a Skipper with his crew. I had one guy, his wife's mother was at him. He was chopping the electrical points down with an axe, Oh dear, so I got rid of him quick. I passed him to another guy who was going home. (Jack Tripp - Hull)

I mean everybody used to have a dram. But you couldn't drink that much. We was away three weeks and there was twenty men aboard the ship and in Northerns you could only carry twelve bottles of Rum, and six bottles of whisky. That was just eighteen bottles of spirits. And you carried about twenty cases of beer. Well that was a case of beer each. But that was for three weeks. So it wasn't much. It used to be marvellous a dram when you was gutting when you were freezing. It gave you that kick for a few minutes until it wore off and you started freezing again. (George Mussell - Grimsby)

There were some characters. It's surprising how many are dead now though. Like "One Eyed Zoop." He had a glass eye and he used to go in the mess and push his eye on the table to keep his eye on his dinner! - 'cause sometimes you had to leave your meal to get the gear aboard, so he'd just keep an eye on his tea. What made me laugh with him, he's still alive, it was his brother that died, we was in the Vivaria as Deckies, we was hauling and she used to haul that fast that sometimes all the turns can come out the warp. Well this warp sprung and

caught the top of his frock and tightened up on his frock and his glass eye shot out over the side, and he lost it. He didn't have a spare.

We'd got an engine room job so we had to go in Kirkwall to get it repaired which was going to take two/three days. The crew was short of money, so what they was doing was pinching the meat and flogging it to get their beer money. The first time we was there one of the lads got the meat and tied it so no one would see it. He was walking all nonchalant like with his meat and he'd got it attached to a rope and he pulled it up when he was clear of the ship. We twigged on to what was going on. All the meat just went. I was on the Bridge having a yarn with Penny and these Deckies come along and had got all this stuff smuggled round them and he says, "Look at these buggers." He blows the ship's whistle. "I've seen you." 'Course they dumped all the meat in the dock so they couldn't get caught for pinching the meat. We didn't mind them pinching the meat. What annoyed us was that they wasn't giving us a cut of it. (Graham Howard - Grimsby)

There was one time, heavy fishing, and I'd wanted to go to the toilet, and I'd put it off as long as I could to carry on. In the end I thought, "Well, I'll have to go." I was strolling along the deck, they were all gutting, and the Skipper poked his head out and said, "And where have you been?" I said, "When nature calls I go. When you want to go nobody asks you where you've been, so just get your head in." And I carried on going. Of course I got sacked for that. (Clive Finn - Hull)

I remember the first big pay-up I had, in 1947. I was in one of Marrs big old Corvettes, coming home for Christmas and the new year. I was only an apprentice - a brassie. We'd been to the White Sea and we was full up with fish. We landed and I picked up £22. I'd never picked money up like that before. I snatched it out of the cashier's hand, signed me pay slip which I never even picked up, and I ran home. I only lived about ten minutes away. I run in the house and my mother and dad were sat there. I shouted, "Look at all this money I picked up Mam," and I threw it up in the air. She picked it all up and gave me £2 back. She said, "Here, now you can go out and spend that." She kept the rest for me to stop me spending straight away. As the

SALE NOTE
CONSOLIDATED FISHERIES, LTD.
FISH SALESMEN, GRIMSBY

S.T. *Grimsby Town*   28 May 1968

Skipper *D. Luter*
Mate *Kirk*

Days at Sea *17*
Fishing Ground *White Sea*

Voyage £ *7446 : 15 : 9*
Average per day £ *446 : 5 : 7*

		10 STONE KITS	STONES	HIGHEST PRICE	LOWEST PRICE	£	s.	d.
Halibut		7	3½	530/-	340/-	49	18	
Haddks	S.	6		78/-	74/-	22	14	
	Bulk	354	3	80/-	56/-	1086	6	6
Cod	Shelf	76		96/-	80/-	376	2	
Codlings		10	5	90/-	76/-	42	16	
Cod	Bulk	969		82/-	71/-	3,591	13	
"	Contract	96		75/-		360		
Codlings		331	5	68/-	64/-	1109	16	
Colay		44		82/-	72/-	172	8	
Redd		15		82/-	74/-	107		
"	Contract	77		33/-		36	6	
Catt. etc		15	4	44/-	35/-	744	11	3
Mix Butt		8	5	82/-		34	17	
		1959	5½			6 957	15	9
		17 Days Subsidy @ £17				159		
						£ 7446	15	9

What the Catch made.

years went by money started getting a little bit better but not much. It was a pittance really. It was only when we went on the share basis in the 70's that you really started seeing something really big. In the 50's and 60's it was pisses really. By the time you'd paid your dues and demands to your wife there was very little left for yourself to enjoy - but you did enjoy it. (Peter Wright Wilson - Fleetwood)

We all used to smuggle the odd bottle of whisky and a few fags ashore and things like that, that was part of the entertainment. Trying to store your 'bacca in some unsuspecting place. It used to make me laugh, looking back in retrospect, you'd be smuggling a couple of hundred cigarettes ashore - you had an allowance - I think it was a hundred cigarettes and half a bottle of spirits, something like that, or a bottle of whisky opened, but I mean the customs came aboard regularly - nowadays you can walk a ton of cocaine in and nobody knows about it, do they? But then the Customs were very keen on the trawlers. You put the Customs light up in the mast and when you docked and hit the quay they were there, waiting for you. (Stephen Drever - Grimsby)

Old Henry he was a sod and half at the lockgates. By he was a stickler for fishermen. He'd stop anybody. He was the old school. There used to be a little box at Humber Street and there was always some police on duty there and they would stop you. "Where do you think you're going?" Especially if it was night time. I used to say, "I'm going to meet the Everton," or whatever it was coming in. And he used to say, "Who's on it?" And I used to say, "My husband" like. "What is he?" But then you'd get to know some of them and they'd say, "Don't forget a packet of fags on the way back." So I used to give em a packet when we came back. (Flo Balls - Grimsby)

You always gave a few fags to the Customs, to the Berthing Master, Watchman and the Runners. It was the usual thing. This new one he says, "And what have you got Skipper?" I says, "Well I've got a carton" like. He says, "You're not allowed to have a carton." I says, "Well I've just give you one." He says, "But you're not allowed to take two hundred off." I says, "Right." These fellers was all stood in the cabin. "Lets have 'em all back." "Your carton an' all." I says, "If I can't have any nobody can. Put 'em all back in the bond." The next trip the other Customs had put him wise like! It wasn't smuggling - it was just giving everybody a smoke. (John Meadows - Grimsby)

Skippers and Mates used to get a turkey from the firm at Christmas. I mean Bill was a top earner out of Consolidated. We gets this turkey given us for Christmas and I'm not joking when they delivered it I said, "Where did it come from?" And he says, "It's your Christmas present from the firm." I said, "I think it walked from bloody Belsen." I was never so disappointed. So I says to him, "You can take it back." He said, "We daren't do that." I rang Jack Mawer up the Outside Manager there and I asked him where he got these turkeys from. They was that paltry another Skipper's wife, Nellie Thrower, went to this Jack Mawer's house on Christmas morning. She often used to pop round there. And he had his turkey in the oven and it was a Yorkie Great. (Flo Balls - Grimsby)

You was allowed three haddock or two haddock and two plaice, and you used to go down and collect that, but later on, when they started getting refrigerators on the trawlers you used to generally bring a bit home. The thing they used to like is when we were fishing on the east side of the 'Westman' Islands when we used to catch the prawns. We used to bring them home and boil them in salt and pickle them. (Graham Howard - Grimsby)

We always called 'em, it was Lumpers this and Lumpers that. I think it was all too easy for them. Where we used to get two haddocks and two plaice they were taking loads of fish home. It would be down under the whaleback or down the fish room. It was all so easy for them to do it. Temptation was there and it was easy for them to do it. People would knock fish off-left, right and centre they did. (Ray Jones - Grimsby)

You did two or three months. And then you'd think, "Oh, I'm a bit tired, you know, Gaff, I'll have a trip off," which is a fifteen day trip. And after about four or five days you used to get fed-up - "I'm going down dock, I'm going to get a ship." Go down in the office and they'd say, "What do you want?" "Give us a job?" "Well, your ship's at sea, there aint no ships in the book, but Consols want one, a Deckie, to

sail in the morning. Do you want to go?" "Yes," so you'd walk round, go in Consols. Do a couple of trips there and go back to B.U.T. Same would happen, couple of months later, trip off, Bostons want a Deckie, you was told to go round there. They could turn round and say, "Right kangaroo court for refusing a ship, twenty eight days suspension." They say you've got to work for one firm for two years before you are entitled to redundancy payment. But every fisherman was doing this, apart from the odd one which stayed in one ship for years, but you were still under the British Fishing Federation which, if you jumped, you went to the kangaroo court, and you've got all the Gaffers from them firms in that court room and they suspend you for twenty eight days. You virtually worked for the lot of them. So how they can say you worked for one bloke, you don't. You work for all the Fishing Federation. (John Burton - Grimsby)

We used to get crews not turning up. Either they'd had a row with the wife, or they'd had a row with their girlfriend, or they'd got drunk and we couldn't find them. And then invariably sometimes the ship wouldn't sail short-handed, so we had to delay the sailing for twenty four hours. We used to take them to court. Invariably in them days it was a court proceeding and they used to get fined £2. But you see £2 was a lot of money. They'd signed a Ship's Article to say that they would be there at the time of ordering and if they failed to appear without producing a doctor's certificate then we was at liberty to take them to court. (Gordon Cockerill - Grimsby)

If you were a naughty boy they gave you walkabout. I remember, years ago, I'd been a naughty boy and they wanted me to go on this ship that never earned any money. Those ships were a waste of time because they were managed by a firm but they belonged to somebody else, so they were always the last to be 'shipped up.' So if you were a Deckie on one of these ships and they were short on one of their own ships you'd be taken off for their ship. You could get stuck in port a fortnight. Anyway, at about two o'clock in the morning the Runner came knocking on my door, wanting me to go as Second on one of the bad ships. I told 'em to get away from my door at that time of the morning, but I agreed to go down later to speak to them. They said they'd put back the sailing

Fighting for a Fair Deal : Fleetwood Wives and Children. Copyright : Fleetwood Gazette.

for twenty four hours. I went down to see them and when they told me which ship it was I said I wouldn't take it. I think she'd been in port a fortnight looking for a crew. You couldn't afford to be on a ship like that. The next morning, about 3.00am, I'd been out drinking all night with three Skippers, drinking cider with a brandy in it - murder - in one of the clubs down the road. Walking home I daren't bend cause I was full up to there. If I moved I'd spill it! I got home and the door was suddenly being banged enough to nearly knock it down. The Runner was there. I started to say I didn't want to go, but then I was sick, splattering him. The Runner said, "No, I didn't think you would. The gaffer wants to see you tomorrow morning." (Chris Fisher - Fleetwood)

We had a code among ourselves whereby if Bill Bloggs had missed a ship we used to notify the other firms that Bill Bloggs was on the spares and he didn't turn up. It was a code of practice among us that we didn't sign him on unless we was desperate. In other words if Jim Smith hadn't turned up that day and Bloggs was in the Humber pub then I just grabbed him and threw him aboard and he would probably get a pair of boot socks from one, and borrow an oil frock from another. Many times they've gone without anything. We've just took them into Dobbies or Colebridges or Vincents, into the shop there, and got them their essentials - toothpaste and some gutting gloves or something like that - and put 'em on the bill and said, "There you are," and the rest of the lads would sort him out with something. We would go round and tell the wives. We would go round and take her a pay card and he would probably say, "I'll go if you give me wife a £2 sub." So he went to sea in debt but we said, "You're not having it but we'll take it round to your wife." So then the wife would have a bit of money to buy some food for the kids or whatever she wanted to do. (Gordon Cockerill - Grimsby)

We did go on strike in the 1960's, and I remember the children and the crews and the wives walking up and down Dock Street. Skippers and Mates didn't go on strike; we was told to stand apart from this strike, neither impede nor encourage it. I think they were going for an extra six pence on the poundage and an extra five shillings a week on their wages. When you think what they was doing then it was a pittance - a grain of sand they were after, and even then they had to fight for it. This was encouraged by the Transport and General Workers Union. Really, if there been someone guiding you proper, which other industries had, they should have gone for a proper work contract. (Derek Reader - Fleetwood)

I remember Ernie Hall, and the chap who started the United Fishermen's Union. We met at the hostel at Riby Square. That then amalgamated to the Transport and General. Then when I went as an Engineer I joined the Firemen's and Engineers Union. Alf Sandford at that time was in charge of the union and I always kept in with Alf, and he said, "What shall we do, we've been put to by the T & G?" I said, "What we gonna do with you Alf?" He was more or less promised that if the unions amalgamated he would still look after the fish, the engineering side of it. John Ibbot just put it to the vote. We were lost on our own. We were only a small union. We only totalled about 150-200 members at the most. The Engineers Union never really did any good on its own. There was never clever enough people in charge really. The unions didn't do much else because it's such a hard thing to try and organise. No matter what happened, if you called a strike, it might be three weeks before it was full, because of the ships at sea. They probably got us increases in pay. (Graham Howard - Grimsby)

The Trawler Officers Guild had a strike in the 1950's when there was a lot of Icelandic fish coming in. We've had two or three strikes but, generally, it's been the Transport Union that's organised it. The one when the Icelandic fish was coming here. In Hull we went back to sea after about two or three weeks, but in Grimsby they stopped out for quite a long time - six or seven weeks - and it soured relations between us for a long time. The last strike we had, first off was pretty general in Hull, everybody was on strike. This was just in Hull, not in Grimsby. After about three days they started sending ships to sea. I think the strike was over cod liver oil money. We went to sea but we had to do it in real secrecy because they were picketing the docks. I went further up towards Ferriby to where the taxi was. We all got into a bus in a field at two o'clock in the morning, from there they rung the central police station, and then we came to Hull by an indirect route onto what we used to call the new bridge (it's not there now) because the police said the pickets weren't there but were further along at the tunnel end. Some of the ships in that strike were in dock for five or six weeks. I can't really remember why we didn't agree with the strike. The Stella fleet, Charlesons, about four or five of their good new ships stopped out the full length of the strike, but that was mainly because their Chief Engineers wouldn't go to sea in the strike. I'm not certain what it was they were demanding but I think it was something to do with cod liver oil. When we were gutting we used to take the liver out and boil it on the ship and the Owners used to sell it to the cod liver oil manufacturers, but it had to be a good end product. It was mainly the deck crew who got something out of that, not the Engineers, but they wanted a full share of it for providing the steam to boil it with. The first strike, regarding Icelandic fish, was in the early Sixties. There was again a lot of controversy because the Icelandics were coming here to land their fish and just swamping the market, so it was almost a waste of time us going fishing. They got that fed up with it that they called a strike. The Owners beat that. People thought they were striking for everyone, the Owners and themselves, but after about three days the Owners made anyone who had a Skipper's Ticket take the ship if the Skipper had refused to go. (Sid Morrell - Hull)

Hull had one Deck/hand strike that I remember, but no strike ever lasted very long. One time they had a Skippers' and Mates' strike, and it was the very day I got my Skipper's Ticket, and I daren't tell Tom Boyd I'd got it in case he gave me a ship. That was in 1961. Hull wasn't a militant port, nor are fishermen in general the world over, and Hull in particular, they wouldn't stop for coal breaking on their heads. They'd maybe do a lot of shouting but that's as far as it goes. You can't make an impact anyway because, as I've said, you'd have to be out for three

1974 : Fleetwood Docks. Trawler Fleet in port during Fishermen's Strike. Copyright P. Horsley

Heaving the Bellies In. Copyright: Grimsby Evening Telgraph.

weeks until the last ship came back. So after three weeks off, for some, they are still only on day one of a strike. (Jim Williams - Hull)

One time we actually went on strike. We were on strike for quite a while trying to get more money out of them. We'd gone to the union complaining and we'd had discussions and that was it. Long before we'd decided to go on strike if we had to. We were one of the lowest paid ports amongst the three big ones, and we wanted to be one of the highest, I think it was in 1974. The unions organised the strike. What was the matter was that we knew we was being robbed and we was determined to get more money out of them. We had a couple of meetings and then we picked a strike committee. I was on the strike committee. The strike went on for a while. All of them on the big Iceland boats went on strike. Not the small boat men. It was nothing to do with them because they were all on shares. It was all right for the Skippers. They weren't on strike and they were getting ten times what the lads earned. We went on strike for about eight weeks. I didn't want to go back. There was three of us on strike in the house. We got £5 a week off the union. The wife was working in the Fleetwood Arms as a barmaid. She had another job at the same time. Holding two jobs down just to keep me and the two lads while we was on strike. It was a bit of a drag for her but I never heard her complain about it. We had dockers down from Liverpool to support us. They gave us £100 towards the strike funds. We'd miners. They sent us a £100 to help. They all knew the conditions we worked under and they wanted to show their support. We were asking for a substantial rise, I can't remember what it was, but in the end we settled for a lot less than we asked for. (Chris Fisher - Fleetwood)

The pool office was like a registration office. If you wanted to stop in the same ship for any length of time the Runner would sign you on the log but if you didn't have a ship you went to the pool office. Every June the pool office issued the holiday money and you went there to get it. In Fleetwood that was a good time. The shops and the pubs were full. The women would be down docks saying, "Come on, where are you?" looking for their husbands. They knew where to find us 'cause we all went in the same pubs and clubs. It was a comical time. The most you would get then was between £45 and £50. That was good money then. (Peter Wright Wilson - Fleetwood)

If you went to sea and you made a bad trip, you've very little money to come, so the Owners didn't have to pay you. While you was catching fish and earning money you was earning their money as well. There has been times when ships have gone to sea and the Skippers and Mates owed the company money. It's happened to me twice. I was in a ship in Boston's, a stern trawler, it was a newish ship, only about four/trips old, but it had a lot of teething troubles. We went to Faroe and then we had a smashed cylinder head and we had to go in to have it repaired. We lost about forty eight hours, came out and did two or three days fishing and another cylinder head went. Then we had problems on the deck. Eventually, we went away about twenty one days and we only landed about 300 kit instead of having 800 or 900 kit. So we settled in debt. I went to the office and I finished up owing them £30. The next trip we had some similar problems and we finished up, I think, about another £30 in debt. I wouldn't go any more. I said, "No, that's enough. It's cost me £60 and nothing to come for all that work apart from the wages that the wife had earned." I went back Third Hand in one of the other ships but fortunately we made a good trip but when we got to the office they deducted the £60 I owed them. So I finished up coming out the office with about £4. What other industry is there where you can go and do three weeks work and come home and they say we haven't made enough money out of you and you don't get paid? (John Gilby - Grimsby)

As a Chief Engineer, at the end of the day, I was on quite reasonable money. Wage wise. We was never big poundage people us Chief Engineers. I was £10 for every £1,000 the ship made, but my wages was quite high, I was on over £90 a week, whereas a Deckie was only on £20. I was on good money. The Skipper was a lot different. He was a shareman. He was just on a share. Usually, after deducting the ship's expenses the Mate got three percent and the Skipper five percent, then the Skipper got bonuses if the ship earned so much a day. So he could be on really big money. I remember the headlines in one edition of the Evening Telegraph where a Grimsby Skipper was earning more than the Prime Minister; he earned £100 a week. That was in the 1950's. Big money. For me, I'm not saying I always picked up a lot. I've picked up as low as 4s.6d. but I've never settled in debt. You sometimes get the impression that the fishermen used to go to sea and come home and go back with no money. They're not that daft. It was a good living. You're not going to go to sea for three weeks for nothing. We're not that simple. I know we was thick, us fishermen, but not that thick. (Graham Howard - Grimsby)

They had a different principle of pay in Hull compared with Grimsby. We used to get a share of the gross what the ship made. If the ship made say £10,000 gross the Skipper in Grimsby would get 5.2% of that and the Mate would get 3.75%. But in Hull they worked on what they call the net earnings of the ship. After the expenses have been taken off for fuel, ice, water, they settled on 10% of what was left. So, if you'd gone to Greenland, probably taking six-seven days to get down there, with bad fishing, or if you couldn't get to where you wanted because the ice was down, you finished up with a long trip. With a bad market and very little fish you only just made your expenses. Therefore the Skipper had nothing to come. He had an allowance sent to his wife each week, but he would have that to pay back. So he would be in debt. Even the top man could settle in debt. That happened more in Hull than it did in Grimsby. We'd a better system in Grimsby. Before I ever went to sea, they were on the net, but gross was the best. I mean if you had these calamities or broken down jobs at least you'd have something to come. (John Gilby - Grimsby)

The least I've ever picked up was seven shillings and six pence. Another one was three pounds twelve and six. Me mother said to my wife, "I shouldn't take his word for it. I'd check. You don't want to believe him Val." (Ray Jones - Grimsby)

I think we made about nearly £7,000 on my best trip, in 1962, a lot of money in those days. I can't remember what I picked up. Anyway the wife was breathing over me shoulder so she'd take the settling sheet. But it gave us a good Christmas anyway. The kids had everything they wanted. I had three kids and they were growing up and wanted things, gear and toys and what have you. I never made a better trip. I might have made more money but I never made a better trip because it came at just the right time. With us being laid up before that it takes a bit of getting back when you've been off for a couple of weeks - you've got to get your suit out of pawn and all that sort of thing. That's the way that fishermen and their families lived. It was hand to mouth. When things were tight the wives would give you a couple of hours to get out to sea before they nipped home, got your suit and took it into the pawn shop. They'd get about a pound for it, but it would have to be a good suit to get that much. It happened all the time, and it wasn't only the fishermen, it happened to Gaffers and Mates and Skippers. (Chris Fisher - Fleetwood)

I think the Skippers and Mates of the Grimsby ships were on five percent of gross - the Skippers - and Mates were on something like three to four percent. Out of Hull Skippers were on ten percent of net earnings, and the Mate was on around seven percent. So on a £10,000 trip there'd be £3,000 or £4,000 expenses, so the Skipper would get ten percent of the remainder. In Grimsby the Skipper would get five percent of the gross earnings, whatever the fish sold for. It's hard to say who would be the better off overall because it depended on the differences between one trip to another. It was never the same. It was just accepted, more or less. We didn't really discuss it much. A Skipper, in particular, out of both ports, had one additional incentive. That was trip money. That varied slightly. Out of Hull the trip money for a Skipper was slightly more than for Grimsby - I'm not too certain now. I believe that on trips earning over £10,000, which was a lot of money then, the Skipper would maybe get double trip money. And if it is a really exceptional trip they might get maybe an extra £150 on top of everything. Managerial incentive I suppose you'd call it ashore. (Jim Williams - Hull)

One particular trip I remember. We caught 150 tonnes of fish in two and a half days. I think we made £11,000 in the early Sixties. It was a hell of a lot of money in those days. But the best trip, money wise, was when we made about £50,000. That would be nothing now, of course. They'd probably get the sack now if they only made £50,000. What few ships there are. The Owners were forever telling us that we were the best paid men in England. (Sid Morrell - Hull)

I was only Skipper with two firms. I was with Tosh Robinson's for over twenty years. A lot used to go on that you didn't know about. I can remember one instance when we landed a load of plaice and there was about fifty kit unsold. In them days the Trawler Owners of every kit of fish you landed would take a small amount of it, perhaps only about ten bob a box. It went into a fund. Now the Trawler Owners made a deal that there'd be a minimum price, so that if you had a kit of plaice, we'll say the minimum price was £15, if that didn't fetch £15 on the market it went to fish meal and you got £3 for it, not £15. But the fund that the Trawler Owners set up got that made up to £15. But the crew never got that. You only got £3. You got paid on the three quid. Then, this time, we'd got fifty kit of plaice left - minimum price I think it was £15. I had a pal who was a big Fish Merchant. We went to school together at Elliston Street School - Tommy Rudland - he came to our house. He said to me, "What did you make today like?" "You had fifty kit of plaice left didn't you?" I said, "Yeah." He said, "I said I'd take the fifty kit. I offered them thirteen quid and they refused it." So I said, "Thirteen quid?" And he said, "Yeah." Anyway I was a bit annoyed about this because we'd been paid on three quid which was fish meal price. So I steamed down dock the next morning and I went in Tosh's office and I was playing up hell and I said, "I want to know why you're robbing me," which in a way they was. And then they ummed and ahhed in the office and I had to go and see the secretary and all this business and the outcome of it was that I found out then about this fund. They wasn't losing money. It was only the fishermen that were losing the money. That was the sort of thing that you was fighting against. (Peter Newby - Grimsby)

My best trip made about £6,000 and after tax and expenses I think I made about £1,900. That was the biggest pick up of my career. In the latter years you never got your bonuses because it all went in tax. You was really taxed heavily. Like the last year I was in that ship I earned £40,000, but I only picked about £13,000 or £14,000 up, the rest was tax. I got into a pension scheme with Legal and General. I paid so much a year in them latter years and it helped to reclaim some of that tax money. But if we'd have been tipped off with a lot of things we could have saved tons of money, but we weren't in the know. Nor did the Trawler Owners want you in the know. They wanted you under the thumb all the time. (John Meadows - Grimsby)

We earned all our money out of the country. As soon as we come back in we paid full taxes. What did we pay all our taxes for - ambulance service, fire service and the police? When we went to sea out if you was badly you couldn't ring a doctor up, you had to go through the Skipper and nine times out of ten he used to give you two codeine and a bottle of 'flu mixture. It didn't matter what was wrong with you, that was your prescription. And then if fire broke out you couldn't ring the fire brigade, you was your own firemen. When fights broke out, arguments over fishing, you was your own policeman. We never got no tax concessions for these but we come home and paid our full taxes. But we didn't get the benefit. It was wrong. (Clive Finn - Hull)

The Trawler Owners owned the stores of course. Naturally, they wouldn't miss out where the profit was going. Don't forget you used to buy everything including your own bed. That used to be a straw palliasse in the beginning. Skippers and Mates was always in debt to the Trawler Owners when they went to sea because they more or less hired the ship and then settled up when they'd made the trip. So if they didn't make a trip they would certainly be in debt. But it was still a good life fishing, I enjoyed it, the majority did. (Jack Tripp - Hull)

The lowest money I ever picked up was three pennies, then seven shillings and six pence. I'd gone in all spivved up, collar and tie, immaculate, and you get you three half crowns. It was always like that. Spivved up. You was king for a day.

Especially in Grimsby or Hull. You read in the papers where these fishermen had picked this money up, picked that money up, well off and all that, I don't know where they got all that from. I always used to say that though. King for a day. When you get in you get all spivved up, smart as paint, and picking about ten bob up or summat. You still got drunk but then you could go in any pub and get drunk for next to nowt. You never had nowt to save to get out of it. So you carried on doing it because there was nothing else. I tried a couple of shore jobs but once you'd been on that job, fishing, it's hard to settle down to a shore job. First of all you can't afford to knock about with all your mates all the time, and you've got to get used to working. I mean I started a job where I was working and digging, that's all it was, labourer, and a day seemed like a week to me. It seemed to drag and I thought, "I won't be able to stick this long" so I went back to sea. (Thomas Bagnall - Fleetwood)

Chapter 8

The Fisherman's Dream of Home

"Abandon home all ye who enter here" wasn't inscribed over the fish dock, but should have been. With two to three week trips, forty-eight to sixty hours in port, the period at home allowed little time for either rest or domesticity so fishermen could go back to sea as tired as they'd arrived home. Some were even recorded as working more days than the calendar offered and between five percent and ten percent spent over 350 days a year on their vessel's register and at sea. Most British workers spent more time at home, even if asleep, than at work. For fishermen home life was rare, and intermittent. Several even worked Christmases to make up their money.

Some were misogynists, loners or drifters. A lot of young men were unmarried. Yet most of those who stayed in the industry had homes, wives and families and all the impedimenta of a normal life. Except that of being home every night. Fishermen didn't need to follow the working-class habit of escaping home or wives in allotments or pubs. They weren't there enough for that. The sea was their escape.

The result was a male industry at sea but female dominance on shore. Everything depended on the woman's efforts at balancing the budget, running the home and bringing up the kids. Wives raised the families, fathers spoiled the children on their "visits." Holidays were rare, usually crammed in during a break in service or while the ship was in dock for maintenance and survey. The masters of the sea were strangers in the home. Hard bouts of work followed by a burst of living crammed into their short return made shore-side a pressure cooker escape from reality not its substance.

I always went to meet John at the docks after a trip, unless it was at night then I wouldn't have been able to because I couldn't leave the children. When they were due in you'd get the kids all dressed up, but sometimes the boat would miss the tide and they'd not get in until twelve hours later and the kids would get very upset. We was down at Cleethorpes when it was still in its heyday, and they had telescopes that you used to have to put a coin in to operate. Debbie wanted to look through, so I put 6d in and also had a look through. I saw a tug and there were people coming off a boat and into the tug, and I said to the kids, "Come on, that's your dad getting off that boat." We went up the station and got a taxi and said, "We want to be wherever the tugs come in," and he took me there. When John came off the tug he was absolutely amazed to see me there. Those two / three days in shore were like a honeymoon each time. You tried to cram so much into those few days but you also had to get all the washing done and dried, ready for him to go back again. That took a day. At first he had only one set of work gear because he couldn't afford two sets. Later on he did have two sets. He never came into the house in his sea gear. He used to walk through the back way and drop it on the floor to go into the washer, because it used to smell so badly of fish. For entertainment we used to go to the Gaiety, Winter Gardens or the Café Dansant and later on to the disco. Freeman Street was always heaving with people, and you would always be sure of bumping into someone you knew down there. All the fishermen went there and you'd start at one end, have a pint at Riby Square and be drunk before you got down the other end. A lot of people tried not to talk about the job when you were at home 'cause you could get bogged down with it. But there used to be some pubs where we used to say that you had to gut your way to the bar there was that much fish around in the bar. But they were one offs. A lot of people didn't talk about fishing when they were on shore. It was just a job. (Beryl Pickett - Grimsby)

The best moment at sea is when you came home. You was a millionaire for, say, twenty four hours. I mean, me mam used to say to me, "You live in a taxi." Well you were always that short for time. Time went by like that, and you weren't ashore for say three weeks or two weeks. The only time you

The delights of Grimsby to come.
Copyright: Grimsby Evening
Telegraph.

All spivved up.

did that is if you didn't go back or if you were surveying. In them days they used to survey for about three weeks once a year, but when you came home from sea after three weeks, in thirty six hours you were away again. So there was no time - you'd just time to get your sea bag off and your clothes washed and you were back at sea again. (Bill Ellerington - Hull)

When you went out you'd say, "See you in so and so." When you came off dock you all used to go in the Subway Club for an hour, then you used to go your different ways. Or maybe in Andrews Club, it's still there, Andrews. Then have an hour at Rayner's, the nearest pub - you generally would go there to wait for settling up, 'cause you didn't while twelve. So rather than wait if they were a bit late settling you'd just go off to Rayner's, nearest pub you see, and meet all the crew in there. Then the Fish Room Man would get his money. Then he used to treat the Deputy Fish Room Man and the Ice Crackers. (George Waudby - Hull)

In the summertime say we'd been away three weeks and we arrived in the river say ten o'clock in the morning, and it was high water, tides out, and they used to say, "Stop out," 'cos it was too warm to be laid in the dock. So the next tide was ten o'clock at night and you was all day laid in the river. Oh, it used to be heart-breaking. You could see all the lights and you'd been away three weeks, a young bloke full of life, and you're just laid there. They used to do that regular. We used to have shore parties. We used to have a tug in them days and send half ashore. The other half had to stop. It was horrible. Two days later and off we went again. It was ridiculous when you think of it for young people with young families. Your kids - it all depended when you come in - but that day you landed they was at school that morning, you was down the dock and you might not have come home 'til about five o'clock at night. I mean you want a day out with your wife don't you? Even if you weren't drinking you was shopping and all that business. They was in bed that night so you never see 'em. Sometimes you only see 'em a couple of hours. And back to sea again. I can't believe it myself and I did it! I did it voluntary. I must be crazy. (George Mussell - Grimsby)

I hate being hemmed in. We lived out in the country at North Thoresby for a few years, then Ludborough. They were good years. Good happy stable years. Wife and children and meself. Great years. I used to come in and not go out me first day in dock. Then the next morning I'd get a phone call from the Mate saying the trip had turned out all OK, something like that, about ten in the morning. About eleven o'clock I'd be at the office to see the boss. By about two o'clock I'd be finished with the office, re-ordered the bond for the next trip - all sorts of things like that - and I used to either go out to Louth or to the Humber Royal and just sit and relax. Say it was the Humber Royal, you could see the golf course there, and I'd just have a couple of pints and you could feel the lead dropping off your back, just unwinding like and I'd order a table for the night. We'd have a meal and the next day I'd stay in with the family so you hadn't had too much to drink for sailing. That was like the pattern of my life. Your first day in stay in, the next day your landing day was your day when you enjoyed yourself but the day before I sailed stay in again. So you only had the one good day. (John Meadows - Grimsby)

I was born in King Edward Street where they used to put the plant pot in the window. It meant the husband was gone or he'd come back - the ship hadn't sailed. It was a signal. And a lot of kids had uncles while the husbands were at sea. It was a man's world. I used to do his washing, pack his bag. But there was the romance through it as well - he never, all the years we was married - never forgot to send me my flowers for my birthday or our anniversary - never forgot. It was funny if I'd missed him when he come in the door, if he'd come early tide, I'd say, "Hello, had a good trip?" He'd say, "Not bad." I'd just kiss him on the cheek, we'd have a cup of tea and a chat. He'd say, "How's things?" And this is how little they noticed in the home. I bought a colour television and I said to him - we was watching it - I said, "Well, aren't you going to say anything?"

He tipped up every penny from the day we was married. And I mean every penny. He gave me his settling sheet, his bond would be on, and if he'd sent flowers and that. I gave him so much to spend. Some of the fishermen were devils. They'd keep taxis going all day, spend up, wives would go with them, boozing. They're very big drinkers, a lot of them. But I mean no worse than the miners. We went everywhere together. We went walks on the beach with the dog, and go out for the day with Russell. We'd go to the races for the day, Market Rasen and Catterick, because I like a £1 Round Robin. When he'd come in he loved going in the country, and with me not drinking we'd take him all over. He'd just have a pint and sit and look around the countryside, looking at the cattle and the cornfields and that - loved going out. (Josephine Gibney - Cleethorpes)

If you was in the North Sea you would come in one evening, say six or seven o'clock. You would land the following day as we called it. In other words the ship would be emptied of the fish and it would be victualled and it would sail the following day. So you could virtually say they was getting thirty six hours in dock. And when you've been away from the drink for ten days your system isn't the same as if you're having a few pints every night. So consequently the first few pints they had they was the worst for wear. And some of the fishermen in the early days after the war I don't suppose they remember anything that's happened after landing. They was just drunk virtually all the time. It wasn't a case of buying homes in those days. It was just a case of live for today and drink and a fisherman always wanted to get to sea in debt. He would land and settle up with his money and probably have £30 in his pocket which was a lot of money in those days and the following day he would go down to the cashier and get a £2 sub. It was always an omen. You should never go away not owing money. (Gordon Cockerill - Grimsby)

I think every fisherman in the town used to use the Humber at one time or another, when they were in dock. They'd call in when leaving or landing. Of course they'd still smell of fish. They'd get washed but you could always smell the fish, but you got so used to it you hardly smelled it. Fishermen were very well dressed when they were in dock, but when they were going fishing they would have on their jerseys and trousers to go away in. When they were in dock they liked to wear the suits with pleats at the back. They were all made at Goldstones the Tailors. You could recognise who were the fishermen in dock by their clothes, the pleated jackets and the flared bottoms on their trousers. They'd come in all togged up, have a drink or two then go around the other pubs to see who was in, then finish the night with us, then go home. They didn't talk about the job, certainly not to the women. They used to tell Eric about work but they'd never speak about it to me or the barmaids. We used to ask them if they'd had a good trip and they'd just say, "Yes", but they'd go into more detail with Eric - but then he had been to sea. (Eric & Joy Reynolds - Grimsby)

You might just have had two days in dock. It went too quick didn't it. Half the time you was groggy - you didn't know what you was doing. Plus the fact, I mean, we all liked a drink. The idea of the drunken fisherman was a load of rubbish really because the shoreman used to drink equally as much or in fact more than us but we had ours in such a short time and we had three weeks at sea that you never had a drink. So you used to come in have two or three pints and it used to affect you quicker. It wasn't all booze. I mean you had your family to see to. (George Mussell - Grimsby)

We opened at 10.30 in the morning and shut at 2.30 pm. The Clee Park didn't shut 'till 3 p.m., so they could dash from the Humber and get a quick pint at the Clee Park. When we had the Prince of Wales you could serve in your bar but all the foreign seamen had to come out your rooms at twenty to ten because the police wanted the pubs clearing down Freeman Street by quarter to ten. We opened in the evening from 6.00pm to 10.00pm. Every night at 9.40pm a couple of police Inspectors and a couple of bobbies walked down Freeman Street clearing the pubs of foreign fishermen to make sure they got back on the docks onto their boats. You could still serve in your bar but all the "Scrobs" had to come out of your rooms. The Bobbies made sure they'd have a quiet night that way, and they had more power then to sort things out. They wore them leather gloves and would smack 'em across the face with them and say, "Now just get on your way," and they just used to go after that. There was never any real bother in those days, not like there is nowadays. (Eric & Joy Reynolds - Grimsby)

Years ago when we'd all been down dock there was thousands, literally thousands of people. Say we'd all been down looking for a ship, hundreds of us, and there was no ships, they all used to come up the dock and the first place they used to head for was The Humber. They used to open about half ten in those days so from about ten o'clock the side of The Humber to right round the front was full of blokes waiting for opening time. And Eric used to torment us. He'd open two minutes late or something like that. Of course he might have three or four hundred blokes stuck out there. As soon as he opened the doors it was just one mad rush. And he used to have all the pints pulled and all the spirits pulled. He took some money. In Grimsby then there was hell of a lot of rum drunk. You don't see it now. We used to drink rum at sea. I don't know whether that has 'owt to do with it. Every seaman or fisherman used to drink rum. So we'd had a pint and a dram with it. A pint and a dram. It was either The Humber (that was Humber Street) then at Riby Square - that used to be The Lord Raglan, a pub called The Lord Raglan. And that always used to be full. That was right on the corner where Orwell Street comes out. When I was Deckie, the Skippers seemed to have their own pubs. They had the Oberon and the Royal Hotel, the posh ones. They didn't mix with us much. But what you'd call the latterday Skippers we all used to mix together. I used to go to the Humber a lot with the crew. Because the crew actually were my friends. (George Mussell - Grimsby)

A lot of people remember fishermen as a lot of drunkards. They were contemptuous of us in Grimsby. But if you was ashore for only three days you did it to blot out what you'd just been doing for three weeks. When I was in my twenties I was a heavy drinker and I just did it to blot out what we'd been through for three weeks. It's terrible the way fishermen was tret and looked down on in this town when they made it what it is today. (Tom Jacombe - Grimsby)

We had the Prince of Wales in Freeman Street. The pub had four rooms a bar and a snug and it was mainly Danes and Grimsby fisherman that used it. We used to get a few Icelandics in but then we had the trouble because the Icelandics and the Danes clashed when the Danes had to pay extra income tax to keep Iceland, because it was once a Danish possession. Well it's still Danish but they've got their own independence now, Iceland have. Anyway the Danes had to pay more tax and that was the source of trouble between them. We used to send the Icelandics up the road to the Red Lion, we never got many Icelandics. The Danes got on well with the Grimsby fishermen because there were a lot of local Danish people as well. It was a good community. They called them Danish Danes and Grimsby Danes. For the area we were in we didn't get much trouble at all. But he's been a strict landlord all the time and he used to give them just one warning then it was out. There were two at the other end, Jock MacRobert, he had the Lincoln Arms Hotel, and Big George Langham, he had the Red Lion. They got all the trouble. Big Jock just used to stand at the door and say, "Oot" as they came round.

Then, of course, we used to have the ladies of the night. They used to come more for the foreign fishermen than anything. We had the characters. One used to come in and Eric used to say to her, "You're drunk," and she would say, "No, it's just my shoes Hen, it's the high heels." We had some laughs with them but they always knew, when he told them, "Pack it up," it was that or get out. Then there was Woodbine Betty. She was an old lady then, but a character. When we first went there it was strange for me, I hadn't known much about ladies of the night. They didn't give us much bother. They just used to come in and then go off to the houses that they used to go to, we never had any bother that way. It wasn't a meeting place for them, the law says you can't serve a known prostitute but that means to regularly serve them, to let them stop there all night, things like that. But then, you can't just say to someone, "You're a prostitute you can't come in," because then you'd be at the law courts. You have to work your way round things like that. (Eric & Joy Reynolds - Grimsby)

The drunken fishermen thing is not as it seems. There was always some who were like alcoholics, but the majority of fishermen were just family men like other people. But you was in for just three days so you went out together, it was all taxis everywhere, you stuck together because, as fishermen, nobody else knew what you was talking about. Skippers always used to meet together. They used to meet in the Royal, the old Royal that used to be near the docks. My kind, we used to meet in the Freemasons Arms which is now the Rainbow, on Freeman Street. At night time it was always the Black Swan, the 'Mucky Duck.' When we was flush we used to go to the Harvest Moon, they had Rock and Roll on. Sometimes we had an outing with the Skipper and he'd always buy the ladies their drinks. Champagne on a good trip. Johnny Linford, he got killed in a car accident, but he was a nice bloke. He always bought the ladies champagne. We used to go out to Caistor and that - the Red Lion. It was a long way on an outing on the bus in them days. Just country roads. (Graham Howard - Grimsby)

There was a sort of dividing line when it came to drinking. All the Skippers and Mates went to the Conservative Club or the Bowling Club, the Chiefs and the Deckies would probably go the Working Men's Club, the Gasworkers Club or the British Legion Club. I preferred the Working Men's Club 'cause I've always gone there and my family always went there and I used to meet my father, who was retired, for a drink there. Then, after a few drinks, we'd all disperse, maybe take the wife shopping or whatever. Sometimes I'd go on to the Marine Hotel with the lads to play snooker. After that, at about three o'clock, a taxi would pick us up and we'd go over to the Conservative Club because that was the only place open after that time, and the Skippers and Mates would have gone to the Bowling Club. You had to have a ticket to get into the Bowling Club. To buy membership of the Bowling Club you bought a share, and the Skippers and Mates were the only ones who could afford that. The wives weren't allowed in the club, they had to sit in the garden. (Wilf Cartmell - Fleetwood)

There was a lot of good places. The British Legion, the Gas Workers Club, the Working Men's Club, West End Club - them was your four big clubs, you had to be members of them. Mainly, you drank more in pubs like Dead'uns and the Kings Arms, the Prince Arthur, and there used to be a couple of right dives on Dock Street, the Blue Flamingo and the Wyre Social. That was a room with a great big stove in the middle and a pipe going through the ceiling. It was run by an ex-seaman. He used to always get smashed. Them days the Icelandics used to come in here. They used to be in their big

Fedoras. There used to be big fights, it was a giggle more than 'owt. You'd all go down dock to see what jobs were on the board then your mates would be landing so you'd be in the pub. Once you'd got in the pub there'd be pints coming from all over. (Thomas Bagnall - Fleetwood)

The fishermen didn't have it very nice. I realised that my father went away and came home and had a hard life. I always wanted to be there when he came home. I always wanted to be around him. We had a big family, we had a big house, and my mother, in the middle of the night whenever he was coming home would put a big fire in the grate. The table would be laid and she'd have a hot toddy ready for him, but also there would be poultices ready to poultice the salt water boils that would be up his arms and round his neck through the chaffing of the oil frocks, and the salt water. Also they would have a 'lance' boiling so that if they were in a very bad state the wives used to lance the boils for them. I saw all this. (Dolly Hardie - Grimsby)

I've got two girls - I never seen 'em grow up in me life. The pride was when I used to walk through that door - my front door. In them days we used to have a big kit bag on our back and all the bond, which was the chocolates and things on top. My little kiddies used to run up this hall and grab me and kiss me and then they used to dart straight in this kit bag and we used to have Quality Street and things like that, and to see their little faces! That's what kept you going. I never seen my kiddies grow up at all because when I finished fishing my kiddies was in their twenties. They was getting married. Fortunately, I've got four lovely grandbairns and I intend to see them grow up. I didn't realise at the time but to not see your own family grow up is something that you miss in later years. (Tom Jacombe - Grimsby)

There used to be a place on the docks where he used to make Deckies' suits. They were all trendy and you got one off him and you paid him so much a trip for it. I never did but lots of blokes did. I know two brothers - both about the same size - and one of them went down and ordered a Deckie suit. He was only a young feller who'd just started going to sea. He was a Deckie Learner. He had this younger brother who was still at school and he wanted to borrow this suit for the school dance. The two brothers were so much alike that it was hard to tell the difference. So the younger brother went down to the tailors and got it out. When his older brother came in from sea he went hairless - but they were all right because they were two good brothers. I know because they were both my sons. (Chris Fisher - Fleetwood)

You'd perhaps have £40 or £50 in your pocket and you'd think let's go out and have a good spend up, whereas a man ashore perhaps had only £10. You used to go in dock, pay your light bill, pay your gas bill, little bit for the mortgage and the rest was yours. You used to buy your wife clothes, buy yourself a new suit - I mean you could buy yourself a new suit for about £8, £9, or £10. We always had pleats and bell bottoms. The Navy tradition is bell bottoms and we always had pleats in the back. Everybody knew you was a fisherman. You used to have half moon lapels. That was the mark you was a fisherman. It was just tradition, what you grew up in. I could come home and get changed twice a day and I had a different suit for every day of the week. It was just fisherman's tradition - always smartly dressed. When I first started going to sea, tradition was a long mac with a white silk scarf. That was a trademark in them days. As times got better so your spending power got better and you looked for better things to spend your money on. Nobody had a car in them days, nobody could afford a car. Couldn't afford to go on holidays. You couldn't say to the wife, "I'll have next trip off, we'll go to Spain on our holidays," pure and simply because you didn't have the money. But you always managed to get through. (Tom Jacombe - Grimsby)

We wore oilfrocks. My mother used to do all ours with the old wash tub. We didn't have no washing machines then. She wouldn't wash the day we'd gone away - she believed in that superstition. She'd never wash on any of us going away. After that boot stockings - you always had three or four pairs of boot stockings. You always had two sets of gear so when you came in that other gear was all ready for you, more or less like. And then you had to get your oilfrocks yourself down the dock, or from Beadles or Tiplady's. My father used to buy a load of cloth from Beadles and have his own suits made.

Sometimes three or four of them would get together. They had someone who made suits for them, then they'd buy this big roll of cloth and have three or four suits made off it, a suit each. They were like an ordinary suit, but they also used to wear a thin coat, a long coat, very light, but the same cloth as your trousers and suit. Oh! they looked very smart. What they used to call a 'two piece suit' 'cos you had your top coat with it for bad weather. A lot wore the old style suits with watches and chains in. That was the older people. (Roly Webb - Grimsby)

When I first started, if you wanted to get in a better ship your best time was at Christmas when people wanted to be off, so you jumped in then. I think in the first ten years of my sixteen years of fishing I spent nine of them at sea at Christmas time, for the simple reason I wanted to get into a better ship - so I missed all those Christmas's with my kids. (John Pickett - Grimsby)

I did find time to father six kids. You always found time for that. I did miss my kids growing up. It's only since I retired seven years ago that I've got more contact with them. But during my forty years working away at sea I didn't have much to do with my kids. I never really saw them growing up. I was home for the birth of one of them. Karen. I was at sea for the rest. But I enjoy the fruits of it now, especially the grandkids. They keep me occupied and out of trouble with the wife. (Peter Wright Wilson - Fleetwood)

I always used to try to have two trips off a year but really if you're a fisherman you don't fetch your kids up - your wife brings 'em up. My lads are grown up now. I never ever hit my kids. Never. When I came home and they'd done something wrong I only used to say something. I'd sit 'em down and as soon as I started talking to 'em they'd start crying. I didn't have to hit 'em. A fisherman's wife fetches the kids up. We've always gone on holidays, Audrey and I, but we was fortunate in that. Aud's mother, or my mum and dad, always had the kids. We used to take the kids away and then we'd go off on our own somewhere. (Peter Newby - Grimsby)

I used to knock about with proper boozers and plonkies and I could have easily have got trapped into that kind of thing. When I got married it was a case of having to, but I did the right thing and married. It was, "Oh you won't be going out with us." I still couldn't get used to being married. When I landed I never come straight home. I'd land and have two or three of me mates with me and we'd go to the office and then we'd go drinking. I wouldn't bother about the wife. We'd go drinking. I used to come home absolutely sozzled, sometimes in the early mornings, and my wife would be waiting for me fast asleep on the settee. And she used to say, "Have you had a nice time?" And I'd say, "Why don't you say summat?" But she said, "Oh no, you're alright." I couldn't weigh it up. I thought, "I'm out all day." I used to give her money. I used to live with my mother in law when I first got married. I lived down Pollit Street. It's as you come on to Riby Square docks, there used to be a row of houses there. I used to walk off the dock or we'd come off the dock in a taxi and she'd be probably be stood near the door. And I used to say, "Stop the taxi a minute." I used to whip out the taxi,. "Here you are. I'm just having a drink with the lads." Give her some money and get in the taxi and we used to float off having a good time. After we'd had the first youngster she started getting a bit stricter. (Les Bowden - Grimsby)

My wife lost twins to me after eight years. Then she told me to pack up. I got a shore job. I didn't realise I'd chucked the Mate of the Truman away for her as well. That was my last ship in 1965. She had two children when I married her, they was three and five. I had to go away when she was expecting twins but she lost a lot of blood and when I came in she'd lost them. I didn't bear no malice or anything like that. But she gradually got on with this man that had a kidney and a lung out. I couldn't believe it. Our love life changed just like that in bed. "Get it if you want it," that style of thing. I thought, "There's something wrong here." (Roly Webb - Grimsby)

I did like it. I do miss the sea. I do miss it very much. I lost my wife through it. She hated it from the start. Never even went down dock for money when you had to go down for the wages. Sometimes she'd go with me when I had to go down in a taxi to settle up, and we'd go for our dinner somewhere or for a drink and do a bit of shopping and go home, but she used to hate the docks. She had no time at all for fishing. (John Kirk - Grimsby)

My father was a Third Hand, a Bosun, a Trawlerman. He had been in the 1914 war. He had the honour of the DSM and Bar. He came back to fishing and my life revolved around trawlers and trawlermen. All my uncles and aunties, everyone I was surrounded by as a child, was trawlermen and fishing families. It was a frightening life at times but it was a great life. It was warmth. Your mother protected and looked after you. She gave you a good home life. Of course your father had to go to sea for the money to provide all this. They didn't come home very often. They were not very well paid, not very well looked after but we had a close knit community and everybody helped each other. No backbiting. If anyone was in need through illness, or they were in trouble, or if a fisherman had not gone down to sail on his ship for some reason or other, the police would be chasing him to arrest him and everybody would be hiding him. He'd be in one false roof to another false roof, it was quite hilarious really. (Dolly Hardie - Grimsby)

There were some very funny tales really. I can remember an incident of one particular fisherman and it's always amazed me that he met this particular girl of easy virtue and he used to go round to this place and he would sit downstairs while she was upstairs with a client. He wouldn't go with anyone else and I remember he was in a ship called the Coventry City. He came to me one day and he said, "When I come in I want a trip off. I'm going to get married." And I said, "Who you marrying like?" And when he told me I just couldn't believe it. He was a well educated man. I spoke to him because I knew him very well and I said, "Well you want to be careful because when you're at sea she's going to be doing this anyway." And he said he knew but he couldn't help himself, that he was absolutely madly in love with her. He was infatuated. She was the only woman in his life and I felt sorry for him really and yet I could understand what he was saying. He did marry her and he was married to her up to two or three years ago when he died. They had big bust ups and what have you and she carried on on the game and yet she always looked

Waiting for Dad.

after him in her way. And I've spoken to him many a time since, as we've grown older and seen him out and I've always said, "How's Grace?" And he'd say, "Oh yeah, she's fine." He had some beautiful children by her - whether they was all his one doesn't know. But it was sad and yet it was a happy one. It was hard to explain. (Gordon Cockerill - Grimsby)

I've come in dock and me wife's said, "Your daughter's had pneumonia, your daughter's had this and your daughter's had that." I wasn't there to help so I couldn't do anything about it. But I did think about it and I thought to myself, "Well why aren't you there?" but you just couldn't release yourself from the grip of the sea. The sea is in your blood and it's hard for people who've never experienced it, it's hard for them to realise what you're trying to tell 'em. (Tom Jacombe - Grimsby)

It was bloody terrible for the wives. They had a hard enough job as it was. We had three youngsters and my wife was like mother and father to them. The women are the unsung heroes of this lot. I don't know how they put up with it. They had to be a special breed of a person to be a fisherman's wife. (Jim Quinn - Fleetwood)

You used to be away a long time. When they were little I was away seven Christmases on the trot without one off and that's when it comes hard. But you see your wife if she comes from a fishing family she's used to it. I mean you've got your family. We've got eight grandchildren. No I don't regret anything. (Mick George - Grimsby)

I used to worry a lot about John. I never watched the news or the weather. I still don't watch the weather forecast when he's away. It was terrible when a ship was lost or someone was killed. When he was fishing we had three but he was never there when they were ill and very rarely there at Christmas or birthdays or anniversaries. The worst thing was when they were ill. You couldn't even tell him they were poorly, you had to cope with all the stress yourself. I didn't like him being at sea but he enjoyed it and it was at that time a good living. He was earning more then than he is now, and that was twenty odd years ago. So I put up with it for the money and because he enjoyed it. It meant we could have holidays, and you have to put up with the bad as well as the good. The main thing was that he was earning a good living. I'll never forget the first time he came home with a thousand pounds, all still in a banker's envelope. (Beryl Pickett - Grimsby)

When it was windy or icy weather you always thought of your father at sea and later, when you were married, you thought about your husband. You thought of the ships icing up. They ice up so quickly with black ice. Of course you'd want them not to go, you'd have loved your father to work ashore like the other children at school. But they were fishermen, that was their life. They wouldn't have been happy working ashore. My husband wouldn't have been happy ashore. My son, he passed to be entered into Trinity House which was going to cost us a lot of money, but he came in one day when his father was in dock and said, "I've joined the Nautical School and I'm going for my Deckie Learner's ticket." What do you do? Everything fell on the mother. She had to do everything. If anyone attacked her child she would have to go and have a go at somebody's husband, and that husband never used to come off very good I can tell you. He would have a skipping rope wrapped round his neck in no time, or he'd have a nasty kick. You'd have to fight for your children, of course, because there were some rough characters - but there were no characters around in those days like there are today. It was just kids falling out and parents falling out to protect their children, but then soon after you'd all be friends again. (Dolly Hardie - Grimsby)

When they went on the freezers they were gone nearly ten or twelve weeks. You never got on each other's nerves. It kept the marriage fresh. But there's something different about a man who goes to sea. He's a man. But some of them, I think "Whimps!" Fishermen looked after you, they were strong, they were different.

When the weather was bad, you worried a bit. You knew every time he went out that you might not see him again, and that's another thing me mother taught me, never let the sun go down on your anger, because everybody has a row. We used to argue now and again which every marriage does, but we always made it up. (Josephine Gibney - Grimsby)

You all pulled together. The same if you was out of a ship. You'd go down to the docks and have a look at the landing list in the little paper shop at the dock gates. If a ship had had a good trip and you had a pal on it you'd go down to the Legion at opening time, get a pint and stand there waiting. Next minute he'd come in on his way down to the office. You'd sit there yapping. He'd go pick up his money and be back. Shorts all round. "Here, put that in your pocket". That's how it was then. We all did it for each other. That was the routine. You give to them and they give to you. (Peter Wright Wilson - Fleetwood)

Missing You.

Say it was your wife's birthday you used to go on to the Bridge to see the Sparks and say, "Can you send us Interflora?" And the Sparks used to say, "Yeah. What do you want sending, flowers or fruit?" A lot of the blokes, they'd been at home, been drunk and arguing, they'd come to sea and after a couple of days they started regretting it then. "Oh, I'll send her some flowers... we had an argument before I come away." So that would smooth the thing over. Well, hopefully. 'Til the next time they landed. (Les Bowden - Grimsby)

I had two children. I was happy enough. You couldn't go to sea successfully if you didn't have a happy relationship with your wife because if it wasn't right it was unsettling. You saw plenty of people pack it in without even realising what was doing it. But if they wasn't contented or they felt something was wrong, whether it was their fault or their wife's fault, or their children's fault, that was enough to destroy a man at sea because it would play on him. Your mind had to be clear. You couldn't be home-sick. If you went to sea home-sick it was no good. I'm not saying you shut it out of your mind, but you had to be completely relaxed in your idea of things, that they were all right. If you thought that, you could get on with it. (Harold Dawe - Fleetwood)

Chapter 9
Power in the Ports

"Down Dock" was a unique world of its own where the hunters, the fishermen, met market forces in the auctions, where Owners asserted crude power and Merchants mediated between catchers and consumers. Here was a powerful interplay of basic instincts and economic forces and a mystery few could understand, none control.

It, too, was a male world where men were men and women were supposed to be glad of it, though they, like the rest of the town, were largely excluded. The Owners ruled, a tightly knit financially motivated group of men, like a cosa nostra *of powerful figures. Each port's score or so of Owners were like Kings, courted by Skippers whom they kept dependent because there were too many for the ships available, by Mates wanting promotion, and fishermen wanting trips. Nor was there any countervailing labour power in the form of strong unions. Strikes were rare and almost impossible to organise, though they did occur in both Fleetwood and Hull. Fishermen were independents who wouldn't be organised, didn't want to be decasualised, and paid little attention to questions of pensions and redundancy because they assumed that the good times and the big money would go on. They didn't join unions in any number, even in Hull. Only the Engineers and the Officers, in their own Guild, were effectively organised.*

Already powerful figures, the Owners tried to make themselves more so by forming collectives to run the ports and their services and by building up all encompassing businesses ranging from repairs to provisions. The trend of the time was the concentration of ownership in ever bigger mergers, with Hellyers merging with Associated in 1961, and Associated with Ross to form British United Trawlers in 1969. The result of that concentration was that where twenty-six Owners had controlled eighty percent of the fleet in 1959, by 1968 ten controlled three quarters of a fleet which had shrunk from seven hundred vessels to about half that number. As a group, the Owners ran the port through the Exchanges and the Owners' Associations. They controlled the fish meal plant which took the unsold fish as well as the suppliers, the ice factory, the box company. They even tried to control prices and manage the market through what amounted to a restrictive landings committee mis-named the Distant Water Development Scheme. Later they attempted more modestly to smooth out fluctuations through the Planned Landing Committee. Yet they could never master their own fate, for Owners were dependent on the Merchants for good prices while Merchants depended on retailers and consumers, who were conservative in their tastes and were being offered an ever wider choice of alternative foods as they became more affluent: chicken, prepared meals, fast foods. The consumer society was as much about eating as possessions and in it fish, tainted by memories of school dinners, did not begin too fare better. Until it was too late.

Thus, though Owners were Kings in their own world and fishermen jealously eyed their assumed enormous wealth, fishing was never particularly profitable. The rate of return on capital was consistently lower than most shore based manufacturing industries. Indeed, the yield declined steadily as competition increased, fish prices fell, particularly from the mid-Sixties, and consumers turned to alternatives. The result was intense exploitation of capital, equipment and crews but it was also and paradoxically improvement and investment. No-one could ever be big enough to control a market in which all competed and on which all depended. British United Trawlers merged several companies for strength. Ross opted for vertical integration from fishing vessels to processing factories. Birds Eye built power on the market. Yet no-one could tame the beasts in the competitive jungle of the fish docks in their prime, so all had to compete ever more energetically. If only the consumers had responded and experimented with new species of fish the whole industry could have moved up market and upgraded. But consumers didn't.

After the War they started building up and different firms started opening. They was in caravans. Little caravans along the dockside. One was an old railway coach. Then they built the offices. Bigger ships came and then you got all your different firms starting up again. They didn't want no offices before that because there was only one firm, and there wasn't many ships out of Hull because they'd taken them all in the war for mine-sweeping. Then we started getting the trawlers back when the war ended because the Ministry of Food didn't need them. That's amazing isn't it. Starting with just six ships out of the dock, just one firm, Hellyers, and it grew from there. And now it's picture houses and Chinese restaurants. That's fifty odd years. Where Hellyers office was now there is a Chinese restaurant. (George Waudby - Hull)

The amount of fish that was brought down there, Grimsby docks, you couldn't credit it. The fish market itself would be two miles long, starting at Len Kemp's which was 'Pneumonia Jetty' - and well named because I think the first stop was Siberia it was so cold - and then it come along under the Ice House clock and up the jetties, Chapman's jetties, onto Doughty's jetties and into No. 1 Dock and you finished up at Jimmy Johnson's. And many a regular time 20,000 ten stone boxes of fish was landed. And if you was on the 'Pneumonia Jetty' and you looked from one end, Len Kemp's to Freddie Rock's, you were neck high in fish. The Lumpers, they packed the fish in twenty fives, five fours and five. And then they squared them up in hundreds. (Joe Linfitt - Grimsby)

The two ports were entirely different from each other. Even the landing, they call them Lumpers out of Grimsby and Bobbers in Hull, was slightly different for the two ports. In Grimsby you always did the landing in boxes, whilst in Hull it was in barrels - kits. Even in the way the fish was swung ashore there were differences. The Bobbers in Hull, as the basket was swung ashore it went straight into a kit on the scales, whereas in Grimsby it went up onto a platform that ran ashore where the fish was sorted out and then put on the scales. (Jim Williams - Hull)

A gang of Bobbers was ten people. I think they were allocated on a ship to land about 300 kits. Say the ship had about 1500 kit, they would put five gangs of Bobbers on board. If they landed over 1600 kit they used to get a bonus. They'd get the equivalent of another gang's money to share between them. So if they took fish away they'd be losing out. We used to think that was a good safeguard. Plus the fact that they used to start landing at about two o'clock in the morning and the Mate used to be on the Humber Market from about 5.30 in the morning. So there was very little could be moved around that time that shouldn't have been. (Sid Morrell - Hull)

In the busiest period we started at nine o'clock at night and we sometimes didn't finish while nine o'clock, eleven o'clock the following morning. I enjoyed the work, but sometimes you had to work hard. But your normal start time was midnight. I started my career off in the fish room, the donkey work, because there was no method to it. We had a man actually filling the baskets with fish and sending it up. There was another piece of machinery that took it ashore, and then they were sorted and graded. It was what we used to call 'one wheel,' that was one hatchway man and four down the fish room, and then ashore you'd maybe have about twelve or thirteen men to do the actual grading, which was more delicate than what we used to do. We had a chargehand aboard and a chargehand ashore and then there was an overall foreman for the ship. Sometimes if you had a big boat in you could have four or five wheels which amounted to about fourty eight men or even more, it all depended on the actual amount of fish on the ship. (Peter Broomhead - Grimsby)

The Lumpers were a race apart. They were a very integral part of the dock. They could unload ships, by God they could. I think the trouble with them was that they joined the elitist group, like the miners, the dockers and the car workers, and there was such a big gap between them and the others, that the jealousy was always there. I think they were overpaid for what they did, and they got the same stock answers from me. About turning out at night to do the job. "Well," I says, "Unless you can point out to me a chap with a gun in your back making you go, you go for one thing only," I said, "The money." (Joe Linfitt - Grimsby)

Getting ready for the Market.
Copyright: Grimsby Evening
Telegraph.

There was one saying that Lumpers was always midnight millionaires. To a certain degree we got good money but we earned it because of the nature of the job. You was always pushed to a time scale. You had to have every fish, if at all possible, out for the sale at seven o'clock. Now when we had a lot of ships in we were late to sale. I've known sales be eleven o'clock when there's been that much work that they was the last ships on turn, but you were still working to a time scale to get it out. I should say ninety nine times out of a hundred you did it. I can remember once when all the hydraulics froze on a night time on the mechanical landings so we had to revert back to what we used to call 'the whip', that meant two or three men pulling on a rope, getting the fish ashore. It was hard work but we managed to do things like that. And I can remember blokes coming down when we had a big flood in Grimsby, coming down to land ships. The ships was actually on the pontoon but all the Lumpers turned up for work, and this is what the gaffers used to like about them. They didn't used to like having to pay us but used to like us if we turned up. (Peter Broomhead - Grimsby)

Every Owner had a Foreman Lumper. He was responsible to go into the National Dock Labour Pool and requisition the number of men he required to unload the trawler. He had to be there to see that all the gear was rigged up to unload it, so he was there when the hatches came off, and he was responsible for seeing that the fish was put on line and laid out properly, and he was also responsible for making a tally out because the Lumpers were paid basically but they were also paid per kit landed, as far as I remember. So they would want to know how much fish was landed. Then, when the Fish Salesman came down, he got the tally from the Foreman Lumper and, because he was responsible for selling the fish, he had to tally out exactly how many kits there were of each variety. (Bill Letten - Grimsby)

When I started lumping the workforce was about a thousand men and when I finished after the demise of the Scheme then there was about sixty, so within a matter of about twenty two years it was drastically reduced. We had our own special funds what we used to call fighting funds because we

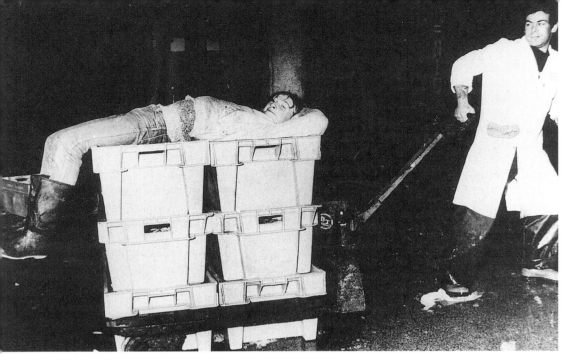

*It's a man's life on the fish docks.
Copyright: Grimsby Evening
Telegraph.*

*Midnight Millionaires.
Copyright: Grimsby Evening
Telegraph.*

never used to like the gaffers and they never used to like us. So we had a fund just in case we needed compensation, if we were out on strike or a bereavement in the family, or anybody was off sick. The company would pay a certain amount sick pay and we'd attempt to top it up wherever we could. We were like one big family, we used to look after one another. We all worked for one company but were hired out to individual firms that owned the ships. For instance, we all worked for Grimsby Landing Company and Tom Sleights could have a ship, Bannisters could have had a ship or Ross's could have had a ship or Northerns. So we were lent out to a ship owned by a certain company. It was a funny system. The Landing Company was a non profit making organisation but all the directors of that Landing Company were all Fishing Vessel Owners, so basically the money that our Landing Company made over a year was just passed round the Fishing Vessel Owners. (Peter Broomhead - Grimsby)

We came back one Christmas and were supposed to lock on Christmas Eve. We didn't make it in time and the locks shut down, so we just laid in the river until New Year's Day and they wouldn't let us off the boat. We docked on New Year's Day and got off, and the docks opened again on the second of January and we unloaded the fish. Half of it had gone off and went for fish meal. It was about the that time that the Lumpers who were casual were made to join the National Dock Labour Scheme by the Owners, who at times hadn't got enough labour to land the ships. Casual labour couldn't do it, so they made them join the NDLB to get regular labour to unload the ships. When there was any problem with the Lumpers refusing to land ships they still asked us. I've unloaded a ship many a time. We always did it when they were on strike and we were better than the Lumpers because we knew what we was doing. But when they were made redundant they got something like £35-37,000. We got nothing. (Tom Jacombe - Grimsby)

We earned a basic wage plus a price percentage divided amongst the men that was working. So if you had a thousand kit, just say for instance you got a pound a kit, it was a thousand pounds shared between the number of men. It could be sixty, seventy, eighty men with a big boat, whereas at the other end it could be ten kit and about four men. It depended on the actual amount of work you were prepared to put in because we used to start off with a midnight shift, then a double, which was a local North Sea vessel and then you could have a treble or even a fourth one. So it was all built up. You got your midnight kittage, your double kittage and your treble kittage all clubbed together. If the work was there it could amount to a lot of money but we always had a fall back guarantee that we was paid even when there was no work. I remember my first wage packet. I left Peter Dixon's to come lumping just after it shut down and my first wage packet, what I actually picked up was £116 and me top line at Dixon's was about £45. So it was a real shock to the system. But it was an enjoyable shock. So that's why we got the tag, 'midnight millionaires.' There was one or two sayings that was locally put to Lumpers. For instance. 'There's only three sorts of people that go out at night, burglars, ladies of the night and Lumpers.' (Peter Broomhead - Grimsby)

My job was a barrow lad. You used to have to go down, take your big barrow with blown up wheels. When the tyres blew up it was like a rocket going off. It's a wonder someone didn't get killed because of the pressure in the tyres. But it wasn't long, even though there was hundreds and hundreds of people, before you got to know faces if not names. When you was going round with your barrow to pick up the fish for your firm, it was your job to take it from where it was bought at to your stand where it was processed. And these were in five and ten stone boxes and that was quite a lot for a fourteen year old lad to lift, but you needn't worry because there was always someone to give you a lift. You never asked for a lift, you always got a lift. Similarly, though, if someone else was stuck you'd give him a lift as well. The camaraderie down there, I wouldn't think there's another place on this earth where people pull with each other. Organised chaos was originated down there because we had to hump all that fish on the barrows and we used to have to go down a double set of ramps which is quite unnerving for a young boy, and you'd be half way across and someone would say, "Come on, I'll give you a push." Old Ernie Harris, he used to put me nine tenths of them boxes on there, and the boxes would weigh over a stone as well so that's nigh eleven stone on a two wheel barrow, and

I had to pull it for two mile and "Don't be long back." This was for thirty five bob a week, six days a week. It was a lot of money in those days. (Joe Linfitt - Grimsby)

I went down on the fish docks at the age of sixteen, in 1926, to work for a Fish Merchant. In those days it was slave labour. I started at nine shillings a week and for that I had to work five and a half days. In those days there was anything up to fifty to sixty trawlers a day, plus Faroe and Iceland trawlers landing. Sales started at eight o'clock in the morning. Then we had to follow the boss round the market, picking up the fish, until the sales finished - at the end of the pontoon with the Iceland fish. The fish all had to be barrowed up on long, iron wheeled barrows, on wood, and then we started the process of packing. In those days there was no such things as plastic boxes. It was all packed in kits, small wooden kits. These were in sizes from two stone, which were known as 'tubs,' to 'babies,' which was four stones, then there were 'smalls' (six stones), then there was eight stones which, for some unknown reason that I never learned, were called 'swindlers'. Then there was up to ten stone, twelve stone and fourteen stone. All the fish in those days was 90% sent whole for filleting. All the fish was headed by hand, winter and summer. Our stand was right on the end of Chapman's jetty and was open to all weathers. We stood there throughout the winter, heading codlings by hand, with no gloves, no hot water, aprons made out of old fisherman's jerseys, and then, after we'd packed all the fish, it had to be covered over with hessian and nailed down with hooks. Then we had to pack all the fish onto barrels and take them round to the trucks that were lined up in the No.1. dock. Everything had to be manhandled. If they were very very busy there were horses and carts available and if the boss did say to you, "Go and get a cart," you wouldn't see my heels for dust. Although it was slave labour I loved my work, and I stayed there right up until the war broke out. And that was my early days on the fish docks when I was a barrow lad. We weren't called barrow boys, we were barrow lads. Barrow boy was a London term. I was also a packer and I also had to do office work on a Friday afternoon, for which I had to learn typewriting, and I also went to night school to learn book keeping. (George Oliver - Grimsby)

When I first went on the pontoon I was at Robert Chapman's and I just used to watch the boxes and all that and I used to get fed up of it. I told the foreman about this and he said, "Would you like a proper barrow boy's job?" I said, "Yes," and he got me a job at Mooners and Kelly's as a barrow boy and I used to have me own barrow. I used to look after it and paint it and polish it and take it to the place where they used to blow the tyres up for you, and all things like that. I used to take a lot of pride in me barrow. The barrow boy used to have to be down a bit early to get the barrow. They'd wait for me fetching the barrow down and then when they'd bought the fish they used to put it on me barrow and they'd all push it. I really enjoyed it. It was hard work. We used to take the fish to 'Pneumonia', put it in the wagons and the trains used to come and drag 'em away. With it being a small firm - there was only five of us on that firm, you only used to get two and a half kit to the thousand. Sometimes we'd finish at dinner time or maybe one o'clock. Very very rare we'd finish less than three. If you finished at three you was late. I started at about seven. Get on the pontoon for about seven, selling at half past seven. Of course there were loads of barrows there because that's when they used to land 20,000 kit at a time. A lot of Icelandic's used to come in. There was not just the deep water, there was all the North Sea's and all the snibbies and everything. In Pneumonia it was all the deep water ships. I was on about £2 - £3 a week - something like that - and it was good money for a barrow boy. (John Kirk - Grimsby)

I was at work every morning, down dock, at 6.30am. I used to do all the buying. We gradually grew and I managed to get larger premises that had been vacated by Ross Group. Then we got bigger so Young's built a new factory on the industrial estate, and I stayed there until I retired. By the time I retired that staff had grown from a dozen to about a hundred. They employ about four hundred now. I bought everything. My son came to work for me. I bought cod, haddock, sole, plaice - everything. One day I was on the pontoon and I'd just bought a lot of soles and a man stood on the top side of the pontoon and I went up to him and asked him if he was Dutch. He said he was and I told him I was interested in buying soles. I started to deal with him and continued to deal with him for thirty years, visiting Holland and Denmark every year buying soles - we had a very big Dover Sole trade. I used to go across to Holland and place contracts for between seventy and eighty tonnes of sole at a time for delivery over a period of time. We had our own freezing plant and I bought fish from here and abroad. I went everywhere where you could buy fish. Most of our trade was the catering trade. The system stayed the same right up to 1939 - by auction - and after the war they changed over from selling North Sea fish to Iceland fish first. By auction, just the same. I used to buy soles and salmon from abroad because there wasn't enough available to buy in England. I did buy salmon from Scotland and Ireland. I used to buy monkfish to sell to Belgium where it was made into imitation scampi and sold to France. (George Oliver - Grimsby)

My father was a Fish Merchant who came over to Fleetwood during the war years because of his fish allocation. Fleetwood fared better than Grimsby did. Even the Fish Merchants worked in bad conditions. Nothing existed then like the superstructures we've now got on the docks. I can remember the Fleetwood docks thick with ice in winter, and all you've got to protect you from the elements was an old bit of tarpaulin and at the side of that, two lots of filleting containers, and fish box lids to walk on, and they had flame throwers to defrost the pipes. You couldn't wear gloves because you couldn't fillet with gloves on. I'd be absolutely dithering in the cold and my father used to tell me to move around a bit quicker and I'd keep warmer. You couldn't go to the loo 'cause they were always blocked - hygiene regulations in those days were appalling. But you just survived. I got a liking for rum at a very early age 'cause my father used to have a flask with his coffee in it with a drop of rum to keep him warm. I thought it tasted better than the coffee my mother made. (Jill Marr - Fleetwood)

I, along with hundreds of others, have done hundreds of hours of work for nothing, where somebody's hurt themselves or is sick. I've nailed down for him and I've iced up and I'm a Fish Merchant. I chopped my thumb badly, I cut the tendon, the lot, and there was two Fish Merchants, Mally Edwards and Bobby Stansfield. They stopped their work and took me to Dr. Renfrew's because my thumb was hanging and he said, "It's hospital for you." He said, "There it is." He grabbed hold of it and he grabbed hold of the tendon, it was a white grisly looking thing and he just pulled it. And Bobby Stansfield took me up to the hospital, saw me in and everything there, and then they cleared my job up for me. That's the kind of thing they did for you. And yet for a shilling they'd cut you out at the sales. The unwritten law down dock was 'Don't be caught.' If it wasn't nailed down it was pinched. (Joe Linfitt - Grimsby)

The auction system was criticised many times and there were many attempts to get away from the auction system. That was one very uncertain element because the price could go up and down like anything and I suppose one could say that that was one area where the industry was disorganised. We tried to go onto contractual systems with people like Birds Eye, Ross, but they usually were fairly short lived contracts ,basically because the fishermen thought they'd been hard done by. Because if they landed on the market when the price of cod was £5 a kit or something, and they saw one hundred of their kit going for £3, it was bad news. They would find it difficult to remember the days when they sold to Birds Eye at £3 and the market was for £2.50, and as it was very much on a voyage by voyage basis - people looked at their pay packet at the end of each voyage. Nevertheless, having said that, we did have a long contract with Birds Eye but that was basically a discount contract. In other words, if they bought 100,000 kit of fish they'd get a discount of x percent. So that was really recognising them as a big buyer but yes, it was market price minus discount. Then we had a very beneficial contract for the industry with Pedigree Pet Foods, the Marrs empire. I can't remember the number of kits we sold to them a year, but it was many thousand. That was a contract to deliver every single day and it was always the worst quality fish, and so that was more accepted by the fishermen. So we did start to move towards a contractual basis. When we went into the freezer trawler era, that fish was all sold on contract. Birds Eye, Ross, and one or two other buyers. That didn't go through auction at all. It was landed in a different place - on the South Quay, opposite the Renovia building. (Bill Letten - Grimsby)

Filleting. Copyright: P. Horsley.

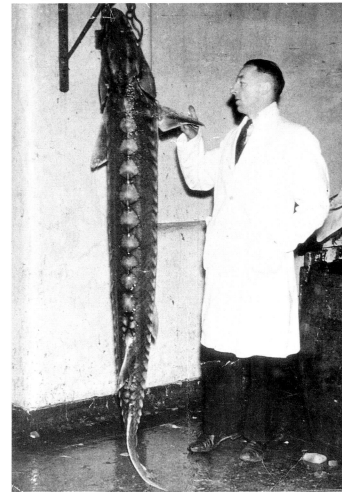

George Oliver and the Queen's Sturgeon.

Fleetwood Fish Auction, 1976.
Copyright: P. Horsley

All the fresh fish trips were landed through the market and sold by auction because it's the only way to get a true value for fish. Later on, when companies, including Ross, started building freezer trawlers, then they were selling the catch directly to processors and not through a market, for the simple reason you could put the fish in store and take it out when you wanted to. There was no reason to sell on the market. Fresh fish is an immediate thing, you've got to deal with it straight away - you can't wait about. Fishermen, anyhow, like auctions. They liked to know that some markets could really hit very high prices and that others are, hopefully, not too bad. The fishermen prefer it that way but it is the only way to market fish. There are so many varieties, so many different sizes and quality of fish, it can only really be marketed in the way it is, through auctions. It didn't make it difficult for Ross's to price their products. Bear in mind that Ross Group was really two distinct halves, trawling and processing. The trawling side of the business was a division of its own. They caught fish, put it onto the market and sold it - and that was that. The marketing side didn't necessarily buy their own fish. They'd buy from anyone, and it's no different now. Anyone that owns a fish business, in the main, is buying on auction markets as well as buying in direct. (Frank Flear - Grimsby)

There were three elements in the reserve system. There was the minimum price element which was to support the price, and then there was the lay-up scheme where you had to lay-up in the summer, and then there was a restriction on the building of ships. It was really to control an absolute free for all. It was all started in 1938 by Owners from Grimsby, Hull and Fleetwood. I suppose it was under the edicts of the British Trawler Owners' Federation, but in fact it was called 'The Distant Water Development Scheme.' It was all the Owners together. There were arguments between Grimsby and Hull and in fact our company stayed out of the Scheme for a while. We abided by the Minimum Price Scheme but we didn't abide by the lay-up scheme nor the control over building, because we felt at the time of the start of the Scheme that Hull had over-developed very much more than Grimsby and they were trying to hold Grimsby down in its capacity whereas they were trying to maintain their own. The majority of the fish that was unsold at the time was in fact that landed in Hull, and so the over capacity was in fact in Hull. We felt that if a balance was to be achieved then Grimsby should be allowed to expand a little bit and Hull should reduce theirs a little bit. So there was quite an argument on that for some time. But in the end we all joined. It did work because the most important thing was that it maintained the price and without that the whole of the industry would have been in very serious financial troubles and you would have had this terrible cycle of building and then no building for years and then a glut of building again - which went on before the war. It was important to avoid that. So the Minimum Price Scheme did work really quite well because it maintained the price, and then there were prices underneath the sale price which was fixed for human consumption. Underneath was the Salters' price which was less and meant the fish had to go to the Salters, and then there was a pet food price and below that there was the fish meal price - that was the rock bottom price in which the fish was sold to the fish meal companies, which were really mutuals. They did have share holdings but a small dividend was paid and the majority of the profit was paid back either to the Owners or the Fish Merchants, because you have to realise that at least fifty percent of the fish went to the fish meal manufacturer in any case - because when you fillet a fish you lose about fifty percent - the head, guts, backbone went to the fishmeal companies. (Bill Letten - Grimsby)

We were supposed to form a ring. There was myself, Richard Jacklin, Rob Bannister and Les Little. There was a double row, probably about 150 kit, of really superb Bank cod. "What are we going to give for them?" And I think it was about £4 then in the days when fillets was nearly a pound a stone. So Les Little said, "Leave it to me. I'll get them. This Salesman's a pal of mine." So the Salesman comes up. "Anybody want a deal, fiver the lot, £4.75 the lot, £4.50 the lot." "These are going to be ours now. Four pounds five shillings." "You've lost them." So I said, "What the hell's going on?" And there was Ernie Macklam and he's sharing them with Les Little, he bought them for four quid and we said we'd pay £4.5s. for them! And Les is one of them likeable rotten buggers, he just lifted his head up and he says, "That wasn't very nice was it?" But he got his fish. Bob Wilson, he could have throttled him! I saw the funny side of it. I thought, "Well, more fool us, we should never have trusted him because we knew what he was capable of doing." (Joe Linfitt - Grimsby)

Bird's Eye contracted to take so many thousand tonnes a year from us and the more they took the bigger the discount they negotiated and they were a very, very important buyer. They had significant primary processing and they used to use our sea frozen headed and gutted fish or just gutted fish to augment the supplies of wet fish when the weather was bad. That worked pretty well, our only hassle that we had with them was that they would use the average price on the market. We ran a sophisticated computer system that told us the average cod price on a particular day, and week, and month. So they would take the better quality fish and expect to buy it on the average price and so they had a buying advantage there, which was quite sensible. If we had been Bird's Eye we'd have done the same. (Tom Boyd - Hull)

When I joined the industry the Bird's Eye Factory was owned by Smethursts. The very formidable but likeable lady who ran it was a woman called Miss Swallow. I had to go and see her because I wanted to do a private contract with Letten Brothers (at the time) and Bird's Eye and I was received most courteously, but certainly was given a fairly keen cross examination as to exactly what my intentions were, why, what advantage it would be to Bird's Eye - she was a great character. The man who followed her as Manager was called Frazer Sidcope who eventually became Deputy Chairman of Unilever, and who I still see around on the golf course occasionally. In those days, it seems incredible, but they used to change over the factory from processing fish to processing meat. For quite a substantial period in the summer Bird's Eye was almost entirely out of the market for fish at a time when we really needed them. (Bill Letten - Hull)

As far as our association (Fish Merchants' Association) is concerned we were the strongest of them all. They had the train drivers, they went on strike, we got over them, no bother, the Lumpers went on strike, we got over them, the fishermen went on strike, ice company went on strike. We was the only one who never went on strike and we were the only ones who could have beat them. And I remember saying to Dick Taylor about going on strike. He says, "What do you want to go on strike for then Joe?" I said, "Just to make a point." The way they've rode rough shod over us, dictated to us, you'll do this, you'll do that, you'll start when we want you to start, and it was us that was financing the job. If you kept them too long they wouldn't sell you fish. But it was our money that was financing the whole industry, because it was our money that was there all the time, we had to pay whether we'd been paid or not. I would think it's fair to say, probably a contradiction in terms actually, greed and kindness was the ruling factor. (Joe Linfitt - Grimsby)

I think one of the main problems that one had was that quite a lot of the fish that was landed was of poor quality. It necessarily had to be because it could be between seventeen to twenty days old and that's getting to the end of the life expectancy of fish stored in ice, the edible expectancy. The British Fishing Federation Ports had a Minimum Price Scheme below which we would not sell and we fought that through the Restrictive Practices Court successfully and we provided a firm base at the cost of the deep water industry which allowed the inshore industry to prosper. They always used to sell just below our minimums so they were always guaranteed a sale and this used to drive my father absolutely mad. There was nothing we could do about it and the alternative was just to have mayhem which was financial suicide really. (Tom Boyd - Hull)

The FMA was a marvellous thing. I mean Ken Beeken, a clever fellow, anything you wanted, he'd do it for you, or see somebody who could or he knew somebody who could. The Beeching Report axe came and we got the Transport Scheme in, I think, the late Fifties. The Grimsby Fish Docks transport bill was a million pounds a year then in the Fifties. And the FMA got it off the ground, a Transport Scheme. It's ever so easy to off-load ten ton to Birmingham but it's a different kettle of fish when you've got a couple of three stone boxes to go half way up a mountain, and there was Merchants started their own transport and then there was other Merchants giving backhanders for other people to take it away. Undercutting the FMA, undermining them. So eventually it went through. They drifted away from the FMA strength. The bank

dispensed out to the Owners who came for them, and an hour and a quarter that's all it took for a cheque to be cleared. And the FMA did theirs and you got a chit back in return of what you'd paid and who'd paid you etc. Marvellous system. They had a legal side for you, they represented you in anything you wanted. I think it was the Merchants who let the FMA down it wasn't the FMA let the Merchants down.

Carl Ross's pipe dream was to catch the fish in his own boats, land it in Grimsby into his own factories and virtually sell it into his own shops. And they tried it with several things. They withdrew lemon soles from the market one time, all the lemon soles went into Ross factories. But if the fishing was good they couldn't get rid of the things, so they was losing money on that so that fell by the wayside. The fish trade will not tolerate interference. Supply and demand, it's feast or famine. (Joe Linfitt - Grimsby)

Our biggest customer in Northern Trawlers, as the biggest producers in Grimsby, was Bird's Eye. In the 1960's, Bird's Eye were buying thousands of kits of fish a day. But come to the pea season, which was a very important milestone in the annual calendar, they just went completely out of the market, which weakened it. It was at the time, in late June, when the warm weather was affecting the consumption of fish anyway. We used to have to try and fit the ships out and concentrate as much of our fitting out programme into the pea season. (John Butt - Grimsby)

Each firm had their own Salesmen at the auctions. Northern Trawlers always used to seem to make that bit more money than other firms. Mind you he had that much fish, see, they could make bargains with the buyers. We always seemed to make that bit more money. It was all a big twist though. He had that much fish to play with. It was the biggest firm. I forget how many ships he had but they had four or five ships landing every day, big deep water ships. And it was, "You buy this this trip and I'll give you so and so next trip." Wrangling all the time. All of them were at it. You never knew what you was going to make. I remember one time I landed in Hull and we landed a smashing trip. Two thousand kit we had, all cod, and we was sailing to come to Grimsby. And there was one of the Hull firm (there was Northerns in Grimsby and Northerns in Hull) and one of the office staff was on the lock pits as we went through and he said, "You've made a smashing trip, Skipper. You've made £10,000." Which in those days was beautiful and I was real fussy. I thought, "Oh great." We came over here and made £9,000. When we went down to settle we'd made £9,000. So coming across the river, about three or four mile, we'd lost a thousand quid. And they was all at it like that. All of them. Thousands of quids. And you couldn't prove anything. (George Mussell - Grimsby)

The 'Ghost Train' was when the ships came in and the Trawler Owners would have so much of the fish taken out which they would sell for cash and this wasn't included in the settling for the trip, so the trawlermen lost out again, for the Trawler Owners pocket money. They could have complained to the Board of Trade, but they'd never have got a ship again, so it wouldn't have done them any good. It was a lot of fish and it was taking money out of the pockets of the trawlermen, and that went on right up to the end of fishing. They had a good thing going. The Lumpers carried it away. The Lumpers couldn't tell Owners what to do. Whilst the ship was at sea the Skipper was in command and the fish belonged to him. But once the ship is anchored ashore the fish becomes the property of the Trawler Owners so nobody tells the Trawler Owners what they can do with their own fish, even though they are stealing it from the trawlermen. You couldn't complain because if you did you lost your ship. (Bill Hardie - Grimsby)

It was Bedlam. Auctioneers shouting. You didn't know what was going. So you had to rely on their honesty. Which they wasn't. They were crooks. You were settled on what they decided to settle on, not what you'd caught. That went on a lot. If you knew you'd got 2,000 kit in, you might land 1,400 kit or 1,500. We used to call it the 'Ghost Train.' In those days the trains used to be alongside. Four or five hundred kit used to disappear. You couldn't prove anything. (George Mussell - Grimsby)

The Mate had to go down at midnight landing. If you were only in dock two days you lost twelve hours there. The Owners emphasised that the Mate had to be down at midnight landing so the Lumpers could get your fish out and you had to be down there while eight o'clock in the morning at least till nearly the sales. I've seen fish go off that pontoon and because you've complained you've got the sack for it. What we call the 'Ghost Train'. I've seen a hundred kit go at a time. But in the finish you daren't complain. (Roly Webb - Grimsby)

In them days there was about a dozen firms, big firms, out of Grimsby and each firm had their office and each firm also had an office that we used to call the Runner's Office. In there was the Runner, maybe two or three of them. And their job was to crew the ships. So if we came out of one ship we used to go to see the Runner. "Owt doing?" If there was they used to sign you on and if there wasn't you used to go somewhere else. It was just looking round all the time. But there was that many ships you had no need to be out of a ship very long. There was that much work. You could go anywhere in the Fifties. (George Mussell - Grimsby)

There's one lad, big Ray Smith, some of the antics he got up to. I don't think he ever had any intentions of going for any Tickets but he was a really good Deckie. He didn't take any palaver from anybody. It wouldn't be the first time he's thrown the Ship's Runner in the dock. A lot of them used to backhand the Ship's Runners to get a ship but Ray Smith wanted to go on the St. Dominic. The Runner said, "No, see me later on Ray, there's no changes." Well apparently there were about four or five changes. So Ray Smith, he gets his seaman's book out and put a ten pound note in it. So he took his book off him and he says come back and sign on in about twenty minutes, so twenty minutes later Ray Smith goes back and signs on. Then he says, "Excuse me, did I leave a ten pound note in that?" He says, "I thought I'd left some money in there." He was only there for the one trip and then he was out. (George Brown - Grimsby)

You were on the job for twenty four hours. I mean I would probably do my day's work, got my ships to sea and everything and I would leave the office and then close the radio down in the office and then all of a sudden there would be a link call and it would be the Aston Villa calling me from

Iceland to say, "What's the market like, what do you think, should I make Tuesday's market?" "Well hang on. We've got so and so coming that day, there'll be a lot of fish. Hang out, or come a day earlier." Or there'd been an accident aboard and they was going into harbour. So your time was never your own. At the end it really was getting me down in as much that I was thinking of leaving but I hadn't got another job to go to. We very rarely met the Owners unless something traumatic had happened, you know loss of life or loss of a ship. Then we would liaise together. All the liaising used to be done by the Outside Manager. "Can we get the ship ready for so and so?" and we would give him the 'OK' and then he would go back to Sir John and the people upstairs. They was just there to put the pen to paper. It was virtually all done by the Outside Manager and us. Later on they did start to interview Skippers. They took that outside the Outside Manager's job. (Gordon Cockerill - Grimsby)

You had what you call these Under Managers come round. You very rarely got the boss come round, well in Hellyers never, but in Lord Line they did. You never used to get much trouble in Lord Line. It's when I went in Hellyers I got sacked twice for fish. These Under Managers come round, and of course they was only young, straight from college, and of course they don't know that first caught fish is gonna go off. You might catch practically nothing, say fifty kit, for the first three days, and the skipper would just wipe that off if you get good fish in at the end of the trip. We're willing to throw that away in order to stay out longer and get more of the better fish, but when you get home these Under Managers don't look at it like that 'cause they haven't got the experience. It'd be, "This is awful, this is no good." It wasn't really from the boss who never saw it, it was these little Under Managers who'd say, "Wait for Mr Hellyer to come," so of course we'd be waiting, and it would be freezing, and the sales would have started because they didn't wait for Mr Hellyer, and of course there was people buying fish and wheeling it away, and when he did come round to look there was no fish there. Another time there was me and Sid Exxon, he was another manager, waiting for ages, and then they told us Mr Hellyer wasn't coming - be nothing for him to see if he'd come. That's how it used to go on. But I don't think those young 'uns from the college had any experience of fish whether it was good, bad or indifferent. (Roy Dobson - Hull)

The family has been involved in the industry for a number of generations and from a very small boy, on Sundays, we used to go to the various shipyards, Cook, Welton and Gemmell and Cochranes at Selby and various other places. Sundays were the time when my father inspected the ships that he was building and he'd built all the ships not only for our own company which was very small at that time, having had most of its ships sunk in the War, but he built all the ships for Associated Fisheries of which he was Managing Director of the Hull office and we always had ships for Hull, Grimsby and Fleetwood. We always had a number of ships building so it was quite an exciting time. From very early days it was always rather exciting to go with my father at weekends to visit ships that were building. I first went to sea when I was twelve and had been a number of times to sea whilst I was still at school and then after University, I spent some time at Heidelberg doing an Interpreters course, won a scholarship to Cambridge and joined the industry in 1968/9. It was our sort of life. I don't think there was very much a question as to whether I was going to go into it or not. I like boats, like sailing, built a number of boats, first built a canoe when I was about ten and then I built numerous boats, dinghies and sailing dinghies and seventeen boats whilst I was still at school and then whilst at University I built two junior offshore group boats before joining the company. So I spent a lot of time at sea. At University I did a lot of time ocean racing and at one stage we represented Britain in the British Admiral's Cup Team so it was very exciting. It was really a pleasure as well as work to come and join the company. (Tom Boyd - Hull)

My great-grandfather started in fishing smacks and then his son, my grandfather, and his younger brother founded three fishing companies, together with thirty or forty other shareholders. The first one was the Great Grimsby and East Coast Steam Fishing Company 1891, followed by the Standard Steam Fishing Company 1896, and finally the Loyal Steam Fishing Company which I think had been called Butt Brothers and Hill before it was incorporated into a limited company in 1906. They operated anywhere between thirty and perhaps forty ships until the beginning of the War. After the War, about mid-1947, I went into the family firm. I was always very interested in Skippers and fishing grounds and which Skippers were in what ships and where they'd caught the trip as we say and when I used to come into the office I used to be introduced to them and talk to them and this more of less fired my imagination. I did all sorts of things. It was just a general training. I didn't go out onto the market and see the fish sold and speak to the Mates and all that sort of thing until some years later, because I really went into the office as a sort of unqualified Accountant and so they wanted me to act as an Accountant, but I wanted to be learning the industry so I suppose there was a bit of a clash in that way. But eventually I was put in charge of the Mates. I did that for the last three or four years. We sold out in 1957. Father and his brothers were all around the seventy mark, I was the only one of my generation. Our family businesses and family companies were sold to Associated Fisheries in 1957, and I went along to work for the local AF subsidiary which of course was Northern Trawlers. I was at that time an Assistant Manager, then I became General Manager of Northern Trawlers. That went on from 1961 and then in 1962, or possibly a little later 1963, Associated Fisheries bought the Atlas Steam Fishing Company, managed by the Letten family, Letten Brothers Limited, and their ships came into the Northern Management, as Butt's ships had done previously. Bill Letten and I were joint Managing Directors, he was Chairman and joint Managing Director and I was joint Managing Director and continued to run the ships and he concentrated on other matters of a more political nature and general management and that went on until I retired in 1978. (John Butt - Grimsby)

When I was working for the family company I used to get up and was always down on the market by about 6.30 am. The job was to go round the fish with the Mate. The Mate was the man responsible for the quality of the fish so I used to go and talk to him about it and any particular problems which they'd had on the voyage, particularly with the gear - winches and so forth - because he was at the sharp end. I used to ask him if he'd got any bright young sparks we ought to be looking at for training up. That sort of thing. Then the auction used to start at 7.30 am and I always used to attend that with the Salesman. The Salesman we had was a chap called Percy. He was a wonderful character. He helped and taught me a great deal. Then I used to go back to the office and see the Ship's Husband. The Ship's Husband was the man who collected the gear requisition, and I'd discuss that with him, whether there'd been any undue usage or any particular problems, and agree, therefore, the orders for replacement gear which would go out. The next on parade was the Superintendent Engineer. He used to bring in the repair requisition and the Engineer's report. We used to discuss the fuel requirements, all those sort of things - the general state of the ship, any special surveys which were needed. We normally programmed the surveys. There was an annual survey which we did ourselves. But all our ships had to be Grade One at Lloyds for which we had to go through Lloyds and the DTI on safety equipment, and we used to programme those during the year so we didn't have all the ships in at the same time. So if there was any particular survey which needed to be done I would have a look and see exactly what they were going to do and how long it was expected to take. If there was a major job we would agree a specification and it would be put out to tender, because we didn't have our own in-house engineering company. Then the Skipper used to arrive at about noon. He always came in for an interview as to how he'd got on and where he'd been fishing, if he'd had any particular problems, how his Mate was doing. We would then discuss where he was to go next, Iceland or wherever, and we used to have historical records as to where the fish was, what bank. We kept those records. Also the Skippers kept their own records but we had a general record. That was a fairly long morning, so then I'd have lunch and, in the afternoon I would normally go round the ships to see how the work was getting on, or there were meetings at the Grimsby Exchange. That was broadly the structure of the working day. Obviously, if we were building a ship then there was the additional task, and we used to take a lot of care about drawing up the specification for the ship because we hoped then that we got the ship right so far as stability and that was concerned. Also, if you specified well in advance you would normally be able to get a fixed price for your ship. But, inevitably, there were alterations as the ship was being built or between the time you ordered the ship and the delivery date, and you had to incorporate these. So all those matters had to be discussed and the building of the ship had to be supervised. Those extras or alterations always involved an extra price at the end of the day. (Bill Letten - Grimsby).

Before the Second World War the company had started in 1936 building three brand new ships. It had five or six ships before the War and they were requisitioned by the Admiralty. At the end of the War, when my father returned from the fighting after a pretty distinguished career, we had one and a half ships left and the half ship was a ship that was on the bottom which had been sunk by a bomb. My father set to rebuilding it and when I joined the company from University we had six ships and we then built that up to twenty two ships by the time Britain joined the Common Market. The family didn't take any money at all out. Very few and very low dividends were paid - it was the excitement of the chase and establishing a position in what was one of the last hunting industries. I've had offers to go and run other businesses, some of them fishing related at more than double the salary I take out of the company. We've had offers to buy the company at a figure which would allow me to sit doing nothing for the rest of my life and live in the lap of luxury. It has really no interest to me at all. I enjoy the industry enormously. I enjoy the people I work with, I admire our sea-going people enormously and I get a great buzz every morning when I set off for the office. I think about fishing, much to the annoyance of my wife, almost twenty four hours a day and I just love it. (Tom Boyd - Hull)

First I went into the Navy for my National Service, for two years and three months. I left school at eighteen. Then I went up to Cambridge where I took a degree in economics, then I came back and joined the industry in June 1952. It was a family company which had been established by my great grandfather. He lived in Gravesend and had a very small fleet there. He had an interest in small vessels - smacks - and they (my grandfather George Letten and his brother William) moved up from Gravesend to Grimsby, in about 1870, and they built up a really quite substantial fleet of smacks. There is a model of one of the vessels which they built, the James

Letten, which I have loaned to the Grimsby Museum. They died in the 1920's and my father took over the family firm. He fought through the 1914-18 War and got an MC and he returned to the fishing industry in about 1920. I joined him in Letten Brothers after leaving Cambridge in June 1952. Letten Brothers controlled the Atlas Steam Fishing Company which actually owned the ships. Letten Brothers was the managing agent. At the time when I joined the company was in fact building a ship and so I went from June to September when the vessel was actually commissioned, to work in the yard. As soon as the vessel had been commissioned I went to sea with Jack Evans in the Vindora and got a little bit of experience there. Then I started off properly. We built in really quite quick succession the Velinda, then the Vianova which was the first diesel vessel which we built. It was quite interesting because at that time the company had coal vessels still in operation, then oil fired steam vessels, and then we moved onto the diesel. I think the oldest coal fired vessel was built in about 1936, and the first diesel vessel which we built was in about 1957/8. So there was quite a substantial building programme. But, there was over capacity in the industry and it's astonishing to think now that there were about a quarter of a million kit of fish left unsold on the markets of Hull and Grimsby during that period. So really you had to scrap a vessel to build a vessel, otherwise we would have had even more over capacity. (Bill Letten - Grimsby)

I think we were perhaps the most successful distant water company in Grimsby. I don't know whether Boston Deep Sea would agree with that or Consolidated or Ross but I thought we were. This was a wonderful set-up that I inherited. The effectiveness of Northern Trawlers as a Grimsby distant water fishing company started really with the fifteen famous old German built Northern boats that Mr. Bennett Senior bought. They had a system called the exhaust turbine which made them very much more efficient in the use of fuel oil and we were able to run them a good deal longer, I think, than most other people with the ordinary standard triple expansion engine. (John Butt - Grimsby)

The last boss in Hellyers that we had, Mr Graham, was a Victorian but he was also a very shy person. If you had to see him about some ship's business you'd walk into the office reception area and a bell would ring for you to go in. If you'd just come out of a ship he would say to you, "Don't bother to sit down, we're having a change. Off you go," and that was it. There wasn't any false impressions that you may be going back. You knew that was it, straight from the shoulder. Other times, if you were happy in the ship you would sit down and discuss the job with him for maybe an hour. So it was the two extremes. With some of the others, everyone had their own impressions of it, but some of them were real nice to you but would go behind your back and suddenly tell you you were finished. I think you knew in your own mind if you were doing a good job. (Sid Morrell - Hull)

The cost of building vessels was escalating enormously. I think that the cost of vessels between 1949 and 1959, trebled. From about a £100,000 cost to about £300,000 cost. When I joined the industry there were two public companies, Associated Fisheries and Ross Group. All the rest of the companies were privately owned family companies. There were pressures with these family companies with this escalating cost of building vessels, because you had to generate the cash or borrow the money, but the shares were by and large owned by families and you did get it. For example, dear Auntie so and so who owned, say, ten percent of the company, suddenly saw you building a ship costing £300,000 and she would say, "Well, rather than you building a ship I would rather have £30,000." That is a very simplified explanation though it has a lot of truth in it. The other thing was the problem of raising the money, as I say, to build these ships was causing strain on the balance sheets. And the other thing was that in the late Fifties, early Sixties, people were getting worried about whether we were going to be able to continue with political problems and such. So there was a spate of sales of companies. I think that Butts sold in about 1958, we merged with Associated Fisheries in 1961, Crampins very shortly thereafter, and there were similar types of mergers or sales in Hull. This was due to under-capitalisation, or pressures from the families for their cash, and political worries. The extension of limits was beginning to loom, and I suppose it could be said that those who had foresight realised that things weren't going to become any easier. Croft Bakers sold out to Ross. Crampins sold to Ross, Butts sold to Associated Fisheries and we merged with Associated Fisheries for cash and shares in 1961. Some of the trawler companies bought their own merchanting companies, because we were suspicious that Ross was by-passing the Minimum Price Scheme by buying his own fish from his own trawlers at the minimum price but selling it down the line. So there was a move to buy into fish merchanting companies. By and large that was unsuccessful because while we were selling to wholesale markets really we were just cutting each other's throats. So that didn't work. Out of that came a funny scheme which was called the Cod Equalisation Scheme under which we all paid a little levy on each kit of fish which we landed, and then if we had fish unsold we were compensated up to the price, so it didn't pay to try and contravene the Price Sheme. Then people sold out because of their losses in the merchanting. That was a short sharp lesson to many of us. (Bill Letten - Grimsby)

I was with the Boyd Line for over twenty years, and Tom Boyd was, in my belief, the best of the bunch. Hellyers were very different. You weren't a name in Hellyers. You were a number. The top Skipper in Hellyers wasn't treated any different to anybody else, he was just a number. One particular time, Norman Longthorpe, it was when the time in dock was up to two days a trip. Norman Longthorpe had won the Silver Cod that trip and he asked for an extra day in dock. The story says, and I have no reason to doubt it, that the reply was, "Certainly. If you want another day in dock Longthorpe you can have one - but your ship sails on Monday". (Jim Williams - Hull)

There were some good Owners and some bad. Marr and the Boston firms were more or less on a par with each other. They were strict, the man in charge of that, Captain Lawford, was a very strict disciplinarian. In Marr if they could diddle you out of a penny they would do. I spent a lot of time with Marr but it was only because they had good ships. (Peter Wilson - Grimsby)

The Grimsby Exchange looked after the ice and did all the boxes. They employed the Lumpers as well, and negotiations with the Lumpers was always a very long and protracted business. Inevitably, we had a committee of Owners who dealt with the Lumpers and at an early stage I got involved with that. That took up a lot of time I must say, an awful lot of time. The running of the Ice Company was relatively simple. Then we had the Owners Association who dealt with wage matters, dealings with the government and those sorts of things. We had meetings, I suppose, once a week, one afternoon a week for those general matters, and usually one afternoon a week with the Lumpers! (Bill Letten - Grimsby)

The Owners just controlled the trawlermen's lives. They told the trawlerman to do something, he did it. If he didn't or even made an excuse not to do it, his livelihood would be taken from him. Then, if they wanted to go on any other ships they couldn't get a start because the Owners had an investment in the Mutual Insurance that insured all the ships. So if you disobeyed a Trawler Owner you couldn't get a job anywhere. You would have had to go to the Midlands or even out of the country. If you wanted to go on fishing you couldn't disobey a Trawler Owner. He was lord and master of all he surveyed. The Owners had a solicitor. They controlled the fishermen body and soul and he was the prosecuting solicitor. He used to prosecute the fishermen, and the Trawler Owners used to tell him, "See that they get a custodial sentence." A lot of trawlermen did get a custodial sentence. They had great power. You can't say that there were any best ones. Consolidated wasn't a bad firm but I can't really say that there was a Trawler Owner who didn't just want to work his trawlermen to death and pay them as little as possible. (Dolly Hardie - Grimsby)

Everybody in the town was terrified of Trawler Owners, of what they could do to even the ordinary man. They just usedto pick up the phone and say, "Blah, blah, blah so and so - sack him", and they had that much bloody power, everybody in the town relied on the docks to keep the trade going. If the trade had gone the town suffered. (Tom Jacombe - Grimsby)

You used to see the Owners on the market, that was all. Used to get a fry when you landed, you know, two cod, two haddocks, that was your ration. Trawler Owners never spoke to us. No. There was only one, he was a good 'un was Tom Boyd. He was the only one though, the others didn't know you existed. The Owners didn't live in Hull. Outside at Cherry Burton in the big houses up there, Willerby, where all the big houses are, where Marr's live now. They didn't ever live in Hull. Maybe their great grandfathers had been born in Hull, Hessle Road, but certainly not in my time. (George Waudby - Hull)

The Owners were hard people to work for because they just wanted the ships in and out all the time and you was only a number. Fortunately, the gaffa of Northern Trawlers, John Butt, I got on very well with him because when I got divorced he took a bit of an interest in me. He used to send for me every week and tell me I'd been a bad boy boozing. He knew everything about me like, until I settled down. But you was only a number. You could be very successful, the top Skipper in the firm, then you made a couple of bum trips and there was no sympathy, you was out. Get somebody else there. It happened to everybody. All it was was money. While you were earning you were alright. If you never earned money that was it. You were out. (George Mussell - Grimsby)

The company I was in it was a family concern, the Marr's. Me personally, I could always go and see Alan Marr or Andrew Marr, more or less when I wanted, or see the managers upstairs, they wasn't stand-offish or anything like that. They was real posh, with the accent. Because I'd sailed with them, they'd come with us pleasure tripping. Not only pleasure tripping. They were experimenting before the big freezer trawlers came out, with freezing plates. And we had the engineers on board, the scientists and all that and we always used to have either Andrew Marr come with us or Alan Marr, so we knew them. Because Andrew Marr's a similar age to me you see. But they were always accessible really. There was none of this that you were a peasant or anything daft like that. (Ray Smith - Grimsby)

Some of the Hull Skippers were great guys but generally the young fellers were all braggers. You always got that they were far superior to us, they always bragged. Generally with the Grimsby blokes you didn't get a lot of braggers. One time I broke three records on the trot and we were at the firm's do and John Butt got up and said, "Top Skipper of the company, top trip of the year and top earnings," and it was me, me, me, three times like. Well I felt like crawling under the table and everybody was clapping and staring but I didn't know where to bloody look. I felt so bloody embarrassed. Because I'd been working so hard and I didn't know. I won a bloody sweet bowl and some candelabras. That was given to me in the boss's office. You know, you had to be careful what you said an' all, because there was all the office staff in there, heads of different departments and there was the Chief Superintendent, Chief Engineer in there, George Thompson, and there was three Skippers for these awards. The other two Bill Sate and Eddy Hall had made a couple of good trips but they got a tankard and a silver cigarette box. Bill Sate was having an argument with this George Thompson and he was saying, "You ought to get down on the ships more and you'd get better maintenance on the ships, better work done, if you were showing your face now and again." George Thompson, the Superintendent Engineer, says, "I have plenty of work to do. My office takes all my time." So I just spoke up and said, "Well, Mr. Graham, the chap who had the job before you, found time for both." I'd made the biggest enemy in the world. (John Meadows - Grimsby)

The Owners were always greedy, avaricious men. They never paid tax like the men did. They invested their profits in farms, and always have done, so they are also wealthy landowners and wealthy farmers. But the trawlermen were absolutely soaked very hard for tax. My husband paid tax at eighty three percent all his time as a Skipper. Eighty three percent and not less than sixty percent. At the end of the day the Government and the Owners tried to say he was a casual worker! (Dolly Hardie - Grimsby)

I always considered that it was my job to look after the crews. I was more of a social worker. I had wives fetching bills down to me, "Can you pay this bill for me?" "Can you do this, can you do the other?" Or, "Could I have a sub?" I'd be here for a week telling you about the crew problems we had, drink and drugs and God knows what. (Don Lister - Grimsby)

I think some companies were pretty feudal. I don't think our company was like that at all. I would have termed it as, I hope, one of the better benevolent employers unlike certain vessel operators. The company policy has been never to send a ship to sea that we weren't totally happy with; its safety, security, its machinery. We are not prepared to accept breakdowns, though of course breakdowns happen, and we've never, never sent a ship to sea which the management of the company or the family wouldn't be happy to go to sea with. So maybe one could say autocratic but people don't have to work for you if they don't want to. People do like being part of a successful team and over the years the company has had remarkable successes. (Tom Boyd - Hull)

Chapter 10

A Changing Industry

The comparative decline of most of British industry is usually portrayed as a complacent failure to invest, innovate, and introduce new technology to stay ahead. Too much was taken out, too little put back. So industries fell further and further behind, in a world of competition growing ever more intense.

Such British norms were not the failures of fishing. Britain's was not the biggest fishing industry in the world for Japan, China, the USA and USSR, Norway and Canada were ahead in sheer scale, but ours was technically one of the best and the distant water side started as a world leader and stayed in pole position up to the 1970's. The stimulus to change was not imports, which undermined so many British industries, but intense competition within the industry, between vessels, between firms and between ports. Fishing is a living example of Michael Porter's theory that competition between domestic industries stimulating each other leads to continuous improvement.

The immediate post-war years were easy. Fish stocks had grown because large scale fishing had ceased in the war. Once this glut was fished out catches became more difficult, vessels had to trawl deeper and further afield and the Owners were losing money by 1953. So they had to modernise. Gradually competition became ever more intense, not only with other Owners and other fishing nations, but increasingly with the countries, on whose grounds Britain depended. The result, unlike textiles, shipbuilding or engineering, was a drive to invest and modernise, as well as to concentrate, unparalleled in any other British industry. Owners who were local not national magnates were proud of their industry, directly involved in it and out of the mainstream of complacent British capitalism.

Immediately after the War the fleet was old. It was quickly enlarged by the conversion of Naval patrol vessels to fishing. Several were oil fired and from 1946, when Marr's launched the first oil fired trawler, oil gradually drove out coal. In the 1950's diesel began to drive out oil. The last "steamers" were built in the Fifties. Today's giants, the factory freezers, were a British innovation pirated by the Russians but which caught on slowly here because consumers preferred wet to frozen fish. Yet, by 1970, Hull had twenty three freezer trawlers. Stern trawlers came in in the Sixties starting with the Lord Nelson in 1961, allowing men to work under cover, not on the exposed deck, and were a major proportion of trawler fleets by the mid Seventies. Their safety and accident record was better than the sidewinder where men hauled, cast and gutted exposed to the elements. Yet, paradoxically, many fishermen liked them less, because they felt less stable than the sidewinders and were unable to 'dodge' storms in the same way. Indeed, in taking storms rear-on they could be exposed to flooding through the doors in the same way as Ro-Ro ferries.

Technical equipment improved in much the same way with more powerful radios, radar, echo sounders, and fish location equipment. The workers, too, enjoyed a steady improvement in food and living conditions. Their gear, which they'd had to buy, began to be provided for them like other workers. Their rest periods, while still short, increased from six hours plus "gash" breaks in the Sixties to around eight in the Seventies. At the same time market prices for fish rose to pay for it all.

Thus, by the 1970's pay and conditions for the smaller number of trawlermen in bigger, safer, vessels were much better. Most vessels were infinitely superior to the battered tubs of old and British fishermen were even getting some of the support services which others, like the Germans and the Dutch, had always provided for their fishing fleets. Like the one horse shay fishing was at its best and its most efficient just before it all fell apart.

The worst ship I was ever in would be a Wyre boat, the Wyre Colonel. She was alive with rats. If you was sailing early morning it was a race to get aboard and help the cook put the grub away because if it was on the table it would get ate. You'd be picking loaves up off the table and passing them up to be thrown over the side because they'd been eaten away by rats. We brought her back into dock once because of this. We thought we'd be going home but no, they just brought some more bread aboard and kicked us out to sail again. They'd get anywhere where there was food. As soon as you moved they scarpered. It was horrible. Bloody inhuman. There were a couple where the toilet was a bucket, in some of the old 'duck' boats. They didn't have proper toilets. Some of them had a toilet that was just like a dugout on the bow, and you had to make it there in bad weather, do in a bucket and chuck it over the side. So you might as well as just done it over the side in the first place. In some ships you did that. You had to sit on the rail and do it over the side. I wasn't in any of those. In fact I was lucky. (Jim Quinn - Fleetwood)

In the War I was just a boy on the dock. It was quite a big dock, we'd had a hundred ships in one of the companies at one time. The East Coast was shut during the War so we got the big Icelandic trawlers coming into Fleetwood. People could work day and night then. There was no safety rules, no limitations, as long as the fish was coming in. The country was short of food. Even the standards of fish quality had to be relaxed because nothing could afford to go to waste. (Harold Dawe - Fleetwood)

There aren't many left now that was fishing in that particular era where there were ships that had no whale backs. We went mainly to Iceland when we got the crews. They weren't modern ships because the biggest part of the trawlers was used for mine sweeping. So we had no whale back, no toilets. There used to be two go at a time. We used to wait at the mouth of the Humber for the big convoys and destroyers. When they passed we tagged on to the end of them, and we had one little Lewis gun on the casing and I used to get, or whoever was doing it, sixpence a day for keeping it clean. We used to go into a place called Scrabster. There we used to stay overnight and refuel with coal which used to go into the

fish room and when that had gone we used to have to wash the fish room out and get it ready for fish. Then we used to have to go from Scrabster right across, right through the channel in Faroes, which is like a small fjord, and we used to have to go across there on our own. The only protection we had was that gun. So we had to fish out there and then we never got no escort home or anything. I'm talking now in late 1944. And the conditions was absolutely terrible and we used to work maybe twenty four/thirty six hours without a break. The Cook used to have a bucket of cold water with a sponge and he used to wash your face so you didn't fall asleep. Then, after you'd been so long the Skipper used to shout from the Bridge, "The last man on deck come up here and look after the ship while the rest have their nap." The Skipper used to spike the clock. Instead of giving you four hours you used to get three hours. The man who'd been looking after the ship on the Bridge got longer. They forgot about him so he got maybe an extra hour or two hours. There was no whale back but you had like sort of a stairway down with a canopy and if it was bad weather and it was tea time, or breakfast or dinner, you used to have to put all your oilskins on and you had a rope. You used to have to pull yourself along the ship. (Bill Ellerington - Hull)

There was some terrible ships - what we call bad sea ships. We had some in Consolidated Fisheries. They were built during the War for the Navy and then converted into trawlers when they came out - we called them the 'fish class'. There was the Blaefell, the Burfell, the Valafell, and they had iron decks and they was the worst sea ships that you could ever imagine. They was terrible, terrible ships. (Gordon Cockerill - Grimsby)

There was a heck of a difference between ships then. The sea handling, you know. Some of them were terrible things. Some of them had dreadful names, you know - "You keep out of her, she's a slushy." You know, you was getting wet all the time. (Stephen Drever - Grimsby)

I was in a ship once where the rats used to run over my face in my bunk. We got rid of them though. What they used to do to keep rats from pinching food was to 'tin it out.' We used to line the pantry with tin. We did have ships cats, but you can't have them now for hygiene reasons. I used to have three or four cats on board. They'd eat fish or a little bit of meat. They never got seasick. (Claude Couch - Fleetwood)

The old-type boats with G.F. Sleights were the Bridge aftsiders. That was the Bridge behind the funnel. I did a couple of trips on the Reporto, open bowed, and if you went as far as Faeroes as some often did we carried coal on the deck which when you got through the Firth you had to open hatches, shovel the coal down off the deck and get everything ready. Some of the Bridge foresiders in Sleights, the old ships, the larger ships, had a tunnel between the Fish Room and the Bridge. It went through the bunkers into the stoke hole and they could transport coal through that. They carried coal in the aft part of the Fish Room. By the time we got to the grounds we'd used that coal up and had to wash the Fish Room out and then it was ready for fish. Now these old things of Sleights didn't have a tunnel. So we used to carry twentytonnes of coal down the Fish Room and fifteen tonnes on deck. You got rid of the deck coal first whilst you went through the Firth, then you steamed to Faroes and in the Faroe Islands you brought the coal up out of the Fish Room, dumped it into the bunkers, then you carried on. That was a heck of a job that in those days. Those were the sort of ships I started on. (Stephen Drever - Grimsby)

In them days, when I was a kid, there was tons of fish, absolutely tons of it just after the War. You'd just put the trawl in the water and five, ten, twenty minutes it was full. This conservation, as they have it today, we never had it in them days and you brought three, four, five hundred baskets aboard for, say, twenty minutes towing time and half of it was dumped because these meshes was so small and the small fish couldn't get through and all we wanted was the big cod, the big fish, because we knew in them days you was going to fill the capacity of your fish room and so you only saved the best. Now if you'd had conservation in mind all that small fish would have got through and it would have saved you a lot of slaughter of fish and hard work for us dumping it all. It was stupid. (John Meadows - Grimsby)

When the big ships started coming from the War I wanted to go deep sea. My first ship was Deckhand in the Syrian in Northern Trawlers. Then when the Vizalma came from the War I went in her as Deckhand. Of course we were heading all the fish in them days, chopping all the heads off. And Jack Evans was skipper and old Tommy Spall was Mate. Them days in that ship we used to fill up every trip with headless fish - 3,600 kits of fish each time we come home. And we couldn't get no more in it. All with their heads chopped off. And that was to get more edible fish. Some of the ships used to land in Germany to feed the Germans because they were starving you see. The biggest trip was 4,700 kits landed in Germany, to feed 'em 'cos they were starving. They were dying after the War. It did pollute the grounds to chop the heads off but we'd shift to another ground, find some more fish. Anyway that was the idea because there wasn't the amount of ships then to catch the fish, so what they wanted was as much edible fish as they could. Now the head is a third waste. You see a big cod and take his big head off and that's a third gone. We used to land three cod to a kit, and there was ten stone to a kit. You see I still speak in kits not boxes. There was ten stone to every kit. You get cod up to six stone don't you? Great big things but I shouldn't think they taste very good. They're too old. (Mick George - Grimsby)

When I first went you used to sleep in the fo'c's'le - all mucky, sweaty socks hung up on twine, and boots laid all over. Most of them used to roll out with their gear on and roll into the bunk because you got called half an hour beforehand and you only had half an hour to get your grub and get rigged, so that saved time if you slept with everything on, just put your boots on. You'd get bathed in a bucket. You used to get the top off the stove, get it red hot, then put it in the bucket. That was the hot water. On the first trawlers the toilets were right outside. When it was blowing a gale of wind and bouncing up and down, you couldn't get into it. (Clive Finn - Hull)

I started in the coal burners, it was all coal burners at that time. In those days there'd be about fourteen of you sharing the living accommodation, down in the fo'c's'le, three bunks high. All you had was a little coal stove for heating -

Grimsby MP, Kenneth Younger with
Crew of S.S. Marano, after his first
fishing trip. Copyright: Grimsby Evening
Telegraph.

It's Been A Hard Day's Night.

plus fourteen jolly men! The bathroom was just a steel bath on the ship side. There was a bath there but no running water. You filled it up by bucket and then you'd go aft and ask the Engineers to put the steam on. You'd put the steam pipe in the water to heat it up. The condensation would just run like rain. It would be freezing. No heating or anything in the bathroom. In the winter time when the ship iced up it was freezing - and even then you only got a bath when you'd finished fishing. All in all it was pretty good comradeship. The biggest arguments used to be if someone let the fo'c's'le fire go out. You'd have the funnel from the fo'c's'le head onto the forward end of the ship and if she's ducking and diving the funnel wasn't high enough and you'd get a bad draught down from it, filling the room full of smoke. That's how you lived. (Ken Robertson - Hull)

They had what they called Firemen who used to shovel the coal into the furnaces and behind that they had what they call Trimmers who used to trim the bunkers and shovel the coal. In the summer months when the North Sea ships went to Faroes they used to go out of the Grimsby dock with the decks full of coal. All the fish room was full of coal. That would be gone before you got there. You had all that to shovel and put in baskets and drag along. Say up to seventeen ton a day was a regular occurrence plus your own work. That was only a part-time job. But you had it to do. (Tom Jacombe - Grimsby)

On the coal burners - you never had a lot of washing facilities. I mean in later trawlers they had bathrooms, but in these coal burners you never had that. To get washed - well you never got washed in the trip. None of the blokes got washed or shaved for maybe twenty odd, or thirty days. Only coming home would they have a shave. When I was Galley Boy you'd see some bloke, they'd come down and they'd had a wash and shave and you wouldn't recognise them. They looked all queer. Pale faces because they've had their beard on for a month. (Les Bowden - Grimsby)

When the steam ships finished there was a lot of these Chief Engineers who were made redundant. That was when deep water was still going and so you got some of these old Chief Engineers coming. They weren't really old - but they came as Greasers. And they were good fellows as well. Once you've been at sea all your life it's very difficult to come ashore and get a job. That's why these old chaps they came back as Greasers. It was quite a good job for them really. I was younger then and when you get chaps twenty years older than you you tend to give 'em a bit of an easy life anyway, so you was doing more than they were. A bit of sympathy I suppose. But they were all good chaps. (Colin Donald - Grimsby)

From the end of the War a trawler was roughly one hundred and seventy to two hundred feet long, that's side-winder trawlers just fishing off one side. Your middle section was the fish room, most of your deck crew lived forward down the fo'c's'le and had to come along the foredeck each time. With the advent of the oil burners they started using that side as accommodation. By the Sixties all the crew had moved to accommodation aft and port side aft. The Bridge was just aft of centre - in between forward and aft. The fish room actually only took up about a third of the whole of the length of the ship. One of the biggest areas taken up on the ship is the engine room and fuel store, whether it be coal or oil. The fuel was tight up to the fish room bulkhead below decks, underneath a lot of the central accommodation - the Bridge and that kind of thing - until it came to the stoke hold and boiler. Then there was the engine room aft. All that lot's below the water line of the ship, the same as the fish room. Most of the crew's accommodation is below the water line because above that there would be the galley, one or two of the officers' cabins and the liver house. The Skipper's cabin, compared to the crews, was comparatively spacious but it was always close to the wheelhouse, and in a lot of ships immediately after the War, the Wireless Operator's berth was in the wireless room. (Jim Williams - Hull)

When I first went in a ship when they converted the ships from coal to oil we used to have what they called an evaporator aboard the ship. We used sea water evaporating and used it in the boiler, and I thought it was a palace. Just the thing. I could go and get a cup of water any time I wanted. I'm not saying there was enough water to get washed with, but at least you could have a drink when you wanted, and that's

*Steam and Diesel Trawlers
landing in Fleetwood. Fish-oil
tender alongside. (FD 60 Dragoon,
Scrapped 1966).
Copyright: P.Horsley.*

*Mending the trawl on the Idena (1958)
Left - Bill Taylor (Mate)
Right - Des Wright (Bosun).
Copyright: P.Horsley.*

something I'd never had in my life at sea. You just went without a drink and when there was no water you melted the ice down. (Tom Jacombe - Grimsby)

The last diesel ships we built as a company were built in 1961, and one of those ships, the Arctic Cavalier, is now in the Hull museum. The first stern trawler, the Lord Nelson, I can't quite remember her date, she would be built about 1961/62, she was the Port's first stern trawler and she was a wet fisher as well as a freezer trawler, so she was the first freezer trawler as well. She was a composite ship, could land half her cargo frozen into headed and gutted blocks and half wet for the market. She was a magnificent ship, built in Germany, the Germans having really started the building of stern trawlers. We built the Arctic Freebooter and then in the late 1960's early 1970's, a plethora of ships were built. Newington Trawlers were really the only company still building wet fishing stern trawlers. They seemed to be locked into the concept of wet fish. (Tom Boyd - Hull)

The first diesel I went on was a ship called the Idena which was a good class ship with engines that lasted right to the end of the job. Of course you then raised your ambitions. You got interested in getting into a new ship because there was always a new development, a slight improvement, on each new ship. Although the ships were basically the same it was a product of continuous refinement and development. The first diesels were controlled with a telegraph on the Bridge and a telegraph down below, and the obvious development from that was to have complete remote control from the Bridge, which they did do. That made it possible to have infinite control from the Bridge. Therefore, all the problems they'd had before - when they couldn't just get the right amount of movement forward in the water, which was the Bridge requirements - all those problems were answered by remote control performance, provided it was performing well. And they did develop it so that it did perform well. (Harold Dawe - Fleetwood)

In 1971, when Marr's started introducing the new class of stern fishers, that was home from home in them ships. It was a different life altogether. You was a regular watch below,

accommodation was beautiful - it was just like working in a fish house. You was under cover and the only time you came on deck was to get the trawl up and down. That would take three quarters of an hour, then back down below again. We had one freezer factory ship here, the Criscilla, and that really was home from home. It was twelve hours on and six off. I could have stopped there forever. (Peter Wright Wilson - Fleetwood)

Later on they did start to build all the quarters for the crew aft on the galley side. Imagine a 90% roll and trying to hold a mug or two mugs of tea to take to the Skipper or the watch on the Bridge and when you got there it was full of salt water or it was bloody empty. I've attempted a cup of tea and probably gone down half a dozen times before I've got it there. And the Skipper would turn round and give me a blast, "Where the hell you been?" Because you've only gone fifty yards. (Gordon Cockerill - Grimsby)

The big companies had started to invest money in them and they were just starting to get organised. One of the things was of course the fifteen Northern boats - the Germans. They started with those. When I went aboard the Northern Pride I had a cabin of me own and a bathroom - I'd never seen anything like that at all. You could go from the Bridge to the galley or aft without going on the deck. Otherwise you was galloping along a deck in the old types of ships at mealtimes and that sort of thing but these ships - it was just like going into a wonderful wonderland when you went aboard there. (Charlie Board - Grimsby)

There was no comparison between steam and diesel. There was a lot more involved with steam than with diesel. Diesel was relatively simple compared to steam, even though they were probably more reliable than diesel. Diesel made a big difference to trawlers 'cause they gave them much more space for the crew, and water became freely available because it used water for ballast whereas with steam water was that precious the Skipper used to deter people from having washes. He didn't want 'owt as silly like that. (Graham Howard - Grimsby)

As a Skipper, as the ships improved, I got a big day cabin, though as they altered the ships later you still had the same area but one end would be closed off as a sleeping cabin, with a separate bathroom. In a Three Bridge ship the middle deck was generally the Skipper's and the Operator's quarters. Underneath them the Bosun, Chief Engineers, etc., used to sleep. Everything did improve tremendously as the ships got bigger. But then with the later, smaller, ships the extra conveniences were the first thing they did away with. In the small stern fishers that Marr's built I think there was one shower for the whole ship. There just wasn't the space available in the smaller ships. But overall the conditions for everybody improved over time. When we first started all the crews slept forward. That could be a nightmare in bad weather with people having to cross over the open decks, When the ships got better all the accommodation was brought aft so you never had that problem again. The working gear and equipment also improved, as did the radio equipment. At one time it was an occasion to use the radio equipment. It was rarely used then because it wasn't good enough to use for any distance. You had to be well within a hundred miles of coast stations to get telephone calls and things like that. That improved until you were able to call from anywhere. (Sid Morrell - Hull)

Coal lasted until I think 1960, then you had steam which was the oil fired ships. They went out and then you had the diesels, electric diesels, and all that. Towards the latter end trawlers were palaces to what the older fishermen knew it to be. They might not have been palaces to a shore man but to think on the big modern trawlers you had refrigerators where you could put your meat in to last you three weeks. You never had that. You used to bring it aboard the ship from the ship's chandlers, put it aboard the ship, put it down on the ice and leave it there for three weeks. Over that course of three weeks, by the time you wanted it, it was green. But they just used to carve the green and do the rest. The older ships had what they call saltpetre tubs on the boat deck where you used to get big joints of meat, particularly pork which was bad for keeping without refrigeration. They used to put that in these saltpetre tubs. That was used at the latter end of the trip when all the fresh had gone That was the way you used to do it. When you think you used to eat meat and it was green. But there was nothing else to eat. How long does a cabbage last? If you went into a supermarket today and bought a cabbage how long would that last? But you had to last that three weeks. You found your own way of preserving that for three weeks. You used to freeze it on ice.

North Sea ships only earned a few quid. I've been in the North Sea and come home regular and picked about £2.50 up, £3, something like that and you were satisfied. They were proper coal burning North Sea ships. Smaller than the deep water ships. They never had radar. They had nothing. There was nothing on them ships at all. All you had was the Skipper's skill. The Skipper would just set sail, set a course and think to himself, "In four hours at the speed I'm going I know what fishing ground I'm on." He would shoot his trawl, haul his trawl and the first thing he used to feel the fish to see if it was slimy. That was his knowledge that he was in the correct position he wanted to be. If he wasn't he would just steam - drag the trawl behind him - in different directions. But as soon as he felt that fish was slimy he knew where he was. He was happy and that's where he just used to tow round and round and round and catch the fish. That was the skill of the Trawler Skipper. Different banks you fished on. You would get stones, you would get little bits of coal and little bits of shell. All them things he used to look at and that was the skill which made a good Skipper. 'Cos he knew just by looking and he used to think, "Oh another three hours that way, or another three mile that way and that's where I want to be." (Tom Jacombe - Grimsby)

When I first started we had the old dry paper echo sounders, which used to stink to high heavens, but they got better. We used them in Iceland. You were working points to land or towing round tips of bank, or over the tops of banks, working the distance off, because the "decca" was no good over there. A lot of people said it was in the South East of Iceland, but the lanes were that wide that you'd never go back over the same area twice. Whereas, if you went to the Norwegian Coast or right round the top of Norway you got Decca coverage up there, so you could work your different lanes up there. A lot of the old Skippers still worked distances off the land and bearings and all that. (John Pickett - Grimsby)

I remember the first ship in Grimsby that had been built new with radar was a ship called the Rinovia built by Rinovia Steam Shipping Company (which was owned by the Little family) about 1947 - Skipper, Paul Adalsteinson. She had a terrific run, he was a wonderful Skipper, who regrettably was killed in a motor accident in about 1970. That company sold out to Ross and I'd like to say that I knew the Rinovia Steam Fishing Company as man and boy and they really were outstanding trawler operators. If you had a ship landing on the same day as a Rinovia ship you were jolly pleased if you beat them. They had some wonderful Skippers, so did Northerns. The vessel Rinovia was the first Grimsby vessel to be equipped with radar. Butts bought five ships from the Admiralty, called the Military Class and they were equipped with radar in about 1948. By 1949 you wouldn't think of building a new ship without a radar. (John Butt - Grimsby)

Just after the War, I was given to understand the reason for what they call the German Gear. The Germans were short of lots of stuff at that time and there was only natural fibres then, no nylons, so the natural fibres were in very short supply and we used natural fibres for the quarter ropes. The Germans came up with the idea of dispensing with all that and bringing all the full set of bobbins in in one. It took a lot of parting of wires before it was perfected. I was Mate out of Hull with Eddie Woolrich, the man who really got it working - I've got all his drawings here now - and it was much quicker than the old way. Also, you saw all your net every haul to see if there were any holes or rips in it. The trawl itself - anywhere from two hundred feet long, depending on the ground you were working and the particular ideas of the Skipper. On bad ground you wouldn't have too long a length, but on good sandy ground you could have longer and longer bellies to catch more fish. Apart from the actual trawl itself an innovation that came along were cables. These were wires from the trawl to the door, whereas years and years before the trawls were shackled straight up to the trawl doors. The idea of cables was to get an even wider spread of the net so that you disturbed the fish on the bottom. The wider the spread the wider the area of fish you disturbed and swept into the net. (Jim Williams - Hull)

As time went on all these new instruments - echo sounders, the position finders - kept coming in and of course we were the top ship in the company, so we had them first you see. So scientifically there was all these improvements going on all the time. Then we had the depth sounders that you could see the fish at the bottom. They had a tube and you could look on that and you could see the fish on it. (Charlie Board - Grimsby)

The fish came in, was gutted, thrown across to the port side, then when it was all gutted you went across with the hose, stamped it about, kicked it, dropped it down to the fish room by hand. But one Boyd Line Skipper made up a washer out of wooden deck boards and fish room boards. Basically all it was an open ended box or trough that could hold maybe eight or nine inches of water all the time, with water continually going in so that the movement of the water going in whirled it round with the movement of the ship so that excess dirty water automatically went out over the lip at one end. Instead of throwing the fish across it went into the washer. No mechanics whatever were needed to run it. It was invented by Skipper Wally Woods in the Boyd Line. Taking his idea up Tom Boyd had one made out of metal and patented it. The first people to use it were the 'Grimmies'. They quickly latched onto the idea and there were soon a lot of Grimsby ships using that patent before many Hull ships did. That would be in the late Sixties. Innovations were mainly thought up by the men and as some of the younger Trawler Owners were coming along and replacing their fathers, they started to listen to the men and try out their ideas. (Jim Williams - Hull)

Early on we used to be buying our own but then they got to buy gear for you. They also started issuing bedding and blankets later on. Things improved a lot towards the end. They had to because other people's conditions were improving. At one stage you'd never see salad aboard a ship but towards the end - the back years of fishing - you'd have salads, tomatoes, all that sort of business, lettuce, which you never used to see before and there was enough food going on the ships that could be put on the side. On trays on their own. So if you wanted any you could help yourself. Whereas before you was only allowed so much food. We used to have halibut stew at night. A big halibut about that thick, cut it up and put it in a pan with onions and carrots and boil it up and when they used to come off the deck they'd put the ladle in and you could just break through. There was hardly any juice, it was just pure fish. You wouldn't be able to do it nowadays. (Colin Donald - Grimsby)

Different firms had different ships, and they all had different stoves. When I first went to sea they was all coal burning stoves. I went in an oil burning ship and it was an anthracite stove, like an Aga cooker. In a diesel ship you had an oil burning stove. So you had to figure out how to use it. Coal burning was easy for me 'cause that's what I'd been brought up with. These Anthracite stoves had slow combustion and you was supposed to only fill them up once a day. In the diesel ships it was red hot and there was like a tank in the corner of the galley that used to drip feed the stove by gravity. The oil used to drop onto a pan and that was your fire. But, if the ship rolled over to starboard all the oil used to go back, and when it rolled to port all the oil that should have been there seemed to nearly explode when it hit the pan. (Claude Couch - Fleetwood)

At one time if you was getting good fishing you just carried on and on 'til you was walking around like zombies. So we'd say, "That'll do us, we're all packing up and we're all going to have six hours." In the end they come out with a watch system, eighteen and six, something like that, so you got six hours sleep each day. (Tom Bagnall - Fleetwood)

In the early Fifties you didn't get a sleep until the Skipper said so. It was only later on that we started to get watch belows. Even when fishing stopped, the North Sea and the Middle Water ships, like the Ross Tiger, they never got a watch below, all they got was the spare time between hauling and shooting. So they could be up until the Skipper said. When I first started it was not unusual to do twenty four-thirty hours before the Skipper said, "We'll sleep." It wasn't a case of liking it. It just became a way of life. (Graham Howard - Grimsby)

The early days you worked 'til you dropped. That was it. There was no watch below or anything. You fished, you cleared your fish, you hauled, you cleared your fish. In the North Sea you got chance for an hour's sleep, an hour and a half, two hours sleep, between hauls, because you fished twenty four hours a day, but on the deep water ships you sometimes worked twenty four/thirty six hours. Then the Skipper would very graciously give you four hours sleep. But then they didn't have the watch below which was eighteen on and six off. It came in, it was gradually acceptable, because blokes were getting hurt. It wasn't the unions, that is for sure. We never had a union then. There was no union, but those Iceland Skippers that sailed out of Grimsby really started the ball rolling and so once they found that some ships worked them you wouldn't go in a ship that didn't work a watch below. The first thing you ask when you signed on, "Does he work a watch below?" "Yes, he does, but he breaks the watches sometimes." "Oh, well we're not going with him." So all of a sudden these guys realised that they were being ostracised so they had to fall in line with the rest. So that's how it sort of moved on. (Stephen Drever - Grimsby)

First of all you wasn't entitled to anything. In Consol's you used to work what was called 'a tow below.' That was after you'd finished hauling so many men would go below and as long as you got to sleep for over an hour that was classed as your watch below. Other firms, you got to sleep when the Skipper said. If you was up a bit and you got fish the Skipper would let you get to sleep, maybe four hours, maybe six hours. Then we started to work twenty and four. We worked that for about two years then we could either work eighteen and six or twelve and four. The majority worked eighteen and six. B.U.T was always eighteen and six. Then right at the very end when the freezers came in they started to work twelve and six - that was luxury. The deep water trawlers were still eighteen and six right up to stopping (Graham Howard - Grimsby)

The really major step forward in the industry was of course the development of the freezer trawlers. I joined Associated Fisheries when the Lord Nelson was being built. That is a part freezer, part fresh fish trawler. It was the first of ts kind. The part fresh fish, part frozen fish concept, in fact, was soon superseded by the whole freezer trawler. They stayed at sea for five or six weeks. When they caught fish they were profitable. Then we were fishing off Russia, Mermansk. Associated Fisheries built Victory, Lord Nelson, Conqueror, Defiance and one or two others. Letten Brothers always had names beginning with V and ending in A, with seven letters. (Bill Letten - Hull)

I was in what I would call the top twelve, fifteen, Merchants who wanted nothing else but quality fish. These freezer trawlers - they served a big purpose - but they served a purpose that was surplus to requirements, because at that time there was that much fish being caught, backed up by these freezer trawlers, there was fish unsold on the market. Ross's, who had these freezer trawlers, the Victory etc., they had all these stocks to get rid of and instead of buying off the market they were using the cold storage and ended up, unfortunately, lots of times, with good quality fish unsold. (Joe Linfitt - Grimsby)

The Lord Nelson was the first freezer trawler and she was built because of the three hundred odd days that a trawler spent at sea during the year. If she was a distant water trawler, half the time was spent steaming and half the time was spent fishing and if we could increase that ratio, the fishing to steaming ratio, by keeping at sea longer then obviously the economics of the operation would improve because of course ships, very expensive capital items, don't earn any money when they are steaming backwards and forwards. (Tom Boyd - Hull)

As Factory Manager you used to do same as what you'd do ashore. You used to work on the deck when they were first steaming down until your trawls were ready. But that was different again because you didn't have no dragging or pulling nets aboard. When it was hauling time you just started the winch up and the doors came up. You unshackled that, and then your fish came, the trawl came straight up and then the deck used to open and the fish used to drop in the factory, close it, just let your trawl go and all get down in the factory. Well once they started there gutting the fish it used to go along a chute into a washer, then on a conveyor belt and we used to

pack it into blocks and then set each block at certain times for freezing them. Once they were frozen then I used to have to take the blocks out and put them on the conveyor belt and then go into a lift and you had to stow the blocks in the lift and go down on top of the lift with it then start to make a floor of fish, and then you came up so high that you didn't need the lift and you started to build it up like that. And it was all blocks of fish and it was all solid. We used to have films aboard. From where your berths were you just walked up a ladder and you were in the mess deck and everything was comfortable. Different life altogether. Although you were longer away at sea. Whereas a sidewinder was about twenty one days but you were only home for say thirty six hours, but on the freezer you were away for three months, maybe longer. Then you were home for a week or maybe longer. (Bill Ellerington - Hull)

Our own company built the Arctic Freebooter first which was a very, very successful ship. She won the Dolphin Bowl which was the top freezer trophy when she was twelve years old, so it shows she had a lot of good design features and we followed her with two smaller stern freezer trawlers, the Arctic Raider and the Arctic Privateer which were also extremely successful. Raider and the Privateer must have been built about 1968. In 1975 we built two wet fishing trawlers, primarily for William Liston Limited, one of our subsidiary companies which operated out of Leith, Edinburgh and those were two forty-two metre stern trawlers, with twin decks and very mechanised trawl handling equipment, way ahead of their day. They could fish single boat bottom trawl, pair boat bottom trawl, single boat pelagic trawl, and pair pelagic trawl, so they were very, very flexible boats and they had a remarkably successful career both of them. In 1975/6 we built two very successful stern trawlers of something like eighty-six metres each in Poland with 4,000 horsepower engines and either one or the other was the top freezer trawler all the time we ran them until we had to sell them in 1982, with the run down of fishing opportunities in the country. (Tom Boyd - Hull)

The Ross Kelvin broke down every trip for long

Factory Manager emptying Freezer plates. Fish to go on hoist via the rollers to Fish Room. Copyright: P.Horsley.

enough. First trip we broke down, we got it sorted out, then we ran aground, that was a big fit out. The Sec's lad had been killed on a motor bike and we went in to put him ashore so he could come home. While we were ashore we run her aground and damaged her stern and the propeller, and got towed home by my mate Alf in the Northern Gift. Then they found out that they'd got the engines in wrong. That's why they'd been having all the trouble. They found out they'd been going ahead on the astern gears and astern on the head gears. (Graham Howard - Grimsby)

When the stern trawlers came along you could square all your net out much better. Stern fishing was invented by Salveson's. It was a professor who thought that if they could get huge whales up a ramp what's wrong with getting a trawl up. They had a small cargo ship converted, and one of the finest Skippers that ever sailed out of Hull - my father sailed with him before and after the war - Leo Romayn, one of the most unusual characters there ever was. He was either Oxford or Cambridge educated and at one time I think he flew his own plane. Very well educated man but didn't know anything about fear. He was a brilliant man and he became one of Marr's top Skippers. He took to sea the world's first stern hauler. He experienced and ironed out all the faults, the requirements etc. It was a completely new way of hauling and shooting. (Jim Williams - Hull)

Stern trawlers didn't really make life easier because think it was the advent of the stern trawler that brought about all this Icelandic situation. Before stern fishing we always did bottom trawling, then the stern trawlers started developing the pelagic trawl. When we were only fishing on the bottom the fish used to be able to conserve itself. They'd come up after they'd fed and it didn't matter what you tried, you couldn't catch any fish. But the stern trawler developed the pelagic trawl and that caught the mid-water fish and huge amounts. Obviously the Norwegian and Icelandic fleets decided they couldn't stand for that, so they started being awkward and putting extra limits on, and as a consequence the sidewinder trawler's days were numbered. Even the ordinary stern trawler, the fresh fishing stern trawler, would have been accommodated, but the big freezer trawlers were too much to accept. I remember one time, for a couple of months around the Cape of Iceland when there was a terrific amount of fish there and the side trawlers were all getting good trips. At that time the big German stern trawlers and freezer trawlers were fishing off Greenland. One of them came and was quickly followed by the others and in a period of about six weeks they took 60,000 tonnes of fish out. Them alone. I think all our trawlers took was about 5,000 - 6,000 tonnes. That's when the Icelanders said enough is enough. They stopped them before they even put the limits on. (Sid Morrell - Hull)

The change to stern hauler absolutely changed the design of the ship. Some of the earlier ones, to look at them, they looked like pleasure ships. They were beautiful looking ships like the Junella. Lovely lines on her, streamlined. But their wheel house was well forward and unless you were aft you couldn't see them hauling because it was just a ramp, like a factory mother ship, a ramp aft. They could haul and shoot a set of gear in fifteen minutes, whereas, in a sidewinder anything over about seventy or eighty baskets you had to get in two or three heaves. So four hundred baskets in a sidewinder would be eight heaves, taking maybe an hour and a half. Heave 'em in, let it go, tie it up, over the side, come astern, fill that up, heave that up, let them go. All very time consuming plus the fact that to shoot a side winder you had to make sure your gear was well up and, if it was fine weather, steam round, steadily letting your trawl go below, steam round again - you'd maybe have to go round and round twice before you shot. Not so with a stern hauler. He could get the same amount of fish in in one heave, let it go and then just shoot in one straight line. He'd do it in twenty minutes as opposed to an hour and a half. Also, in bad weather there was no huge seas rolling aboard unless it was exceptionally bad weather. The crew didn't bother to wear oil frocks or sou'westers, or a pair of clumpers even, when hauling and shooting. Then all the actual manhandling, the cleaning and gutting of the fish, was done down below on a factory deck. But with a side winder, - some people would say it depends where you were, whether you're on deck or up top - the ideal weather for shooting would be force three or four. That would keep your gear well off the side of the ship and you didn't have to go around so far. (Jim Williams - Hull)

We saw there being restrictions in fishing opportunities within third country waters and we equipped all our ships at vast expense with pelagic fishing gear. We were the first of the deep water companies to fish with pelagic trawls, despite two years of training and tremendous expenditure and mocking by the other companies. We really did suffer from that and I particularly who had been responsible for that investment felt pretty raw about it. But two years later we were sending ships to the North East Arctic to fill themselves up with eight hundred tonnes of fish and no gear bills at all because nothing was trailing along the bottom. Many of the other companies then came running for help and I was unwilling, because of the rubbing up I'd received, to help but my father said, "No. We should always help people," and we handed over our expertise and lent people offices and had them on our own ships which helped the U.K. industry get into the pelagic fishing world. We were the first company to catch sprats and herrings and we supplied Marks and Spencers with sea frozen herrings, must have been in the late 1970's. We were the first to be fishing for mackerel in the Channel (I think British United Trawlers had a ship there) and we expanded our pelagic fishing interest catching blue whiting for Findus and for surimi operation with the Japanese herring and mackerel. Our last four ships we built, Buccaneer, Galliard, Challenger and Riever, were all equipped with the capability of fishing very, very deep water where the blue ling was. Unfortunately due to an absolute shambles of legislation and the Ministry or the politicians being unwilling to provide adequate fishing opportunities for these freezer trawlers they were severely disadvantaged. We had a much bigger freezer fleet when we joined the Common Market. We had three hundred and fifty deep water ships with fifty freezer trawlers. We were denied fishing opportunities by our Ministry. We were unable to invest in those ships properly so the Dutch rapidly overhauled us subsequently by falsifying their landing records, enabling them to establish themselves as the European Union's top pelagic freezer trawler operators. With hindsight I was pretty disgusted at the shambles which our lack of determined leadership caused to the industry and that is something that I shall never forgive the Government or the Ministry for. We had the British Trawlers Federation which eventually became the British Fishing Federation and I think they were really quite an effective organisation. I think the problem was the Civil Servants had an objective or the Treasury had an objective and the Owners were playing cricket. They were just taken like lambs to the slaughter. (Tom Boyd - Hull)

Chapter 11
The End of the Affair

Compared to other fishing powers, Britain's industry was lopsided depending on distant water for the greater part of its catches, while inshore waters yielded perhaps an eighth. This made trawling deeply vulnerable once the world changed and other nations began to assert more control over waters they were beginning to regard as theirs. Depending on open seas Britain long defended the traditional narrow three mile national limits, which had been the range of a cannon ball, along with the concept of the freedom of the seas. These were the basis of both our maritime power and our powerful fishing industry which roamed the northern world. Yet as fishing fleets grew, as vessels became bigger and more powerful and as pressure on stocks increased, other nations, particularly Iceland, began to see the need to protect their stocks and build up their own industries by gradually closing their waters to others. That process, coupled with rising oil prices, killed British distant water fishing.

Trawlertown vessels fished most of the North Atlantic but depended heavily on Iceland whose waters were closed off by four Cod Wars. The first was precipitated in 1951, by the imposition of a four mile limit from baselines in place of the old three mile limit. The second came with the twelve mile limit in 1958, and lasted until 1961. In 1972, a new left wing government imposed a fifty mile limit and the confrontation became more violent as Icelandic gunboats began to cut trawl warps. This was scarcely settled by allowing in a restricted number of British vessels when, in 1975, the Icelandic government took its final step by extending its waters to two hundred miles producing the most bitter and violent Cod War of all with rammings, collisions and warp cutting.

The British government mobilised twenty two frigates to protect British trawlers but the spectacle of a big power using its Navy to protect fishermen in hostile distant grounds could not be long prolonged. In 1976, Icelandic fishing ended. The extension of limits by Norway, the USSR and Canada followed closing most of the British industry's traditional trawling grounds. Suddenly an industry which had developed North Atlantic fishing and stayed strong and competitive by reaching out to new grounds and new waters had nowhere else to go. Some claimed to have seen the inevitable coming. Most of the fishermen, who lost their livelihoods because of political and investment decisions entirely outside their control, didn't.

In the Fifties and Sixties, we had the most enormous amount of distant water fish, a lot of which was not sold and went to fish meal companies. The withdrawal price, the price at which fish was withdrawn from sale which didn't reach a certain minimum price, helped to put a floor to prices, but of course it was financed by the fishermen themselves - the fishing companies. It helped from a marketing point of view but the reality was that we were simply bringing in too much fish for the market, which looking back, was not the most intelligent thing to do. We had too many vessels, unrestricted fishing, and the market simply couldn't absorb it. The Owners did try to regulate fishing but it wasn't easy. They had all sorts of schemes, for example things like bream, which we had an enormous amount of from the Norway coast, was sold to the Eastern bloc countries, Poland, Czechoslovakia, Eastern Germany. Big tonnages - at very low prices, simply as a means of getting rid of it. Overall what you had were price structures that were simply too low. Everyone was grossly over-fishing, which was one of the triggers for an extension of fishing limits. (Frank Flear - Grimsby)

About 1960/61 was when we were getting worried. My father, sadly, died in 1963 very shortly afterwards, but we were all getting worried because of the Iceland wars - that was our fight against the extension of limits and, therefore, we had to try and persuade the Government to fight on our behalf. To be fair they did. They put frigates up there. But at the end of the day the Government told us they could not do that forever,

Captain Gudmend Ernesteid at the Bridge of the Gunboat Aegir attacking the Everton. Copyright: Associated Press Ltd.

and we were expendable from that point of view. They did give us a subsidy for a short while to ease the burden but a lot of ships were decommissioned as a result of the Icelandic situation. Another thing which caused an enormous decline in the industry, which is forgotten about, was the oil price explosion. It has to be borne in mind that a large number of the vessels which were sailing from the Humber were oil fired steam vessels, and they could burn ten tonnes of fuel a day. In those days we had big contracts - I was on the oil fuel negotiating committee for the Humber and we were buying 300,000 tonnes of fuel a year on behalf of the Owners. We had contracts with Esso and Texaco, and we did the rounds. We said, "Here you are, this is the order, you bid us for next year", and I think the price went from £10 to £30 a tonne almost overnight. Instead of having a fuel bill for the a ship of, say, £100 a day, you had a fuel bill for £300 a day. That caused the decommission of a lot of ships. They suddenly became uneconomic. Diesel ships were all right because they were burning only one or two tonnes a day. So the oil crisis caused almost as large an impact on the fleet as the Iceland situation. (Bill Letten - Grimsby)

The Icelanders began to build a fleet of their own and stopped us fishing in these grounds. So gradually we'd nowhere to go. The Norwegians, the Russians, all of them stopped, the Greenlanders, so it got to such an extent that there was nowhere to go except in the ocean where the water was too deep. That was something that must happen. You educate people and it's not long before they are telling you what you know and they know. So they say 'Right' and they stopped all the fishing inside the fjords which we used to go in and catch beautiful fish. You gradually worked all the way round poaching all the time and then they got one or two more gunboats and they'd put lines across. They'd put three miles here and three miles there. You couldn't get in. This didn't happen in a day, it didn't happen in a week but in five years it had begun to tell. These Scandinavian people were earning money to build bigger and better ships so they were competing on level terms with us and they had the benefits we didn't have. They could fish in their waters and we couldn't (Charlie Board - Grimsby)

I was brought up in Isafjordur in the North West during the 1960's and I remember vividly the great number of Hull, Grimsby and Fleetwood trawlers that visited our town, sometimes by the score, including the ones bearing all those football club names, the Ross's, etc. Prior to that I lived in Adalvik Bay where the US Air Force operated an air defence radar station on top of Mt. Straumnes (Straumnes Point). I remember seeing from the mountain top at night the trawler fleet lit up like a city off the coast before or during the "Cod War" of 1958 to 1960. I remember also with pleasure the interaction between kids of Isafjordur and the British trawlermen when we tried our broken Kings/Queens English, that we were starting to learn in school at that time, on the rough trawlermen who spoke practically their own tongue and which was certainly not what they were trying to teach us at school. We all had a lot of fun. I also remember, surely, the tragedies that struck in the late 1960's when it seemed as if every year around Christmas there would be at least one or more vessels lost, local or British, leaving a lot of families without a husband and father. (Fridhor Eydal - Iceland)

In about 1958 it became a four mile limit drawn from baselines so it was not only an extension of three or four miles but, in certain areas, these huge bays and fjords were cut clean off, and all that water or area inside. That was one of the things that ruined the spring fishing at Iceland on the South West side. Then it became twelve miles from the base line and then, of course, Norway did the same and so on. (John Butt - Grimsby)

I did get arrested for poaching. I was poaching on the South side of Iceland and he spotted us and got us. I wouldn't let him come aboard for a start but in the finish - that was a bit diplomatic again - they was on with our insurance and I got a wire from our Owners to let them board us and take us in, or else they were just going to grab somebody else from the same firm. They just took us in and fined us. That's all they did in them days. Normal poaching it was just board you, take you in, fine you and let you go. It was pretty informal really. (George Mussell - Grimsby)

I got the sack. They caught me inside the limit line at Langerness, it was the Odinn that captured me, and I was in there for four/five days. It was a funny situation. Everything was done in longhand and the first one, they got the village postman to be the interpreter. I couldn't understand him, then there was my Agent alongside of me, he could speak good English but he wasn't allowed to interpret. So, as I couldn't understand the postman they got the village schoolmaster - but I couldn't understand him either, so they said they'd have to send to Reykjavik. I wasn't too happy with this 'cos I wondered how long that would take, so anyway, they carried on the case and I got fined something like £5,000. When I came out I went back to where I'd got caught. (Jack Tripp - Hull)

About 1972, something like that, I was Skipper of the Ross Kelvin. Eventually we lost a set of gear to the gun boat. There was a lot of ships and the only way we could actually fish was by riding shot gun. One would do the fishing and another ship would just jog along behind him to stop the gunboat coming in to chop your gear away. They kept close up and the gunboat couldn't get between you. The ship that was towing would have one tow and then when he hauled you shot your gear and then he would ride shot gun for you. We'd just got down the end of the tow and was coming round and I was in the Kelvin which was diesel and the Northern Chief was riding shot gun for me. He was covering my gear, and we just got turned round and going back straight in the line again and the gun boat came in to make his run. I said to the Skipper behind, "You're dropping too far, get in close to me." He dropped back too much, because the ship I was in was diesel, it was Bridge controlled. You could put the revs on and move the ship faster and slower yourself, but in the steam ship you had to blow down to the engine room and say drop a few revs or put her up a few revs. They weren't quite so controllable. He dropped back too far and with that the gunboat he was through. BANG that was it. The recoil of the warps was tremendous. It flew through the air and hit the mast and if anybody had been there it would have killed them. Mind, we'd been more or less expecting it. It was going on all the time, sets of gear going. Both warps went and a full set of gear. That was two sets of gear. The Rio Madrid lost a set of gear about an hour previously, the skipper there was Cocker Mussell. We just got another set of gear there then to carry on fishing. We used to carry about three sets of gear, bobbins, and we put another set of gear because normally when you're towing and come fast and lose some gear you don't necessarily lose the whole lot. But when they chop your warps you've got your warps to splice up, all the doors to move across from one side of the ship to the other. It took us about four to five hours to put another set of gear there. (John Gilby - Grimsby)

I had a tremendous run in the Grimsby Town, and I was caught poaching, taken into Iceland. We was poaching all the time on the West side of Iceland. Fishermen were the biggest liars out. I said, "Oh no, I was just steaming in to take the Mate in." So in the end I got fined for my gear not being stowed properly. I was fishing, but I'd washed all the fish away before they got near me, and I got taken into Iceland. I must have been there about five days. At that particular time it was run by communists, Isafjordur was communist. They tried to get me to admit to drugs, this that and the other. Anyway I tried to ram the Icelandic gunboat, because I wouldn't go in with him and I started steaming out to sea and he fired and he puts a hole in me funnel. I said to the Mate, "Don't worry they're all blanks, to hell with him." And then all of a sudden I turned towards him and chased him off - I wouldn't have hit him - all I was trying to do was to get him to stop following us, and all of a sudden BANG! a bloody hole in the funnel. So I thought, it's about time to surrender again. And I was fined for illegal stowage of gear, not for illegal fishing, and for trying to ram the Icelandic gunboat. I got six months jail sentence. I appealed and I come home and I wouldn't go serve it. I couldn't go into Iceland. So I started fishing a lot at the White Sea and then the Icelandic Premier came here and I got a letter from the Advocate in Iceland, because it was causing hardship for me and me family, etc. saying that it had been suspended for two years. Yes, I could go to Iceland and fish, but if I was caught poaching I would have had to serve six months, perhaps a bit more. (Don Lister - Grimsby)

I was the first one to have both warps cut. We was fishing - we were supposed to keep in a group you see - and we were at the north cape of Iceland and I'd found this fish - there were a couple of bags of haddocks. I could see the ships fishing away there on the radar, about eight/ten mile away or maybe a bit further. I knew the gunboat, the Icelandics, were after them. Anyhow he must have picked me up on his radar this gunboat and I'd just what we called backed round 'cos the warps were flipping a bit. So a Fleetwood skipper, Tommy Watson, he come on. He said, "Who's that over there?" I said, "It's me Tom." Like we never used to say the name of the ship. That's what used to baffle our Navy fellows. "Oh," he said "It's you Mick is it?" I said, "Yeah." They knew your voice, you see. He said, "Well he's steaming up towards you now. But he won't bother you . He'll just come and tell you that you're inside the fifty mile limit." I said, "O.K. Tom." With that he steamed across our stern and chopped both warps, chopped the gear off. And I was the first one to have both warps cut. We still got a trip. We made £20,000 when we got home so that was a good trip. We put another set of gear on. We'd loads of stuff. We had plenty of warps and things. He'd chopped about six hundred fathom of warp off you see. We were blocked up again and fishing by eight o'clock with all the gear and everything there. I thought, "Well somebody will catch me gear and give me it back," but nobody ever found it. It's amazing isn't it all that net, bobbins, warps, doors, everything gone. But you'd think ten or fifteen ships would have caught it on their gear, but nobody did. I think it was the Odinn that chopped the gear off and he uncovered his gun. (Mick George - Grimsby)

The first two Cod Wars was nothing like the last. The gunboat - I can remember once he came along side of us and he said, "Good morning Captain." He says "Do you know you're fishing inside Icelandic territorial waters?" I says, "Yes, I do," and I says, "And I've got another twelve days of these bastards." It was a bit of a laugh in them days. But the last one was pretty savage and we knew we wasn't going to win it. You could see that because the Navy took orders from Whitehall. They was determined to help you when they were getting involved with the Icelandic coastguards. Then all of a sudden they were withdrawn again. It was just a load of bullshit. When you was there seeing what was happening. They never ever got me like. I was always watchful on the radar. You used to count the pings on the radar - the amount of ships that was around.

I came back thoroughly relaxed after a month off. Anyway I was just coming round Langerness corner on me way to the fishing grounds when the ships was scarpering and I called one of them up and I says, "What's going on?" They said, "Oh the gunboats chased us all away from different places." I says, "Well I'm on me way to a place called Red Head, that's the place I fancy for fish. If you'll come with us and if you want to shoot first I'll cover your gear 'til it's my go and that." While I'd been on me holidays instead of two ships, one covering the other, there was three of you. While the ship was towing the gun boat would go across his head and lay his cutter on the sea bed and when the trawler went across it he'd go full ahead and get it that way, so you'd have two ships on your quarter while you was towing, one to stay there to protect the stern and the other one to charge and make the gunboat keep moving. You know - all the tactics. We got there and the two lads said, "Well it's your choice of fishing ground. You have a go first." Anyhow we had a bloody good haul like, two hundred and odd baskets and we eventually got about 1,500 kit for about three days from there. Terrific fishing but it's hard ground and with a lot of ships in the area we presumed that the vibrations, the banging of the trawls, the bobbins and the doors on the seabeds - hard ground - disturbed the fish and you could see it all come up on the sounders. So I called the Captain of the frigate. I said, "Any chance of moving this haven to the North Cape?" I said, "All the Skippers here are interested in going up to the North Cape" I said, "Because all this fish is off the sea bed now and it won't settle. It needs a few days to settle itself down again." He says, "Right, I'll come back to you in a few hours," because he had to get orders from Whitehall. Anyhow he came back again about four hours later and he says, "I'm sorry Skipper. Our orders is to keep the haven here." I says, "Well with respect, Sir, can you see the point in protecting ships in an area where there's no fish?" Well, it's right though isn't it? I says, "Well you can bloody stuff your haven. I'm going to the Cape on me own." We all steamed to the Cape and of course the gunboats came with us and when we got in John Butt, our boss, he got a meeting of all Skippers that was ashore at his office and he said, "Any Skipper that disobeys the Navy from now on will get instant dismissal." He says, "Whether it's a top Skipper or a bottom Skipper you will be out and that'll be the lot." And we finished up with 3,400 kit that trip. This is when we got the message that we wasn't meant to win. We was still doing our job what we was brought up to do - catch as much fish as you possibly could - fill the fish room if you could and all that lot - but now we were doing the wrong thing. We realised we was fighting a losing battle but we never stopped. The very next trip we goes round and there's a place called 'The Whaleback.' We went into that haven like we'd been told. All this information what I'd got over the years was useless. You had to go into the area where the Navy was protecting you, fish or no fish. It was all coleys. Just a little bit of white fish, cod and haddock. But we finished up with about 3,000 kit again, but only about eight hundred of white fish. So when I got in that trip it was Ron Martin the Under Manager who was in charge. John Butt wasn't available. He says, "What's the idea of all these coleys Skipper?" I said, "Well I was told last trip by Mr. Butt that if I didn't go to the area protected by the Navy, top Skipper or bottom Skipper would get the 'infernal'." I says, "I've gone and done as I was told," but I says, "I can't choose the size and quality of the fish that's in the bastard." It was stupid, bloody stupid. (John Meadows - Grimsby)

I've been in three Cod Wars and in the last one it was the company's decision that all their home water ships had to go down to fish Iceland as a show of strength. We were sent down to Iceland and fished there until Iceland was shut down to us. I did have two or three clashes with the gunboats when they took a couple of runs at me. It was a bit scary because they were going along with big slicing gear which just cuts your wires behind you, and they had to get within twenty metres off your stern in order to cut it. We developed ways and means to avoid it and I was lucky. I never lost any gear. Quite a few did get banged, but not me. I was lucky. (Derek Reader - Fleetwood)

British Frigate Leander rams
Icelandic Gunboat Thor.
Copyright: Associated Press Ltd.

I was in the Viveria when we got rammed by a gunboat. Tried to cut across and chop our warps, and she hit us midships, smashed all the Bridge in - in fact I've got a photograph of it somewhere. Smashed all the rail down. She hit us on the port side. She was a fast ship an' all because the Viveria is no slow coach, she was a big ship, fast ship. (John Kirk - Grimsby)

The first two was all right. They was harmless. It was the third was serious. That was one of the reasons that made me stop. At that particular time they had an eruption on the 'Westman Islands'. We was fishing in a box and the Icelandic gunboat came over and asked for help to get the people off the island 'cause it was just being engulfed by ash. All the ships knocked off fishing and went to help. All started to steam. After about three hours the gunboat came back over to tell us there were enough ships there and they didn't need our help. We turned back and started fishing, and within two hours of shooting our gear the Thor came and chopped our gear away. That finished me. I knew we were never going to win. I could understand the Icelandics. They was fighting for their survival same as us. But what I will never, never forgive was how the Government sold us down the line. They was offered 90,000 tonnes of fish, we'd never caught 90,000, and they just give up. (Graham Howard - Grimsby)

The Owners' hands were tied. It was a case of go and do the best you can. Some of the Northern boats were having a break from Iceland, going down to the White Sea. It was like Heaven to go down there knowing that there was no gunboat chasing you. But the Skipper of one of the other ships said, "We're getting a bit fed up of the riot down there. Can we go down to the White Sea for a trip and have a break?" The gaffer said, "No. Our firm has always found its fish at Iceland. We've done very well out of it, and we've got to fight this Cod War. If we lose it that will be the end of the company. You get yourself back down there and fight it out with them." A poor attitude to take really. (John Gilby - Grimsby)

We were steaming from Iceland on our way home and, in between Iceland and Faroes, we were attacked by two aeroplanes which were firing flares at the ship just to harass us. They were just firing flares at us. We were under orders by the British Navy not to take particular notice. When we did actually get back into British waters we steamed into Scarborough Bay. The Owner of the ship lived in Scarborough and he came off in a small dinghy, and boarded the ship and congratulated us all. He gave us a pound each for doing well, and the Navy ship that had been with us invited us all aboard for a drink. They said they could not understand why the fishermen went through the life like they did to actually catch fish and be harassed by people like the gunboats, and not retaliate. When the gunboat was in the area it was an all day, twenty five hour a day job. Your job was to protect the ship at all times. If they was with you two or three days you wouldn't get any sleep whatsoever. You was just there to protect the ship, make sure that you wasn't boarded, 'cos if you were boarded and taken into Iceland you would just have been treated like robbers. (Tom Jacombe - Grimsby)

When I got captured in the Kandalosit I was in standard issue and the crew had to get the gear ready again - because everything had to be lashed up, and I saw this Third Hand, and I thought, "What's he got on?" He'd got on a fur collared coat. I asked him where the hell he'd got the coat from and it turned out it was the Captain's of the Odinn that he'd pinched. I said, "Bully for you". (Jack Tripp - Hull)

The Navy were marvellous. They were restricted in what they were allowed to do. One of the chaps was promoted to Commodore while the Cod War was on, and he said to the Icelandic gun boat, "I'm twenty miles away but I can sink you as easily as If I was only two miles away." But he couldn't, could he? He wouldn't have been allowed to press the trigger. It's much like the atomic war. Hands are tied. The Navy had old railway lines tied on the bow, and they'd run alongside the Icelandic gunboats and these railway lines would go straight through the plating. When we finally gave in to the Icelandics they only had one gun boat left that was any good. Our Navy had ruined the rest. Really, we had won the Cod War but Kissinger came over and told us to get out. (Bill Hardie - Grimsby)

I think what annoyed us more than anything about that report was that the TV and Radio people were on the Icelandic gunboats chasing us about. That got up more people's noses than anything else. We was made to look like the bad guys when we wasn't. We were just doing a job which had been done for years. But it's always the same, you can see it in the reporting in Bosnia. I thought we'd had a bad deal out of it. We were made to look like the bad guys and the Icelandic gunboat Captains were made to look like heroes. I think we were doing the hardest job. That was the way I looked at it anyway. (John Pickett - Grimsby)

I didn't ever get boarded, other than when I was in the Hull City and we had our gear on the bottom and the Icelandic gunboat said he was coming to board me, and I said to the crew that if he comes to board us we have to stop him, retaliate. The Chief Engineer and the Mate and several of the crew said, "We're not going to get hurt." So what could I do? Our own gun boat said, "Lock yourself in your cabin," which I didn't do. What I did eventually was to chop the gear away so I could steam at full speed to get away. I had no choice because the crew weren't with me in retaliating, and unfortunately two of them were my brothers in law. That was really disheartening. When I came home the Owners thought I had been locked in my berth all the time. When I was on the Aldershot, at Redhead we called it, on the north side of Iceland, and we couldn't fish so we all hauled our gear and decided to hassle the gun boat. We steamed all over the place. The Arsenal thought I was steaming when in fact I was stopped, and he went hard starboard, and his stern knocked my bow in, and the Icelandic gunboat came up by me on the other side and touched the bow the other side. He came up in the darkness. We had to be escorted back to the Faroes and they put a full new bow on. The worst thing to me of the Cod War was the lack of backing from your crew. Most of them, they didn't want to know. They would have given in because they felt they wasn't getting anything out of it. The ship was getting £80 a day. From that the Skipper would get 5%, the crew about 1.5%, very little and no risk money, so the crew couldn't see why they should put themselves in danger. As Skipper all we had to look forward to was the sack because we hadn't caught fish. Some of them did, they rigged nets up to repel boarders, but most, 90% of crews were against the Cod War. And I can't say that I blame them. (Bill Hardie - Grimsby)

There are two things which are fundamental. One is the negotiating stance taken by the Foreign Office which is unlike those taken by most other European States and means that industry advisers are not involved in negotiations with our Foreign and Commonwealth Office, as for instance Norwegians, French or Germans are when they are doing negotiations. Our industry advisers are outside the room and summoned in like small schoolboys or visited when advice is sought. I think this has proved over the years a severe weakness in our negotiating position. There is no doubt of the intellectual abilities of our Foreign Office people, but as often as not they threw tricks away because they didn't know the finer details of what was being negotiated. Before the last Cod War we had many friends in Iceland and we'd had Icelandic children staying with the family and going to school with my sisters and they, I can't remember what the tonnage was, but they told us that the tonnage on the table at that time offered by the Icelanders was 'It.' There was no way that the Icelandic Government could give any more. It was politically unacceptable in Iceland, and although that message was passed through to our negotiators they had already decided that they had got the Icelanders on the run and that they would beat them with a stick and of course we all know the result. (Tom Boyd - Hull)

In the last Cod War I was on this committee which included representatives from Hull, Lowestoft, Aberdeen and Fleetwood. We used to meet at York and discuss how we could survive as an industry. I went to Iceland, to the Embassy, and the first time we went Roy Hattersley had already met the Iceland Foreign Minister and there were a number of Civil Servants there and the Minister of Agriculture. Roy Hattersley was in the Embassy and he gave me a report of the meeting, and he'd demanded 110,000 tonnes. We had told the Government that we could survive on 70,000 tonnes and had provided charts that we'd had drawn up by experts to show where we thought ships shouldn't fish because they were breeding grounds etc. I looked at Roy Hattersley in astonishment. I said, "A hundred and ten thousand tonnes!." He said, "Yes, but that's only for starting negotiations, but I have instructions from Harold Wilson that I shouldn't leave Iceland without an agreement for 100,000

tonnes." I told him we hadn't got the ships to catch anything like that amount of fish. He repeated that that was his instruction. We went to a lunch being given by the Icelandics and, on that morning, they'd chopped another ship's warps. He noted that this had happened even though he was there. I said, "Look, it's not like in England where people do what they are told. The Icelandic gunboats please themselves. It's just a small country. The Government tells them not to chop warps but the Captain of the gunboat, if he wants to chop warps, he'll chop them." He arranged for somebody from the Embassy to come while we were at lunch and give him the message that he already knew about, and we were all to stand, en bloc, and walk out. Hattersley got a Queen's Flight back to England, and we had to wait to come home ourselves.

So next time, Friday night, Austen Laing rang me up to tell me I had to go back to Iceland because negotiations were going to start again. I caught the early 'paper train' to London where I met the other people attending the negotiations, and we flew from Heathrow to Copenhagen, then on to Oslo and from there to Reykjavik. It took us twenty four hours to get there altogether. Roy Hattersley was already there, along with the head of the Civil Servants, whom I knew very well, who told me he was pleased I'd come because the Minister (Roy Hattersley) was going home. I said, "Going home! I've only just got here!" They'd just finished their meal in the Embassy and I went to speak to Hattersley. He told me that he was sorry to have caused me any trouble but he was going home because they'd chopped another ship's warps. I repeated that it was the Icelandic gunboats that were acting on their own accord, it doesn't have to be their Government who are ordering it. So Hattersley decided not to leave. I asked him if he had taken into consideration that the British Trawler Owners would be happy with 70,000 tonnes, since it was doubtful that we would be able to catch even that much. The deep water fleet could survive on 70,000 tonnes. We then went into negotiations where we shouted at one another and went over the charts etc., and I decided that I was really wasting my time being there. The Icelandics said they'd give us some of their fish if we gave them some of our oil. But our negotiators wouldn't agree to that. So we came back home again and the Cod War continued. (Don Lister - Grimsby)

I think we was the last ship to leave Iceland - in 1976. We was lucky, we were near the end of our trip when we got the wire from the HMS Andromeda, that all ships had got to leave by 1800 hours. So we started to steam about two o'clock. Barry McCall, I think he'd only had an hour's tow, he said, "I've shot. I've got five bags." So we shot where we were, but when we hauled the winch conked out. We left about 5.45 and Barry was hauling at 6.15, 'cos it wouldn't take him long to get outside the limits. I knew it was the end when they pulled us out. Iceland offered us so many thousand tons but the Government turned it down. They should never have turned it down. (Fred Quinn - Fleetwood)

We thought we would have won in the end but in the long run the Navy ships just couldn't do nowt with the Iceland ships. They out-manoeuvred our ships. Then the job just stopped. I was there when it did finish. All the ships were laid - they just couldn't shoot. They were surrounded by the Thor and the Igor and all them. That was the cruellest blow I've ever felt in my life. To think you was being slung out and the Icelandic gunboats were steaming alongside of you blowing their whistle, sticking their fingers up, and you couldn't do anything. Your own government had withdrawn the Navy . You was just there on your own. Every ship got a call from the Owners saying, "So and so, in the morning withdraw all the trawlers. Steam out." You couldn't do anything. That was the cruellest blow I've ever felt in my life. They couldn't have done a crueller thing to me because I was a fisherman. It's unbelievable how you felt. How can I put it? If somebody said to you, "I'm going to pinch your wife, I'm going to pinch your house and I'm going to pinch your car, take your family away, and I'm going to drag you out of fishing." That's just how you felt. We came home to Grimsby. Nobody in this town had any sympathy whatsoever for you. They just didn't want to know the fishermen. They knew that the good times had gone. There was no more spending big heaps of money, so the whole community broke up. There isn't no community spirit ashore like there was at sea. Everybody looked after each other. (Tom Jacombe - Grimsby)

I was solely concerned with distant water operations in B.U.T. Extension of limit lines and one thing and another and quotas made it so that we could not operate the ships. The fleet had to be very severely curtailed. There wasn't time to adapt to different types of fishing so the distant water operation virtually came to an end overnight. So I retired at 55 years of age. What I knew was coming to an end. Had it carried on in full cry and I'd been pushed out of it for one reason or another I'd have been very miserable but it wasn't like that. We all knew that the distant waters days were numbered and all the ships that I'd known were going, and the prospect of building new ones to fish the grounds that I was interested in, it'd all gone West very quickly. (John Butt - Grimsby)

Seine netting.

Chapter 12

The Strange Death of Distant Water

The loss of Iceland was the industry's death warrant. Distant water fishing died not with a bang but a whimper, at the whim of the bankers who foreclosed, the government which betrayed, and a European Union which prevented any prospect of recovery. The rest of the world followed Iceland in taking 200 mile limits and built powerful fishing industries within those waters. In the EEC, however, the Common Fisheries Policy, stitched together just before Britain entered, prevented that by making fish a common resource to which all had equal access. So when we took our 200 mile limits in the Fishery Limits Act of 1976, we could exclude the Russians and anyone outside the EEC but not European "partners." In return for providing three quarters of the EEC "pool" we were allocated an eighth of the catch by value - hardly enough to sustain a powerful fishing industry, and certainly not enough to allow Britain to rebuild its fishing fleet once the big distant water vessels had nowhere to go.

Some, like B.U.T., kept fishing into the Eighties but with shrinking waters and catches. Some went bust, like Consolidated. A few opted to run small seine-netter boats - the only survivors in Grimsby and Fleetwood. A handful of firms under family management, like Marr and Boyd Line, kept going to distant waters catching what they could where they could in an increasingly regulated world.

As a group the Owners eventually got compensation, some of it fraudulently by claiming for vessels already out of fishing, profitably sold or decked up with fishing gear to sail round the North Sea for a hundred day pretend. Most took the money and ran. The fishermen got nothing. Fred Peart, Fisheries Minister in 1976, promised compensation, re-training, decasualisation. None of it happened. Grimsby and Hull got development area status because a by-election was pending but the fishermen were cast adrift with neither redundancy nor compensation, deemed to be casual workers in an industry which had treated them like serfs. The betrayal was particularly vicious because those who lost their jobs as a result of political decisions beyond their control numbered no more than five thousand at the end, so the costs of a fair deal would have been minimal.

Some fishermen, particularly in Fleetwood and Grimsby, did carry on fishing in seine-netters or pair trawling which was very profitable for a period. Others went into North Sea supply work, or worked as ticket holders on Spanish vessels and on the increasing numbers of flag of convenience vessels on the British Register. A few went to fish in Australia, New Zealand, Spain, Africa, anywhere where jobs were available. Most stayed shorebound, unemployed or in low paid jobs. Horizons and incomes contracted proportionately.

The poor bloody infantry of the fishing industry had been dumped on-shore. It was not until 1993 that they won even minimal redundancy payments after clever legal work by Humphrey Forrest of the Humberside Law Centre showed that they were legally employed, not casual. Even then, those who could not show two years service with one employer got nothing. As for other compensation no-one has ever received any. Not for them the generous terms miners, steel workers and car workers got. They had been employed as fishermen. The Owners' associations had imposed common pension and holiday pay arrangements. They had been moved from one Owner to another to suit their own convenience and that of the Owners themselves. Yet the Owners' associations who had ruled their lives and employment prospects had cleverly worded their deeds so as not to be employers. Unless fishermen had worked for one Owner for two years continuously they were deemed not to have been employed.

When the end came I was in the last trawlers to be booted out of Iceland where their gunboats said, "By seven o'clock in the morning all Grimsby ships out. Otherwise we'll sink you." Five to seven we all steamed out the waters together but with me being in one of the top earning ships the Trawler Owners thought, "Well we'll run you as long as we can." So we went to the White Sea 'til in the end they did the same at Norway. The gunboats attacked us, stopped us all fishing. We went to Bear Island to try and start fishing there. The gunboats followed us there. I think my last trip we'd been at sea about twenty eight days and we had about three hundred kit in. We came home, we all landed in debt and the firm just said, "Sorry mate, that's it. Cheerio." When I said, "Why? What's happening?" they said, "Why, you're just not going to sea no more." I said, "What about redundancy pay?" "Well" he said, "You're casual labour like. There in't none for you." I said, "How can I be casual labour? I've paid my insurance, I've paid my tax, I've paid every other thing what a shoreworker gets." And they just said, "No that's it." Two or three of us stood outside the office demanded to see the boss upstairs and they just laughed at you. "Go, we don't want you. You're finished." So I went to the Labour Exchange. I think it was the very next day I went to the Labour Exchange and I signed on the dole and I said to the feller behind the counter, "How do we claim this redundancy pay?" He said, "Sorry mate, you're casual." He'd been told by the Trawler Owners to say that. (Tom Jacombe - Grimsby)

Going into the EEC - as it was then - from a fishing point of view was bad news for Britain. When countries were extending their limits to two hundred miles, if Britain had been able to do that we'd have drawn a median line down the North Sea and the Channel and gone two hundred miles out into the Atlantic, and we would have had about 66% of the total EU catch. Now we've got under half that, 31%. So from that point of view there is no doubt that British fishing suffered very badly from going into the European Common Market. With hindsight, there is no doubt that if we'd negotiated properly we would have done that differently, and that was and is, in my opinion, bad news for British fishermen. We could not have done anything about other countries extending their limits but there is no doubt that going into the Common Market was bad news for fishing. (Frank Flear - Grimsby)

When Britain joined the Common Market we then engaged in a ten year wrangle to sort out the outstanding issues of the Common Fisheries Policy and while that wrangle went on no decommissioning was paid. The EEC had the responsibility for negotiating fishing opportunities for its deep sea fleets and practically none were negotiated. So the industry bled to death and it was a desperately traumatic situation. The Banks decided that the industry was to be sacrificed and looked to whatever security they could get and quite unnecessarily put company after company into liquidation and we ourselves were absolutely touch and go so I feel particularly bitter about those ten wasted years. We were told to behave and toe the line and all would be well. In my opinion there was a deliberate policy within the Treasury that if they could strangle the industry, the deep water industry, into non-existence then by the time the Common Fisheries Policy was settled very low decommissioning grants would have to be paid. (Tom Boyd - Hull)

I met Lord Peart, he appeared "pissed" up every time he came to Grimsby. When Silkin came I took him all round the docks. They seemed to come, listen and then forget it as soon as they went back. I thought Silkin might have listened better, but although they've got to show a little bit of interest in the fishing industry, they don't really care. The fishermen were lucky to get the bit of redundancy compensation that they did get. The Government is waiting for them all to die off before they give it to them. There's lots of things that I just don't bother about now. When I first came ashore I sung out from the high trees, I went onto programmes and told everybody. I said on the programme that the North Sea was being raped and we would suffer for it. And that is what has happened. The North Sea has been raped. (Don Lister - Grimsby)

They didn't tell us at the time that they were laying us off. They just told us we'd be in dock for about a fortnight because there were some new quotas coming out. At the time I thought that was lovely. New Year at home, couldn't be better. A fortnight passed, got to three weeks and I was either down the dock each day or ringing up to see if there was any news about a ship, and they just kept putting me off. After over three months of being at home I said to the wife that we weren't going to be going. What quotas were available were being given to the same trawlers all the time, leaving the side trawlers with nothing. Nothing for us. It was as simple as that. We didn't go again. Two weeks became forever. I felt very bitter about it because the last three or four years we'd been just starting to get a bite of the cherry. The fishing markets had improved and you were getting something out of the job at last. It was supply and demand. The fish wasn't there so the prices went up. You was coming home with a lot less fish but making two or three times the money. (Ken Robertson - Hull)

We didn't get to know what was happening. They was all passing the buck. We still signed on for ships and went down dock asking when we were sailing and were told, "Oh we don't know anything." Nobody told us anything. The ones who didn't get to know anything were the trawler crews. So I didn't even know when it was my last trip. I finished up, I went out to the Middle East to an American company, three months on and one month off. Bear in mind I was Skipper of a trawler, I went out for three months, came back home and I went on the dock to ask what was happening, and they didn't even know I'd been away. They still didn't know what was happening they said. (Jack Tripp - Hull)

Every time I came in from sea, every ship I was bringing in, they said to me, "When you go down to the office for your money it may be sold, we don't know." And most of the time, when you went down to the office, it was, "You'll have to sign off, it's sold." They were taking them away. Ship after ship. This was through no fault of mine. The ship was making good money, but they were selling them. Of course they got the money for it, the firm did, but we never saw anything. At the time you didn't realise what they were doing. It was only later on when you said to yourself, "Well hang on." If a miner finished because the mine shuts down, or a firm gets rid of workers because it's closing down or getting computerised, the worker gets compensation. My brother in law hadn't been employed on the docks for many years but he got £30,000 odd redundancy. The day I walked away from that office I got nothing. I feel let down. (Wilfred Cartmell - Fleetwood)

You knew what was going on. I finished up at what they call the West'rd, off Scotland, where we'd never ever fished before. We never made much money because we were that used to Iceland. But we just got chased out of Iceland and that was it. Our money went down a good half. Really we just didn't have the experience. An Owner wasn't prepared to wait while you got the experience because you was losing money. If you took a ship away all the crew had to be paid, you was burning fuel, you was using gear and if you never made much you could lose thousands of pounds. So no gaffer was prepared to wait while you got that experience. It would have cost them a fortune. I was depressed that last trip. I thought, "Well, what are we going to do now?" I mean I was in my forties when we packed up. Never done anything else. When you was a Skipper you was a very important person but when you came ashore you were nothing. You can't get a Skipper's job ashore. You're just absolutely nothing. (George Mussell - Grimsby)

I did get a redundancy payment. I got the maximum twenty years, which was plus interest. £2,200 plus interest - which takes it to about £5,000. If I had to do it again I would be more knowledgeable now than I was when I was twenty five years old with my Ticket. I would have got a better work contract. I would have looked for that, and then carried on doing the job. We've been tied up with this twelve monthly log agreement. As I was signed on vessels, even though I'd been in a ship a number of years, the log book only run for twelve months, so consequently that is your length of employment. We had to go in, sign off the old log which was then sent away to a government institution in Cardiff, and you then signed on a new log, so our length of employment never exceeded twelve months - even though I was in the Wyre Majestic for seven years. That meant I signed on for a contract of employment seven times for the same ship. This is all due to Merchant Shipping Acts that go back to the year 1888. (Derek Reader - Fleetwood)

I was thirty three years fishing. I got no redundancy at the end. Nothing. I went through three Cod Wars. I never got a penny piece. I think that was bloody rotten. The problem is this ludicrous two year rule. In 1966 in Fleetwood, I remember it like yesterday, I went into the Pool Office in the morning and we had our photograph taken and we were given a book. So therefore you're in a pool. If you're in a pool and you walk in and are out of a ship and they offer you one, you have to take it or they'll put you at the back of the queue. If you were a fisherman, you were a fisherman, you worked where you was told to work. Never mind two blooming years. This two year thing for redundancy payments, it's wrong. If they pin it down to two years with one employer what was I doing for the other thirty-one years? I wasn't a coalman or a milkman, I was a fisherman fishing. (Fred Quinn - Fleetwood)

If the Government hadn't sold them down the line John would still have been fishing now. In 1972, he was on over £1,000 per three weeks. If he had been able to continue fishing what would he be earning now and, not only that, what's it done to our children's lifestyle? Our eldest three were used to getting what they wanted as they wanted it and all of a sudden that all stopped. He was out of work. We had to give up our home because we could no longer afford it, so we've lost a lot. This is what the Government don't realise. It lost him his job and his self esteem for a long while because he couldn't get another job - fishing was all he knew. John was out of work for a year then he got a job with Courtaulds. He was there three years. He settled in OK. He was working shifts and we were comfortable. Then in 1982 they took him off shifts, put him on days and his take home pay was just £45. I got on all right but the kids took some settling because I had previously done the disciplining while John was away and now, all of a sudden, John was home twenty four hours a day and he started disciplining them and they found it hard to accept. When John was at sea and only home for two or three days he wouldn't have wanted to be giving them a belt when he was soon to be off again, and I never said to them, "Wait 'til your dad gets home." So when the fishing stopped we were struggling to adjust, living on savings and, when he did get a job, it wasn't paying him as much as he had previously been paying in taxes. The change was unbelievable. (Beryl Pickett - Grimsby)

The Cod War affected my father's fish business badly. The fish wasn't coming in, the customers still wanted the fish so, as happened to most of the Fleetwood Fish Merchants, ten/fifteen years ago, their customers were going to other ports to get their fish. My father, like a lot of people, supplied fish as far as Leyton Buzzard, Luton, little towns round the Oxford area. So even though they tried to remain loyal to my father, his customers would complain that he hadn't sent as much fish as they'd ordered, or it was too dear and they were going to have to go somewhere else. In the end, although my father tried to keep it going, mainly because he didn't want to put his workers out of a job, he had to close the business. I saw it from the side of being a Fish Merchant's daughter who had never known any financial problems until, suddenly, everyone was going under. My father was fortunate in that he'd had a long time at it and was of an age to retire, but a lot went under. (Jill Marr - Fleetwood)

They were just dismissed. You'd get a fishing family whose father went to sea and the grandfather went to sea and suddenly that didn't matter, they were finished. There was no consideration given to help them plan the future. Who could re-train them for another occupation? Who could talk to them? There was no golden handshake, there was no redundancy. Whether those in authority felt for them or not I can't answer but the impression being they didn't. Thousands were involved in the fishing industry in Fleetwood. They were abandoned. And abandoned in a way that was as callous as you would find anywhere. They had developed a way of life over a hundred years and suddenly a man who could only think of going to sea, who felt after two or three days ashore that he was in prison. We would regard being on a trawler as being in prison! He saw it the other way about. And suddenly he's sitting at home and there was never any understanding of that. (Father McMahon - Fleetwood)

I saw the end of the industry. It was a strange sort of system when the Scheme went and we was all paid off I was on the dole for about six months after I left lumping and I couldn't get used to sleeping at night, just one of them things, just laid awake trying to listen to the sounds of people dropping tins on the pontoon and echoing round the town which would happen a lot if the wind was blowing in the right direction, and I just couldn't sleep. But now, personally, I've come full circle, I've come back managing a company. I think things are picking up in the industry with this new dock

Seine Netting : Let 'em out.

starting to take off. A mini revival at the moment. I think that it's more geared to overland fish. I'd prefer to see it the other way, have the boats coming in, when it's bigger it's more money for the town. If you get the Icelandic people in they spend a hell of a lot of money. Danish people do too, if it's only in the local supermarkets and pubs, it's revenue to the town and spin offs. (Peter Broomhead - Grimsby)

When fishing stopped we had just the one child, a daughter, and when I went to the dole office because the wife was working and earned over six pounds I couldn't claim anything for her, I could only claim for the youngster and myself. I was getting £26 a week. So you were constantly drawing on what little bit of savings you had. It all got on top of you, being out of work after you'd worked all your life, and using up all your savings. It made you hard to live with. I was picking on them for every little thing without even realising it. After three months or so I realised we couldn't carry on like that and I would have to do something. I'd been in Hellyer Brothers for more than thirty years so I could have gone on the side trawlers, but I just didn't fancy being on them because of the length of time they were away. I just got addresses from anybody I could find and wrote all over the place for jobs.

Then one day I walked into the Unemployment Office at Hessle - I'd been going in there for three months by then - and they told me the supervisor wanted to see me. He said, "Do you realise that you have been claiming benefit for three months now?" When he asked if I'd ever thought of doing something else I lost my temper. I said, "We've worked year in and year out and never claimed anything and you've got the audacity to start talking to me like this, yet there are people who've been coming here for ever and it's all first name because they've been here that many times."

Eventually I did get a letter offering me a relief job, just for a month, from a coasting company. I said, "Yes" straight away. I'd no idea what it would be like on the coast, totally different from deep sea fishing. (Ken Robertson - Hull)

People had respect for Skippers in Grimsby but that didn't count for work. There was no work. Where could you go? All that experience for all those years - it was all finished. There was just no ships. Afterwards I went fishing out of Spain. I was eight years out of Spain and we were fishing the West coast of the Bay of Biscay and the West coast of Ireland and making a terrific amount of money out of Spain. We could have done that but our gaffers wasn't prepared. Our gaffers got a big pay off, de-commissioning. There was millions and millions of pounds and that's all they were bothered about. They took their money and ran. They was all millionaires so they didn't care. I think they was pleased to get out of it and we was just chucked on the heap. (George Mussell - Grimsby)

When we were forced, because we had lack of fishing opportunities and tremendous pressure from the bank to sell the U.K.'s top two freezer trawlers to New Zealand (that was the Arctic Buccaneer and Arctic Galliard), we had the crews in to this boardroom and told them we'd got good news and bad news for them and I was going to give them the bad news first, and that was that their ships had been sold and the good news was that they had got a job on the ships in New Zealand and would they please go home and talk with their wives about it and there was a job there if they wanted it. I couldn't tell them what they would be paid but they would be paid a reasonable wage and under the best terms and conditions I could negotiate for them, because we'd been retained to manage the ships and every single man in the ship, having discussed it with his wife, sailed with those ships to New Zealand and we proceeded to operate from New Zealand for ten years. (Tom Boyd - Hull)

One of my school pals said, "Do you want a job?" I said, "Yes." "Well," he says, "There's a labouring job." I'd never worked in a factory. And as soon as the wife got to know the next day all me sea gear had gone, she'd give it to the rag man. I said, "Do you know how much that all cost?" She said, "Yes, I'm making sure you never got back to sea again." I thought, "I'll never stick it here," and then I went on a government course and I ended up as a machinist. The Shop Steward was saying, "You can't do this and you can't do that," so I thought, "If you can't beat them I'll join them," and then

I was Convener, then I was District Delegate, Confed. Delegate, and I'm still President now. I've had twenty-two years with the Engineering and Electricians Union and I thought, "Have I wasted my time at sea?" But it was an experience. I'm really proud of the fishermen, what they went through, what I went through. They were great chaps. (Bill Ellerington - Hull)

Having started right from a young lad and gone up right up through the ranks to the top I was sawn off at the ankles. Just finished you like bloody cannon fodder. At the same time as the career ended, so did me marriage after twenty two and half years. My ex-wife was used to money like and I think that's what she was doing jumping from one boat that was sinking onto another one that looked all right like. She went to a Fish Merchant. Then I met this other lass and went into the knitwear for eighteen months. Talk about out of the frying pan and into the fire. I met me uncle and he was all smart with his case. I said, "Where you going Uncle Jim? Anywhere nice?" He says, "No I'm going to work." And he was joining a Spanish ship in Cairn Ryan near Stranraer. He'd just signed on as Master of the ship. So I says, "Any chance of getting me in?" So he says, "I'll mention your name." About a fortnight later they'd got a ship for me. So I went in and I said to the girls, "Well that's it girls I'm going back to sea." All the machines stopped. A couple of 'em started roaring like. I said, "I'm sorry girls I can't stand it." That was 1981 and I started on the Spanish ships then. I went there 'til 1990, and I started on these standby boats and two and a half years I went with Cams. They laid me ship up. Sold it and there was nothing doing at the time so I went back to Spain for a year and I'm just back again now with Novis. But instead of having a regular job its been up and down all the time, nothing regular. (John Meadows - Grimsby)

I couldn't go to sea. When all the big ships was finished I went to seine netting, and I tell you what, you've only got a crew of three on a seine netter and I never thought I was going to be poor again. For the first few months they only went on short trips. I thought, "God, I like this." Mind you, very very hard work. Then after that the prices started dropping, the weather was too bad, you wasn't catching enough fish, and you finished up being in debt. All the crews are share-men in a seine netter and I think I finished about two and a half thousand pounds in debt. You're just going to sea to pay off your debt. I thought, "To Hell with it." Any road, I got a shore job but jobs ashore were nearly all casual jobs, part-time, temps, like the factories round here, like Wold Farms. As soon as they found out you were a fisherman they grabbed you with open arms. They knew you were used to hard work. Nearly all our shift was fishermen and I finished up temporary Chargehand. We knocked more out for one shift than had ever been known. But what was really heart-breaking, you was working alongside of people there that was full-time and they was getting a hell of a lot more money than what you was getting for not putting the work in. When I was temporary Chargehand they got me in the office. They said, "Smithie, for Christ sake you're not at sea any more." Because I sacked five of them and I didn't know you had to give them warnings and letters and all that. I'd just say, "Hey, you, you're no good. Up the road." So I had to pull my horns in. I worked on the land for three years. I did everything, pulling spuds, cauliflours, cabbages, sprouts. There you are, we earned a lot of money on that for the simple reason you was a fisherman, used to hard work. Mud up to the eyeballs and all that, everybody else was crying because it was raining, it was snowing, it was cold, and we was still out there. (Ray Smith - Grimsby)

Seine netting gives the most beautiful fish when it's caught, and it's not marked. A beam trawler can mark all the fish, but if you get a gill net the star fish will attack. Once the fish is dead in that net the star fish will move in and start sucking blood, but you look at the difference between towed cod or towed plaice to a seine netter's fish. There's nothing on the gear to harm the fish, there's no dollies, there's no chains or 'owt like that. It's just a big open mouth. But it's beautiful fish. 'Til you get it in that ice. (John Burton - Grimsby)

I went pair trawling for a while, not very long. We sunk on that. They were wooden ships, no older than some of these seine netters that are still going out here now. The conditions were terrible. You could be up twenty four hours a day, seven days a week really, if you was catching fish. We hit each other fishing up the West coast of Scotland. We were shooting away the gear - because you shoot the same gear but one wire each so you have a good spread - and we were shooting away at full speed. The other ship, the Paul Antony, his steering went and he came straight across us and we went straight stem into him. And of course they are wooden ships so he went down with his fish room with a hole in it. We went down with our stem in. We got picked up easy enough. We threw the life-boats over. They were those rubber ones. I nipped down quick to get my tobacco and cigarette papers. Can't be without a smoke can you? I've always had a plastic bag just in case the ship went down with my tobacco and papers in. It's the first time I've used it though. I lost everything on that ship. I came off in a pair of wellingtons, a wet suit, and a boiler suit underneath and that was it. The Mission were really good. They fitted us out completely from head to foot with new clothes. We went to the shops, the local shops, shoes, even handkerchiefs, collar and tie. Then we flew back from Sundra, 'cos Lerwick's on the same island, and they took us by mini bus and two six- seater planes flew us back to Kirmington. And that was my lot at pair fishing. I never went back. (Colin Donald - Grimsby)

It is unprofitable now because there's no fish left in the blooming sea but we sailed on the 14th December, about nine years ago, and the cod quota was on but we didn't know. We only had two hauls. The gaffer said, "How much fish you got?" I said, "Would you believe 370 kit?" He said, "You're joking." I said, "I ain't joking Bob." He said, "I've got summat to tell you. There's a cod quota on." I said, "You're taking the piss." He say's, "Dig it all out and dump it." I said, "You can fuck off." So he goes to the top gaffer. He said, "I've got 370/380 kit of the unmentionables. What am I going to do with it?" He says, "Esjberg." Did, straight into a factory. We made twenty seven and a half thousand that trip. Beam trawling is the easiest form of fishing I've ever known. Because you've got to get all them chains in. You've got the chain, and then you've got the open gear. The open gear you've only your chains across. Like that, eight chains. And they are killers. They bring all the fish off the bottom. Nothing survives once that's gone over - shells, everything. Smashes all the shells. It just scoops everything off the bottom. (John Burton - Grimsby)

Seine Netters inherit Grimsby.

It was hard to adapt. Hard to understand how petty folks could be at work. I mean, I'd been used to if the Skipper said, "Jump" you never argued. As a Deckie I jumped. You didn't do the childish things they'd do on shore. Mind, I've adapted and I'm just as bad as what they are now, really. But you have to adapt, don't you? And a lot of fishermen never would and never could adapt. (Graham Howard - Grimsby)

We went mackerelling after fishing, finished up mackerelling round the coast itself, Scotland all the way round, follow the mackerel round. Then I went to Australia. We tried fishing out of there, and they went bankrupt, left us stranded there. Then the Victor went to the Falklands. That was my last ship. The Government took her and she went to the Falklands and I thought well that's it, and I went on the standby boats. (Clive Finn - Hull)

Fleetwood became a depressing place, particularly for the deck crew because there was nowhere else they could go. The ship was the ideal training ground for their own job but they didn't have anything else they could go to. At least people like me, Engineers, could get a job of some description just because of your skills. So you didn't really lose a lot of money coming ashore if you could get in on a job. But there were so many deck crew - the majority of workers in the trawling industry was deck crew, and they were a good type of feller, but there was nothing for them. (Harold Dawe - Fleetwood)

I've been small boating for a long time, in-shore fishing and that's a good little number, but that three week away business, I didn't like that. I've been fishing for forty years. I did have a spell of five years on the oil rigs in the Eighties, then I went back fishing. We got our own boat then. We saved up and got one of these little boats but it gradually got worse every year. There were jobs to do on the boat and you couldn't afford to pay your end. So we lost that. But we enjoyed it while we was on it. A lot of people bought their own small boats. We caught mainly plaice and sole, a few codlings and whitings, roker, things like that. It used to be good fishing but more and more boats came with bigger and bigger nets and modern gear, and they scoop up the fish like hoovers. At first you could go out there and you'd be lucky if you saw another half a dozen boats all over Morecambe Bay, but now they're everywhere. Not only that but you've got all these Spaniards - you pass them and they look like a big cruise liner or something. Like a big city they are. Massive things. They just scoop up everything. Nothing goes back in with them. Ruined the ground. (Tom Bagnall - Fleetwood)

I came home and I cried. It broke my heart to think I could never go to sea again in my life. I was fortunate because the feller who lived next door to me - he was a supervisor at Salvesen's - he said, "Come on Tom, I'll get you a job." I was about a month out of work and he got me a job and I've been there ever since. (Tom Jacombe - Grimsby)

We were running twenty-two ships so the cash generation by the company was pretty significant. But if you look at the return on capital invested and our current two factory trawlers which are the UK's only factory trawlers, those have been remarkably successful but they are financed by two different Norwegian banks. One of our Norwegian banks has said to us on a number of occasions that our ships are the most successful in terms of return on capital invested on any of their ship investments. So I think that that is probably a reasonable commentary on the effectiveness of these ships and the ships we're running at the moment are second hand, they're extremely good models and have been very, very efficient. We have spent a lot of money on them and have improved the factories from being able to produce between nine and twelve tonnes of fillets a day to nearly thirty tonnes of fillets a day and that's with the same crews but taking very careful notice and working with the crews, Factory Managers, Mates, the Officers of the ships, to iron out any problems in design and hang-ups to make an extremely successful factory. The top British filleter trawlers of which there were about half a dozen when Britain joined the EEC or a bit later, would do about six tonnes of fillets a day. That was a pretty good day, so you can see how the ingenuity of the fishermen has helped develop a ship which is extremely successful. Now we need to replace these ships with vessels which have more factory space which will allow us to add more value to the fish and much to my frustration and rage we are currently being prohibited by the government to replace these ships. Under some crazy, self-imposed calculation for measuring our fleet capacity we have to replace the ships with ships of existing capacities. Which is ludicrous when one considers that we are in distant waters quota restricted. (Tom Boyd - Hull)

The point about the Cod Wars, when you look back on it, was that the extension of limits to two hundred miles killed the distant water fleets of those nations that were fishing in foreign waters, and with hindsight there was a predictability about that that was fairly obvious. Grimsby, this port, and Hull, had very large distant water fleets. Indeed, the docks were designed to cope with large fleets. Those went in a very short space of time and, having gone, like everything in this world, things then begin to adjust themselves. Those who are processing in the UK, instead of buying from their own markets and ships, simply bought them from Iceland and Norway. So the business became much more international. For those that look back and hanker after the old days of these fleets it's pure nostalgia, nothing else. The world is in a constant state of change. (Frank Flear - Grimsby)

Chapter 13
Requiem

A dozen freezers, based in Hull, still fish the shrunken, tightly regulated world which remains open to them. That world now includes Iceland for a small and grudging catch of red fish. The once proud Owners' associations which dominated their ports have either gone bust (with their records mysteriously burned) or moved out of their grandiloquent offices into far humbler accommodation where they are now Owners and Agents associations. As an industry, a way of life, a community, deep water fishing is dead. The Trawlermen have gone to other industries and suburbs though a few still fish. The dense areas of terrace housing have been pulled down. The fish docks have been put to other uses. Yachts have replaced the fishing boats.

The former fishermen are as proud as ever but their numbers shrink each year and they are scattered. Many are retired, living on their memories, the companionship of their fellow cast-offs from the industry and the pathetic pensions the industry gave. They see each other, talk and drink together. Reputations built in the industry's prime linger. So do the rivalries. Indeed, differences between Grimsby and Hull have ruptured the British Fishermen's Association, formed in 1981, to fight for compensation.

The communities which bred fishermen have been broken up and today's counterparts of the class from which fishermen were bred now has no comparable employment outlet. The towns fishing built have diversified into all sorts of other industries, few of which pay their workers as well. The ports are marinas, even filled in, all pale shadows of their former selves. A great industry is dead and can't now come back. Its centres of excellence, its training and investment, its sustaining networks and the way of life which recruited its workers have all been swept away. Yet the memories, some of the companionship and the debris, human and historical, remain.

It was a good life and it was a bad life but on the whole it was a happy life. Even in the bad times at sea you was a lot happier and a lot closer to your fellow workers than I am to my shoreworkers now, because over a period of time you built up a trust. You knew that man's capabilities as well as he knew yours, and everybody had to work as a team. If you didn't work as a team you wouldn't make any money. The harder you worked the harder the team worked, the more fish you caught, the more money you earned. But that was also according to Act of God because I've done a lot of trips where I've really worked and worked, and I've come home and the markets have been bad so that when I've gone down to the offices they've said, "Sorry, Tom, you owe us money." But that's a fisherman's life. (Tom Jacombe - Grimsby)

I don't know why we did it really. It wasn't a life. It was an existence, especially in winter time, and you used to say to yourself, "That's it. No more," especially if you'd had a bad trip. But you always went back. You'd get in dock with a few pounds in your pocket and you thought you were a millionaire for a day. There'd be taxis everywhere, you'd get blind drunk, and the next thing you'd be back on your way with your kit bag on your shoulder. I think it was the comradeship that was important. You'd make really good friends. In the later days when the ships improved you could go to sea and live like human beings, then you realised how bad fishing had been. But you still missed the life, the comradeships. Thinking back though I often wonder how an earth we did it. Unless anybody has been deep sea trawling and seen for themselves, they couldn't realise what it was like. There was no other life like that of a deep sea fisherman. The abominable weather and life. (Ken Robertson - Hull)

I don't regret it, not one bit. I regret the end when everybody deserted the fishermen. Nobody stood by them. It was a good life, a man's life, and if I could live it again I'd do the same thing, certainly. It was our life ever since we were kids and it was inevitable that you would join them. When the trawlers used to come alongside and they used to give us ships

"The Heydays"

St. Andrew's Dock, Hull 1966.
Copyright: Hull Daily Mail.

"Death of an Indusry"

St. Andrew's Dock, Hull 1990.
Copyright: Hull Daily Mail.

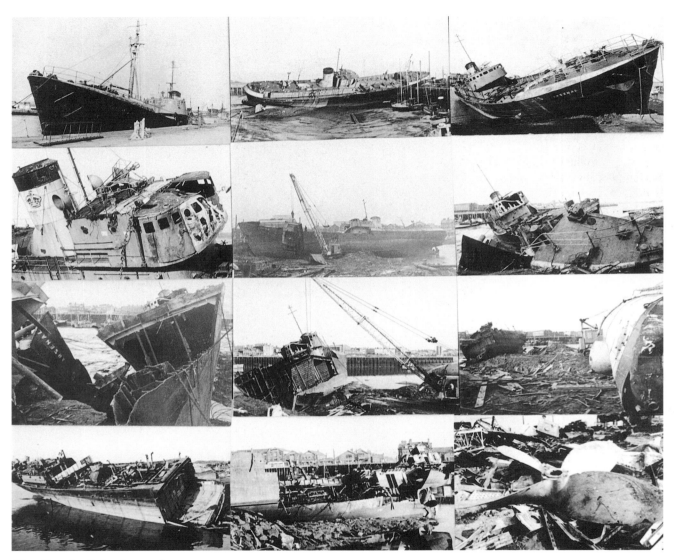

The Death of the Arsenal.

biscuits - they were as hard as hell - but we thought we were doing well to get them. Even the smell of it. At one time it used to be tarry twine they used - you could smell it. It was a good smell that lingered with you. I don't regret it. Not at all. (Jack Tripp - Hull)

I've enjoyed working with people the most. Some wonderfully diverse characters. Many of them were very kind to me. I got enormous enjoyment from working with them. I think I've been very fortunate that during the whole of my life I've never got out of bed in the morning and thought, "Oh Lord, I've got to go to the office." I've always wanted to go to the office and it's always been exciting and there's always been something that's happened. Every day something has happened. That's my overriding enjoyment. Building a ship has excitement. You're creating something. When it comes into the port for the first time - that's a marvellous feeling. I was involved in a very successful fishing fleet out of Grimsby and when I joined Northern Trawlers, Northern was one of the best fleets. It made a lot of money.

I was deeply involved in the re-organisation when Associated Fisheries took over the Ross fleet. That was an enormously exciting period. It wasn't the making of the money, it was the thrill of re-organising the thing so that it could be efficient. That was the thing. That's exciting you know. Re-organising something so that it can perform better. This presents enormous challenges and enormous problems, but managing change is exciting. (Bill Letten - Grimsby)

I was Mate of the trawler Erimo for H.L. Taylor's in 1973, when I was knocked down the fish room while we were clearing the trawl. I fell approximately thirty feet, breaking fish room boards on the way. For the rest of the trip it was all I could do to work the winch. I was x-rayed and found to have a fractured vertebrae and was given pain killers and sent home. I have suffered for the last twenty three years with back pain that is sometimes unbearable. Recently I had to go to Dreadnought at St Thomas Hospital in London, but as the injury had knitted together all they can do is give me stronger pain killers unless it starts to affect the nerves in my legs. (George Drewery - Grimsby)

It was a crazy life. Absolutely mad. Looking back I think to myself, "What a frigging waste." Actually really looking back we all finished up with a house, but none of us actually finished up with 'owt like what we earned. We should have been rich men. But we lived life to the full. I always say it's better to have been there and come back than never to have been there at all. If anybody says 'owt we've been there. Come in the dock with pocket money, going and buying a car, big houses, we had everything. But the majority of people just finished up with the house. No cash like. They'd spent it all. (George Mussell - Grimsby)

I have broken nearly every bone in my body in the course of my work. This has meant that I now suffer from very severe osteo-arthritis in my shoulders and legs. Although I retired early there was no consideration shown by the Trawler Owners - such physical infirmities were considered par for the course. Although many people expect to have joint replacements, that is not for me. My doctor has stated that there is nothing that can be done and that I shall probably end up in a wheelchair. (Jack Collier - Grimsby)

As result of the injuries I did sustain I suffer from arthritis in my right hand, rheumatism in my shoulder and the loss of grip in my right hand. I feel Trawlermen got a raw deal. We were never compensated when off work through injury, unlike the rest of the British workforce, miners, steelworkers, dockers etc., who got compensated and were rewarded with large redundancy payments. I got approximately £2,400 for thirty years as a fisherman. (Norman Steer - Grimsby)

I'm a Grimsby lad and my dad was a fisherman, granddad was a fisherman, all my brothers were fishermen, I knew Grimsby inside and out. When I was sailing out of Hull I used to come back to Grimsby more or less every trip to see my mum, my wife and kids, and when I came back to Grimsby, late Seventies early Eighties, and I walked down Freeman Street I could have cried. I could literally have cried. Because I remember that street. It was jumping, It was just the same as Hessle Road out of Hull. Every day, Monday to Friday, you always had ships landing and when those ships landed you could see the lads coming off. You could always tell a fisherman ten miles away - but that street used to be jumping. And when I saw it I thought, "God Almighty." And when I walked on the dock, Oh, I could have cried because it was exactly the same picture in Grimsby as what it was out of Hull. All the ships laid up and ready for going to scrap, and dropping into disrepair. Oh God. Heartbreaking. (Ray Smith - Grimsby)

I'm now seventy one years old and I suffer from depression, chest pains and I still walk with a slight limp. I never received one penny compensation. (Sidney Cuthbert - Grimsby)

I don't go down the dock. End of story. I've been down a few times fishing off the North Wall with the kids. They all say, "Come on, let's look at the ships." I said, "What ships?" Twenty years ago you could walk along there, there was bloody ships, two or three hundred, and probably a hundred ships out at sea. There's nothing now. It's pathetic. That picture of Les Allen sat on the quay the other day. He was sat there with tears in his eyes when they were breaking his boat up. Twenty three years on that bloody thing, twenty years doing that job. "I've got nothing now," he says, "I'm only 38 years old, what am I going to do? I've been doing that all my life." What else is he going to do? Apart from working in a stinking fish factory. (John Burton - Grimsby)

I was fishing for over sixteen years, nearly all the time with Northern Trawlers during which time I had an accident to my legs and had an operation to have both cartilages out, but over the years they have got worse, and I had to wait for six years for operations to have two knee joints put in. I've had to have a quadruple bypass heart operation, my legs are bowed and I am in pain every step I take. I can't walk very far without my crutch. All down to fishing. (Terence Dunks - Grimsby)

At the age of sixty nine years, I have chronic Bronchitis, arthritis in my hips and both legs are full of varicose veins. Six years ago my spine began to crumble and I was told at Grimsby hospital that my back was bad because of years of fishing. (Charles Quickfall - Grimsby)

You can go out now and walk down Lord Street and you wouldn't know a fisherman if you saw him. But in those days you would have, because the fishermen were the best dressed people you saw, and their wives all dressed up in the middle of the week, or they'd be out on a Sunday night perhaps. Fancy going out on a Sunday night! Every night of the week was like the weekend if you were in from sea. (Jim Quinn - Fleetwood)

When I worked on the market it was like a boom town. I've seen that market - they used to have kits in boxes - with ten stone stacks of cod, so much there was nothing to put them in. Saturday night landings, Sunday landings. They've all gone. All gone. What have we got now? Yachts. It's crazy. (Fred Quinn - Fleetwood)

In March of 1964, I had a very bad accident involving trapping my leg in the trawl wire. My leg was badly broken and hanging off. I was taken into Bodo, Norway, where it was set and stitched up. I went to sea on a ship called MV Gillingham and on going down the fishroom to change some boards over, an iron batten fell from a shelf onto my right arm, breaking it. They took me into Iceland and from there I flew home. I was paralysed in my right arm for six years as my nerve had been severed. Later I had an operation in Sheffield where they put it right. I am now in a wheelchair with a bad back. I received no compensation for either of my accidents, nor did I receive any fisherman's redundancy because I 'had broken my contract'. (Ted Webb - Grimsby)

It's quite nice to look back, as we all do, but most of us, almost without exception, look back through rose coloured spectacles. We always remember the good bits and scrub out of our minds the bad bits - which is not such a bad thing. They were exciting days, but as we sit here at the moment you are sitting in a brand new office block at a brand new fish market costing £15,000,000, looking over a dock that at the moment is landing more fish through its market than it has done for some years. I believe a great deal in self help, that you really need to accept that change is change and then you do something about it. Those that look back and say, "Well, the old days have gone. Isn't it awful? What an appalling situation" - well what we've done in Grimsby is done something about it. (Frank Flear - Grimsby)

I was a fisherman sailing out of Grimsby and Lowestoft for thirty seven years. As a result of this time at sea I now suffer from osteo-arthritis of the lower spine, both hips and knees, and my right ankle. I have had total hip replacement of both hips and the surgeon who did my left one first told me that I am suffering as a result of my time spent at sea. I shall need both knees replaced in the near future. (Robert Sinclair - Grimsby)

I stayed eighteen years working for ICI. Each year was a revelation that I was still working ashore. Christ I missed the sea. I've been trying this last three years to get back. I've written away to different firms but my age is against me. Just today I was given the name of a firm in Grimsby. I rang them up and they are going to send me an application form for the standby boats serving the oil rigs. So, with a bit of luck I might get back to sea again. (Jim Quinn - Fleetwood)

With hindsight it's different isn't it. I would never have gone and done what we did. I spoke a few months ago to a very very successful Skipper. He's a very successful man and he says to me, "Cocker would you have done that again?" I said, "No way. No way." It was just absolutely ridiculous. I mean, when you think of the icy conditions, risking your life. You used to get under land which was the most desolate bleak place in the world, a place called Isafjord, in Iceland. If we was on that North side, that was the worst place Iceland for weather, we all used to steam there and you got shelter. When you got under there you thought it was Heaven. You'd have thought you were at some exotic place just 'cos you'd got under and you was safe. People who say they wasn't frightened they was liars. You had to be. You were risking your life all the time in the icy conditions weren't you? (George Mussell - Grimsby)

If somebody knocked on my door tomorrow and said to me, "Tom, there's a so and so ship for you here," I would go. Straight up and down I would go. I've even told my bosses at work. I've talked about it and I've said to 'em, "Perhaps one day I won't come through them gates at six in the morning and

if I don't you know where to look. I'll be back on a ship." I'd go back tomorrow. My wife said, "You wouldn't would you?" I said, "I would. Definitely." I would go back tomorrow. Even though I know it's a different way of life I would go back tomorrow. It's heartbreaking to think you got booted out for nothing. (Tom Jacombe - Grimsby)

Trawling wasn't all bad. You used to have some laughs and you made a lot of friends. If anything happens, like when Wiggie just lost his boat, you always think about them and wonder, are they all right? We've just lost one of our friends, Trevor Bascombe, he's just died of heart attack. He was only fifty three, but I tell you what, when it comes to the crematorium I bet it's filled with fishermen. You still stick together. (Graham Howard - Grimsby)

Diary of an Unknown Skipper

1977

Sailed 21.8.77
Shot Sunborough Hd. all ships here. But doing no good, wind NNE force 9. Inside 2 cables off land gun boat just steamed into Lerwick so won`t be troubled by him. Ships are laid offside. Just about.

23.8.77
Hauled 200 baskets. Told the ships we are laid for weather. They don`t know I am inside the limit towing up and down, must make the fish up when the ships start fishing.

24.8.77
Wonderful day`s fishing. 800 baskets altogether, ships outside still laid, they think we are (ha ha ha) that`s 450 kit for two days, must remember to make it up when weather fines away - wind still NNE about 7.

24.8.77
Ship's just shot, fucking good oh. I can now (start making fish up). Fuck me, another 250 baskets for the day, 3 days fishing for 600 kits.

25.8.77
Another 300 baskets, told the ship 500 baskets to make the fish up. Leaves me 700 baskets to make up. The lads are looking a bit fucked. Been up forty seven hours now without sleep, must get some soon.

26.8.77
Mate has told me we have 800 kit in, must go in for ice tomorrow, ship`s outside the limits catching between 10 & 50 baskets, stupid ...... dare not come inside, been up now 54 hrs., we have been laid 9 hrs. gutting. I went down the fish room to help the mate, he`s out on his feet, must make all the fish I`ve caught up soon or ships will realise.

27.8.77
Steaming into Lerwick, managed to get 3hrs. sleep, 900 kit aboard, told Keith in the Carlisle about the fish shop and told him to let Jackie Major know through our code (said he would).

28.8.77
Got ice and steaming out, all ships steaming to Papa Bank. Stupid bastards. Keith and Jack still catching plenty where I left them. Phoned Don Lister, told him I had 200 kits in. I`m a crafty bastard. We are 7 days today.

29.8.77
Keith and Jack have had a 200 kit day each. I hope they`re not telling lies like me, no they wouldn`t hold back after me putting them on the fish shop, feel a bit guilty about not letting the other ships know. But fuck them. Wind still NNE force 4, 1000 kits in. Dave Cooper calling me on the 2381, tried to tell him what was going on but too thick to pick up, the dope. Jack said fuck him. But can`t, he`s a pal.Told Dave Cooper to come and get a bottle from me which in code between us means we`re catching plenty, but he said he was too far away.

30.8.77
Just turned out, hauled 50 baskets. Dave Cooper calling me on the V.H.F. Could not answer because I was on low power and if I went on high power the other ships would hear. So called him on the big set and told him to give me a shout when he gets nearer as my V.H.F. is broken. We are 9 days today and the making of a wonderful trip. Keith and Jack and myself the only ships here. Wonder if Dave Cooper will come (he has). Just heard him, gave Dave the dope. He is very pleased because he had a shaky time and only 2 days left.

1.9.77

All four of us have had good day`s fishing, told the other men I am going to let the other ships know, they laughed and asked how I was going to do it. Just called Pete Brown in the Yerso and told him I had just hauled for 600 baskets but I only had 10 baskets, next haul told him 200 but only had 60.

2.9.77

All ships here now all fishing pretty well, all thanking me for letting them know about the fish shop. I said well I just could not let them know, I am a lying ...... but this is it, I`ve had it done to me.

3.9.77

Told ships been laid all night gutting but haven`t. Mate told me we had 1500 kit in. Phoning Don Lister to see if we can land, hope we fucking can, getting a bit fed up now, no sleep yesterday at all, wind East force 3.

4.9.77

Landing with Dave Cooper reported (1600 kits) 900 cod 400 haddock, 100 dogs, 200 coley, must make a great trip. Dave Cooper reported 1000 kit for 17 days, we will be 15 days. Landed 1672 kits and broke port record, made £42,532. Bottle of champers off Sir Nigel Marsden. Dave Cooper made £26,000, Keith Herron reported 1200 kits, Jack Major 1160 kits, the other ships about 900 to 1000 each.

(This Diary was found in a Grimsby attic.)

List of Contributors

Thomas Bagnall	(Deck Hand)	Tom Jacombe	(Deck Hand)
Billy Balls	(Skipper)	Jim Johnson	(Third Hand)
Flo Balls	(Skipper's Wife)	Ray Jones	(Deck Hand)
Neville Beavers	(Skipper)	John Kirk	(Deck Hand)
Charlie Board	(Radio Officer)	Bill Letten	(Owner)
Alec Bovill	(Deckie Learner)	Joe Linfitt	(Fish Merchant)
Les Bowden	(Fisherman)	Don Lister	(Skipper and Manager)
Tom Boyd	(Owner)	Jill Marr	(Superintendant,
George Brown	(Deck Hand)		RNMDSF)
Peter Broomhead	(Lumper)	Father McMahon	(Apostle of the Sea)
John Burton	(Fisherman)	John Meadows	(Skipper)
John Butt	(Owner)	Sid Morrell	(Skipper)
Wilf Cartmell	(Engineer)	George Mussell	(Skipper)
Gordon Cockerill	(Ship's Runner)	Peter Newby	(Skipper)
Jack Collier	(Fisherman)	George Oliver	(Fish buyer (Ross Group
Fred Collins	(Bosun)		/Manager (Young's
Claude Couch	(Cook)		Seafoods Ltd)
Sidney Cuthbert	(Cook)	John Pickett	(Skipper)
Harold Dawe	(Engineer)	Beryl Pickett	(Skipper's Wife)
Roy Dobson	(Mate)	Charles Quickfall	(Deck Hand)
Colin Donald	(Engineer)	Fred Quinn	(Bosun)
Stephen Drever	(Engineer)	Jim Quinn	(Mate)
George Drewery	(Mate)	Derek Reader	(Skipper)
Terence Dunks	(Fisherman)	Eric Reynolds	(Publican)
Bill Ellerington	(Deck Hand)	Joy Reynolds	(Publican's Wife)
Grimsby Evening Telegraph		Robert Sinclair	(Fisherman)
Fridhor Eydal	(Icelandic Correspondent)	Ken Robertson	(Deck Hand)
Clive Finn	(Deck Hand)	Ray Smith	(Radio Operator)
Chris Fisher	(Engineer)	Michael Sparkes	(Bosun)
Frank Flear	(Merchant/Processor/	Ken Standing	(Skipper)
	Chairman Grimsby Fish	Norman Steer	(Mate)
	Dock Enterprises)	Jack Tripp	(Skipper)
Mick George	(Skipper)	George Waudby	(Deck Hand)
Josephine Gibney	(Fisherman's Widow)	William (Ted) Webb	(Mate)
John Gilby	(Skipper)	Roly Webb	(Mate)
Edwin Glenton	(Third Hand)	Jim Williams	(Skipper)
Edwin Hall	(Deck Hand)	Peter Wright Wilson	(Bosun)
Bill Hardie	(Skipper)		
Dolly Hardie MBE	(Skipper's Wife)		
Graham Howard	(Engineer)		

150

The Work

Mate retying Cod ends to resume fishing.
Copyright: Grimsby Evening Telegraph.

Another bag of fish.
Copyright: Grimsby Evening Telegraph.

The Dangers

Stormy Seas. Copyright: Grimsby Evening Telegraph.

But the work goes on. Copyright: Grimsby Evening Telegraph.

<u>Wednesday 6th May 1910</u>

James Parker 54 yrs
1 Garfield Street
Fleetwood
D/Hand
Brought forward from
meeting 22/4/70

7 days
& doctors clearance

Refused duty at sea on the Velia on Thursday 6th April 1970. Put ashore at Ramsey, Isle of Man. Saw Parker Monday 20th April 1970, he said he did not refuse but asked to be put ashore to see a doctor & was put ashore at Ramsey. He has now produced a doctors certificate from Dr J J Devlin 79 Mount Road saying he is suffering from lumbago. The note is dated Monday 20th April 1970 and says he is incapable of work for 14 days. Denies throwing articles about galley.

John Hugh Parker (Jun) 26 yrs
16 Lindel Road
Fleetwood
D/Hand
Brought forward from
meeting 22nd April
1970

28 days
& doctors
clearance note

(34)

Refused duty at sea on Velia on Thursday 16th April 1970 & put ashore at Ramsey. Parker denies throwing anything about galley, says he and his uncle never left crew quarters until Brellin told Parker Jun that skipper wanted to see him about galley incident which he denies. Parker then said he wanted to see a doctor as the accusation made his ulcer painful. Produced cert from Dr Morgan dated 20/4/70 saying incapable for work for 28 days this duodenal ulcer. Has to see doctor again 8/5/70

Have seen Skipper Ward, Mate Laird, Bosun Webster, D/Hands Brellin, Smith, Hudson, 2nd Engineer Warren (with the exception of Warren who was below & saw nothing) all confirm that the two Parkers were drinking from the time the ship let go until 4am the next morning. Skipper Ward accused the young Parker of dumping vegetables overboard after cook complained. Parker was vociferous in his rejection of the accusation.

The young Parker refused to carry on after being accused, and the skipper is inclined to believe Parker. The skipper feels that only the Parkers, the cook or bosun could have done this.

Mr Laird the mate said that the older Parker wanted to see a doctor and both Parkers went off in small boat at Ramsey.

The Bosun says that the young Parker should have been on the second watch but was incapable of keeping watch.

Mr Hudson a deck hand is of the opinion that the Parkers were too drunk to throw anything overboard.

Brellin D/Hand was on watch and does not know who dumped vegetables.

All the crew confirm that the Parkers were very drunk and were drinking from the time the ship let go until 4am the following morning. No one can give any information as to who caused the damage to galley stove or who threw vegetables overboard.

Extracts from the Fleetwood Owners' Discipline Book.

The Rewards

ARSENEL   1958

Feb 12th   Sailed
Feb 16th took chief into Icefjord with stroke
he died Feb 22nd. good start to new ship!
Feb 16 Shot in gully up to 3 bags, 18/25mls
off 110/120 faths. daylight, up to 56 bkts 10 flats
on in & out tow at Adlivik.
Feb 22/23/24th same pos. but in Icefjord 3 times
with engine trouble.
Feb 25th. towing across gully 36mls off 2 bags.
Feb 26th up to 60/10 flats in 55° top of Derry
bank. Feb 27th Bnd home
March 4th   Landed 2048K made £4000

March 6th   Sailed
March 9th Shot on old tow up to 60 bkts
Shep on 21ml tow off Strett up to 120 bkts.
March 11th. towing along line between
Storkie & Duck up to 100 bkts
March 12th. 13 to 16mls S E × E of Horns
up to 150 bkts. March 13th 21 2 off Strett
222 off Horns tow in NW or WNW just to
westard of 50 fath bank you carry deep water
into 19mls off Strett, up to 80 bkts.
March 14th 21mls off each out to 25mls 120 bkts
March 15th on old tow again.
March 20th landed 1500K made £5300
Had week in dock winch went back
to "Fleetwood

Skipper Billy Ball's Log 1958.

BOYD LINE LIMITED, HULL

		"ARCTIC BRIGAND"				Date	12TH DECEMBER, 1972			
Fishing Ground		ICELAND				Days at Sea				
Skipper		J. WILLIAMS				Average per day £				

	KITS		FROM	TO	AVERAGE per KIT	£	s.	d.
SHELF	832	Cpd	16.75	12.70	14.27			
SHELF	571	Codlings	13.00	10.60	12.14			
SHELF	6	Haddocks Big/Small	16.25	15.50	15.90			
	10	Rays	4.55	4.00	4.32			
	24	Cats	10.35	10.60	10.41			
	8	Tusk			9.14			
	8	Ling	11.85	11.50	11.68			
	43	Berrylts			4.45			
	66	Mock Halibut	10.35	8.60	9.99			
SHELF	89	Coalfish	7.90	6.90	6.83			
	2	Mixed Fish			for			
		12 Sts. Mixed Fish			for			
MANURE	4	Rays						
COND.	1	Coalfish			0.89			
		Less Birds Eye Disc. 861		0	0.26			
		Less Allowance for Broken						
		Fish 17/11/72						
	1664	+ 12 Sts.						
		(INCLUDES 4 RAYS @ MINIMUM)						

The Wages of fish.

Name	J Elbrington		14/4/72	
Rating	Spl Mate			
Vessel	R. Trafalgar			
Kits	1950	£	12506	

SHARE MONEY / POUNDAGE		82	53
OIL MONEY		4	49
		87	02

Deductions

Union Subscriptions	4	42	
Sailors' C. Society		03	
Bond	4	72	
Radio Telegrams			
Humber Pension	1	15	
Graduated Pension	1	30	
Poundage Advances		96	
Outfitting Stores	1	87	
Income Tax	34	35	
Skippers/Mates Ins.			
Food	38 22		
N . L . P . S .	14 15		
Advances abroad	56 37	48	80

BALANCE DUE	£	38	22

Relaxing ashore.....and back on board

A thirst to slake.

The consequences.

Bored on board. Copyright: P. Horsley.